D1154375

The Computer in American Education

the Computer
in
American Education

edited by

Don D. Bushnell Brooks Foundation

Dwight W. Allen Stanford University

with

Sara S. Mitter Editorial Associate

commissioned by

THE ASSOCIATION FOR EDUCATIONAL DATA SYSTEMS

JOHN WILEY AND SONS, INC.

New York London Sydney

This book is based on the proceedings of a conference sponsored by the Association for Educational Data Systems and Stanford University, School of Education, under a grant from The Fund for the Advancement of Education.

370
B979c

contributors

Dwight W. Allen
Associate Professor of Education, School of Education, Stanford University, Stanford, California

G. Ernest Anderson, Jr.
Assistant Professor of Education, University of Delaware, Newark, Delaware

Robert H. Anderson
Professor of Education, Graduate School of Education, Harvard University, Cambridge, Massachusetts

Don D. Bushnell
Vice President and Director of Research and Development, Brooks Foundation, Santa Barbara, California

John Caffrey
Director, Commission on Administrative Affairs, American Council on Education, Washington, D.C. Formerly Program Director, System Development Corporation, Santa Monica, California

Sylvia Charp
Director of Instructional Systems, Philadelphia City Schools, Philadelphia, Pennsylvania

C. West Churchman
Professor of Business Administration and Associate Director, Space Sciences Laboratory, University of California, Berkeley, California

Allan B. Ellis
Assistant Professor, Graduate School of Education, Harvard University, Cambridge, Massachusetts

Shelton B. Granger
Deputy Assistant Secretary, Department of Health, Education and Welfare, Washington, D. C.

Peter P. McGraw

Assistant State Controller, Division of Accounts and Control, State Capitol Building, Denver, Colorado. Formerly Assistant Director, Iowa Educational Information Center

Robert W. Marker

Associate Professor, Division of Administration, College of Education, University of Iowa. Formerly Director, Iowa Educational Information Center

Donald N. Michael

Professor of Psychology, Department of Psychology, and Program Director, Center for Research on the Utilization of Scientific Knowledge, University of Michigan, Ann Arbor, Michigan. Formerly Resident Fellow, Institute for Policy Studies, Washington, D. C.

Richard Myrick, *Director*
Stanley L. Cohen, *Research Assistant*
Barbara S. Marx, *Research Associate*

Space and Learning Behavior Research Project, School of Education, The George Washington University, Washington, D. C.

Ottis W. Rechard

Director, Computing Center, and Chairman, Department of Information Science and Mathematics, Washington State University, Pullman, Washington

I. A. Richards

Professor Emeritus, Harvard University, and Visiting Scholar, Center for Advanced Studies, Wesleyan University, Middletown, Connecticut

James K. Rocks

Director, Office of Plans and Programs, National Center for Educational Statistics, U. S. Office of Education, Washington, D. C.

Judson T. Shaplin

Professor of Education and Director, Graduate Institute of Education, Washington University, St. Louis, Missouri

Patrick Suppes

Director, Institute for Mathematical Studies, Stanford University, Stanford, California

Lorne H. Woollatt
Associate Commissioner for Research and Evaluation, State Education Department, Albany, New York

Karl L. Zinn
Research Associate, Center for Research on Learning and Teaching, University of Michigan, Ann Arbor, Michigan

preface

The Association for Educational Data Systems (AEDS) and the Stanford School of Education, with the support of The Fund for the Advancement of Education, joined in November 1965 to sponsor an invitational conference on the present and future role of the digital computer in American education. The three primary purposes of the conference were:

To explore, in the context of a working meeting of experts and educational leaders, the applications, problems, and promising trends in the development of electronic data processing (EDP) in education.

To establish guidelines and criteria for the evaluation and support of future research and development programs.

To recommend areas of needed research and development.

Professors Patrick Suppes of the Stanford Institute for Mathematical Studies in the Social Sciences and Robert H. Anderson of the Harvard University Graduate School of Education were asked to prepare position papers for the conference. By way of response, background papers were commissioned from outstanding practitioners in the EDP field. Conference participants—a select group of educators, educational administrators, technologists, and representatives of federal and private agencies engaged in the pursuit of educational innovation—received the drafts of this material and had an opportunity to prepare their remarks in advance. They reacted during the opening day at Stanford University with candor and enthusiasm. Conferees were actively involved in small group work sessions aimed at developing recommendations for research and development in six areas of computer application to education: environmental control, testing and evaluation, curriculum planning, gathering and retrieval of data on the cumulative experience of education, information sources for the individualization of instruction, and student-subject matter interface.

The conference brought unanimous agreement about the necessity for a clearinghouse for developments in educational data processing. An important role was seen for the National Center for Educational Data Processing, recently established by grants from The Fund for the Advancement of Education within the National Education Association in Washington, D.C. Another fact emerging from the conference was the scarcity of published information about issues and advances in the application of computer technology to education. This book is intended as a partial answer to that need.

Papers of the conference participants were revised (and in some cases expanded) by the authors for publication. These include the chapters by Suppes, R. H. Anderson, Zinn, and Bushnell on the potentialities of automation for individualizing instruction and enhancing learning; Granger and Rocks on immediate and future needs for improved handling of information related to education; Allen, Caffrey, E. G. Anderson, and Woollatt on the state of the art of computer applications in educational management and planning; Charp and Rechard on the introduction of computer sciences in the curriculum; and Michael, Churchman, Shaplin, and Marker and McGraw as experienced and cautionary commentators on some of the problems associated with automation. Two other areas not covered in the conference were identified, and papers commissioned: the educational data bank by Ellis and the role of the computer in contemporary school design by Myrick and his colleagues.

An attempt thus has been made to provide the educator and the general reader with an in-depth report on the state of the art of computer applications in education. In a field that is growing and changing so rapidly, no compendium can claim to be truly up to date. New hardware, solutions to technical problems including those of enlarged memories and high-speed processing, and the growing sophistication of developers and users are bringing about advances almost daily. A solid body of objectives and issues can be identified, however, and developments until now can be examined along with their implications for the future. It is hoped that readers will want to deepen their acquaintance with educational data processing (an extensive bibliography is provided for this purpose) and to become more actively involved in some aspect of its implementation.

An understanding or at least a common-sense feeling about the computer and its capabilities and limitations is urgently needed in the educational community and among persons involved in the arts and humanities. No less necessary is a genuine concern for humanistic goals on the part of computer technologists and engineers. Between these groups an inadequate communication exists. *The Computer in Ameri-*

can Education attempts to initiate a dialogue between technically oriented and nontechnically oriented persons whose interests, for a number of reasons, are beginning to converge on education. Dr. I. A. Richards, eminent teacher, poet, and linguist, provides a critical review and asks some pertinent ethical and philosophical questions. The Honorable John Chafee, Governor of Rhode Island, suggests social needs and goals that should be served by the new technology. It is within these larger contexts that this book should be read.

Transcripts of group discussions at the AEDS-Stanford conference were culled for questions and comments relevant to the material in the formal papers. A number of these selections are included as lead-in statements and as footnotes to the text. *Starred footnotes are the comments of conference participants, and should not be read as statements of the authors.* Conventional footnotes referring to other publications or authors are numbered.

The editors are indebted to all of the contributors who very kindly reworked their papers for publication or provided original material for this book. We are particularly grateful to Dr. Richards and Governor Chafee for their contributions. The Fund for the Advancement of Education was doubly supportive in its generous funding of the AEDS-Stanford Conference and the preparation of this book, and in the person of Mr. G. H. Griffiths, whose personal encouragement and good counsel have been deeply appreciated. The Board of Directors of the Association for Educational Data Processing Systems, and in particular Mr. Jay Fast, Executive Director of the National Center, deserve thanks for their patient backing.

Many hours of typing and clerical support beyond the call of duty have been provided by Mrs. Eileen Clark and Mrs. Joan Johnson of the Brooks Foundation staff. Mrs. Sara Mitter undertook the technical editing of the manuscript and acted as coordinator between publisher, co-editors, and contributors. To all these individuals, we extend our gratitude.

Don D. Bushnell
Brooks Foundation

Dwight W. Allen
Stanford University

March 1967

introduction

Never before has there been such a sweeping commitment to the cause of education as there is today. Education is a primary concern of a majority of Americans. Concern, however, is not enough: it must lead to progress and improvement throughout our educational system.

Of all the "explosions" we have heard about in recent years, one of the most exciting is the knowledge explosion. The world has learned more about science in the last twenty years than in the last twenty centuries. Yet many schools are trying to teach an expanding curriculum in a traditional manner, in the traditional amount of time. In most school districts, children go to school for about six hours a day, five days a week, forty weeks a year, just as they did one hundred years ago. Only at the college and university level have the limitations of the semester system been recognized and firm plans made to operate on a year-round quarter system calendar.

We have learned that a child from a deprived home must begin formal education when he is three or four years old if he is to be prevented from becoming a link in the chain of poverty. Unfortunately, in most states almost every child must wait until he is six to begin regular school. All children whether from affluent or impoverished homes are assigned to a self-contained classroom and are expected to learn the same things simply because they are the same age and are exposed to the same information. Individual instruction for special needs is not available.

The true learning potential of young children may have been badly underestimated. The early years are the most important, and these precious early years must be used to the fullest. Evidence is pouring in that, through new teaching techniques, the process of learning can be moved forward. It begins with what seems the incredible idea of teaching reading, writing, and simple mathematics to children at the age of two and three—and everything else in the same accelerated degree.

What has emerged is a whole new set of experiments and demonstrations for the early teaching of reading skills and the so-called "new mathematics," "new physics," and the like. Many of these innovative programs make use of the computer as a teaching or research tool.

In primary and secondary-school mathematics and science, course materials can be incorporated that will allow the computer to make its unique contribution to the teaching process, that of allowing the student to solve by numerical methods problems which are too advanced for him to work with by analytic means, and bringing to him insights that are difficult to attain in any other way.

In time, every educated individual in American society will come into contact with computers. He should become acquainted with them early and understand their potentialities and limitations, what they can do and how they accomplish it. For this reason we must give special attention to developing course materials that will bring students not majoring in the sciences into contact with a computer and teach them about its principles and operation.

In its short life the computer has been closely associated with the university. In most cases its presence there has been justified initially by its importance for research—first in engineering and the physical sciences, but increasingly in other areas. As a secondary function it has become valuable in university administrative data processing. But only recently has it come to be considered part of the pedagogical equipment; its usefulness as a teaching aid has been discovered almost by chance, and its potential in this area is just now beginning to be recognized.

How the reforms suggested here are to be realized is a matter of immediate concern. Piecemeal efforts are not the answer. A campaign for change requires a gradual and evolutionary program of innovation, appraisal, and systematic implementation. The computer can serve as a valuable aid in this process. Any step toward the automation of an aspect of school operations requires a carefully drawn up and systematized approach to implementation, for each step can affect the entire structure of an educational system. Automation demands systematic planning and thinking: therein lies its promise and its complexity.

And working closely with these impressive technological advances is the teacher—guide, mentor, and partner in the learning process. There is an undefinable magic in the human presence that no computer can ever duplicate. Our schools, facing the challenge of teaching twice as much to twice as many, will be resorting more and more to technology in education. They also will need greater numbers of humane and responsive teachers. The problem for the schools, as for society as a whole, is mechanizing without dehumanizing.

John H. Chafee
Governor of Rhode Island

foreword

THE CREATIVE AIM IN INSTRUCTION

The authorities reporting in the succeeding chapters are at least as likely as any others to be right about what may be on the horizon. This modest claim is a prelude to a succession of doubts that mount into an almost desperate appeal for a concentration of the most balanced and vigorous thinking possible on an imminent and very likely crucial turn in earth's history. The contributions that follow promise new power, power of a far more commanding and transforming kind than has ever been presented to man before. What we are being offered is nothing less than an infinitely great amplification of the effectiveness of our thought.

But what is meant by "our"? *Whose* thought is to be made so much more efficacious? Who is to be trusted with these new powers? What will prevent the new facilities from being used merely to maintain the customary assumptions of this decade as to what the priorities among our endeavors should be? What guarantees can we seek that the best thought extant will not be short-circuited by whatever step-in-quick effort first gets to the control of the switchboards? What guarantees could we obtain that this new source of power will not follow an only too well-known pattern?

The outcomes of technological revolutions are probably unpredictable. Foresight, at least, was in short supply as to what would happen with each of the sudden unheralded accessions of power which have divided the last three centuries into periods more charged with hope and despair than even those marked by the coming of agriculture, metallurgy, or writing. What was done with steam? With electricity? With the automobile? With radio and television? What has been done with the airplane? What is being done with nuclear resources and missile capacities? What is likely to be done with weather control? It is evident that immense transformations of human possibility that may look like blessings can come to seem more like afflictions. Why should we think that a means to the increase of human power in many ways surpassing and transcending all of these together will in fact be more intelligently, more humanely, and more wisely used?

All the foregoing epochal steps may be regarded as extensions of familiar specific capabilities: steam replaced and transcended men's and horses' muscular energy as photography and telephony surpassed and extended the range of our distance receptors. So, more widely, did radio and television. But the offerings of the computer go beyond all such services; they extend the resources of the central nervous system itself. The computer can supply an inexhaustible slave service for whatever we have the wits to instruct it to do. Suddenly, we have a Caliban-Ariel executive that will achieve for us all that we, in our wisdom or folly, can contrive to tell it how to handle.

Wisdom or folly? Some computer aficionados can almost persuade themselves that their monster servants can be taught to tell them which is which. Computers no doubt can tell us much that may be helpful: What most of the background factors are, what decisions have been taken in similar circumstances and with what outcomes. They can be made to show us—with more exactness than our imaginations can —what will probably ensue from what. They can select with magical celerity what other persons have told them will be relevant to our problem. But of the *what else* that may be relevant they are uninformed. It is up to us to be somehow cognizant of and judicious with that illimitable *what else*. That is the testing point. Here lies the difference between living by the book of rules (and the computer is but a book with a built-in selective reader) and living by the judgment instinct, that ultimate responsibility which is seen in all true action and most clearly in the creative arts. This is another way of affirming the concluding declaration of Shelley's *Defence*: "Poetry is the unacknowledged legislation of the world."

Someone will reply that computers, by taking immense intellectual burdens off our shoulders, will free us for precisely these tasks of ultimate choice, these legislative acts. We may hope so, while fearing that they will not. Almost all of us are products of the assistance we can accept. Equally, we are potential victims of those who, for whatever motives, would like to run things for us. Like all power sources, the computer is not going to lessen our responsibilities but to increase them.

The development of the computer has been one response to the increasing complexity in required operations as man's activities have grown in scale and in interrelatedness. The rapid expansion in numbers and in mutual dependencies has imposed problems to which the computer provides a very practical answer: it is the technical means by which man can handle intricacies otherwise beyond him. There is also the economic side. Computers are not inexpensive, nor are those persons competent to brief them for new undertakings. This fact may look, to a hopeful eye, like a useful restraint on applications of doubtful value. But, as so often happens, the new means have rapidly overtaken the original needs that called them into being. After the accounting and the administrative uses have come the instructional uses with which the rest of this essay will be concerned. What is alarming is that neither the superb ingenuity of the technologist nor the purview of the educator necessarily fits either individual for the reflective choices, the discriminative judgments required. There is, however, this comfort. Computers can be made to be exactly observant and critical of their own routines; to collect the evidence of their inefficiency, analyze it, and indicate the needed redesign of their operations. In short, computers, suitably instructed, can become to an important degree self-corrective. It is this feature that affords us our best hope as to their service to education.

At this point two fresh sets of doubts may reasonably assail us. One concerns the extremely solid resistances and obstructions that educational procedures can raise against innovations, however necessary and well accredited they may be. The other comes from certain limitations that may appear inescapable as to what may be expected of even the most cleverly briefed computer. The first are practical, professional-political obstacles; the second are theoretical objections. Let us look at the two sets in turn.

Franklin Roosevelt, writing to Cordell Hull in June 1944, remarked, "If in regard to Basic English, we get the views of 'competent government specialists,' we shall certainly sound the death knell of Basic English or anything like it. I never knew any group of such people to agree to anything really different from the existing system or for that matter anything new. Basic English has tremendous merit in it." [1] These anticipations were more than fulfilled. Churchill's volunteer committee of the Cabinet, which was to concern itself with Basic English, failed to meet; and C. K. Ogden, inventor of Basic English, having refused for years to appear in *Who's Who*, consented at last in order to insert "1944–6, bedevilled by officials" as his summing-up. Basic

---

[1] Quoted by J. A. Lauwerys, *Journal of the Royal Society of Arts*, August 1966.

English, it should be pointed out, was a prototype for many of the inquiries into symbolic similarities and differences that computer programming needs and engenders. Its explorations of "vertical translation" from unrestricted into restricted language are a landmark in the history of an investigation that will be a major concern of programmers for generations to come. The adventures therefore of Basic English in Officialland and deserve sympathetic study.

The obstructions that were raised, however, were not the fault of particular officials, but a consequence of their role, just as certain characteristics of academics derive from the scholar's role. The statesmanship of the instructional development of computer resources will need to be concerned with role psychology, at those highly sensitive points at which the self-conceptions and professional images of academics, administrators, and businessmen converge.

The term "education" straddles a wide field into which have entered in recent years such strong and highly organized interests as child psychology, learning theory, and linguistics. All of these have for some decades been in a condition of considerable polemic excitement. As traditional defenses seem to weaken, factionalism within each of these advancing "disciplines" becomes the more exacerbated. These skirmishings and vendettas are reflected in the textbooks written for the use of teachers and for adoption by school systems. And as business comes more and more into the picture, warfare among publishers hardly seems likely to be replaced by a more discerning rule of reason. Roosevelt's remarks on "competent government specialists" will apply to the chosen advisors of the industrial colossi which are hoping to take over the distribution of educational software, as well as they apply to the traditional panels and committees with whom these advisors will seek to cooperate. The result may well be that innovative projects will be deprived of the criticism that might be useful to them.

This sketch of some of the sources of obstruction will at least remind us of factors—aside from the merits of the project itself—that affect steps toward finding out what should be done. With the possible exception of the entertainment industries, education is the area of activity richest in examples of a principle wider even than Parkinson's Law: the principle that "probable expenditure of effort in any matter is inversely proportional to its importance." It is much more likely that we will let computers hurry the world onward into every sort of further danger than that we will concentrate their resources on the production of enough good minds to save it.

A computer-borne reconstitution of education somehow will have to circumvent all these resistances. But there is a more deeply rooted source of probable frustration to be considered. Why is so much teaching a waste of time in an average school? The answer is to be sought in terms of teachers' roles. The learner-teacher relation is among the most complex, varied, and equivocal of all. There are teachers who, at certain moments and on certain matters, do in the highest degree help their pupils to learn, enabling them to discern both the general nature of the task and the specific phase, opening up the appropriate choices of strategy in exploration. Having said this much about the rare teacher in his rare hour, the token teacher whence the ideal type is derived, we may note that most teaching falls tragically short of and even runs counter to this ideal.

Why this should be so is a matter for very serious study. Part of the failure may be due to the degree in which the teacher teaches as he was taught, does to as he was done to; a pupil become teacher may not infrequently be paying back what he underwent himself. He is normally in a position in which it is extremely difficult for him to know what he is doing. Whatever the reasons, failure is so widespread that a public impression exists that persons who enter this high profession are those who cannot hold down other kinds of jobs. It should be added that the very grave shortage of persons willing to become teachers and able to give even moderately good service in the role has already become a major threat to our culture, especially as the numbers of children requiring instruction inexorably rise. A clear recognition of this situation can inspire both our hopes for better things and our fears of worse: our hopes that the highest capacities for design may take over via computer instruction; our fears that the new powers will—as has so often happened—just multiply mediocrity.

Computer-handled teaching must attempt to match with the vastness of its responsibilities an equally extensive self-criticism. Fortunately, this means of instruction will be on view, open to analysis and comment, as no instruction has been before. Every step in every sequence can be placed on record, made fully replicable, and the failures and successes catalogued and analyzed. It is this that stirs an impulse to be optimistic.

Traditional classroom teaching by contrast has been private, observed only incidentally, except by the teacher and his pupils. Inspections, team teaching, the presence of extraneous witnesses in the classroom, in many ways influence and disturb what most needs to be observed. Such methods do not yield a full actual record. With computer-augmented teaching, on the other hand, the full record can be compiled and analyzed for the appraisal of those who know most about what is being attempted and are most likely to be guided in their redesign by an awareness of ways in which it is failing.

At first, no doubt, this will not be the case. Early attempts will seek to do by computer just what has been done traditionally by select individual teachers. So experimenters with language teaching via film and television have sometimes thought they should just put a teacher in action on view. Such underestimates and misuses, like yoking oxen before a tractor, occur whenever new technical resources become available. Consider, for example, a language laboratory in Africa set up for teachers whose classes had hardly a sentence of viable English among them. It was used to provide the teachers with model pronunciation, via tapes, of such things as "Now, Tommy, I don't want to have any more trouble from you!" "Put your hand up properly!" "Go and stand in the corner!" and other samples of the outcomes of incompetent teaching. That does not show, however, that tape, when its uses are understood, is not an epoch-making aid in teaching.

Let us turn now from obstacles to objections, to what may be advanced as inherent limitations in computer handling. Some of these are not hard to answer. Others look exceedingly recondite, but some sort of elucidation may be briefly attempted.

The simplest of these objections is perhaps that computers are machines, and their students will lose much that they might learn from another human mind. We may reply that a computer, however prodigious its performance, is no more than a medium through which directives put into it by other minds come to the student. These hierarchically ordered messages are intended to supply appropriate interactions with the learner who thus converses via the computer with the minds that have programmed the sequence of requests and responses. It is true that the directives leading to all this are put into the machine in code, operated in code, and decoded in the output into whatever is offered for the student's comprehension and further response. But all this internal code traffic need no more stand between the programmer and the student than does a telephone, in whose operation there is plenty of transformation from message to signal and back.

What can be encoded, however, is only a selection from the resources of language. The objection can be made that the machine must be limited, and so biased, by being confined to the selection. But in this it is not fundamentally different from any other instrument or medium. The properties of the instrument used enter into, determine, and confine the scope of the investigation. The computer is so limiting. It cannot understand or respond adequately to most of the points a student may want to put to it. And it is an important part of the programmer's task to find means in the sequence of the computer's behavior to indicate to the student what he can and cannot reasonably expect from it. Here of course come in the problems of ambiguity and the obliquities and equivocations of language, all of which so often multiply with the importance of the message. The nub of the objection is that the student and the machine will miss one another's points too often for their exchanges to be profitable.

To this there are two answers. The minor one is that communication between live teacher and pupil is rarely so good as is supposed. The more important answer is that there are subjects, important in themselves and as keys to much else, which are simple and controllable enough to be programmed even now so that clear communication with the learner can be kept. From experience with these the programmer can go on to try out more perilous themes.

The chief problems here are linguistic. They require a rather specialized concern with language, with the intricacies of comprehension, with the interplay of cognitive and other than cognitive components in a meaning, with an extensive field of inquiry touching on literary analysis, psychology, epistemology, and linguistics in its narrower contemporary sense. The typical question is: How does this way of saying it differ from that and how may such differences be described? It is to a further exploration of this field—through experimental studies of the samenesses and differences in the effects of variant phrasing—that we must look for the help the programmer will require. Given such exploration, to put limits on what may be programmed is premature.

A far more subtle and abstruse objection turns on a supposed ultimate opposition between men and machines. Men can develop selves; machines cannot: that is the thesis. In part by putting ourselves in the place of others we evolve a personal identity. Machines, it is averred, cannot do this. One might reply that it is not clear why their human creators should not in time contrive to teach machines to put themselves in the place of others. Indeed, this view [2] has not as yet displayed enough of its own real grounds to let us judge it.

The grounds here implied are grounds in feeling. It may well

---

[2] Propounded by J. Bronowski, *The Identity of Man*, New York: Natural History Press, 1965.

be because computers will be unable, probably for a long while, to do justice to more than the plain sense of messages that so many discount or shudder at computer instruction. That computers can be programmed to interpret something as subtle as intonations in any near future will not seem very likely to those who appreciate the ambiguities of the means by which people convey their attitudes.

This much at least may be ventured: those subjects that are most free from attitudinal complexities—those in which the bare typewritten, factual sentence is wholly adequate to what is relevant in the utterance—are best suited to present-day computer technique. Thus mathematics, the factual sciences, and languages (if confined strictly to the handling of plain sense, factual propositions and to conventional formulae) are the subjects through which the development of computer instruction can best be forwarded.

There is fair evidence that first-grade and even preschool children can learn simple typing. Good theoretical grounds exist for thinking that suitably designed instruction in typewriting can be an excellent way of beginning the learning of reading, especially, perhaps, for backward or underprivileged pupils. Reading, it is recognized, is the key problem of instruction. It is the learner's introduction to the use of a systematic notation for a naturally acquired activity. *Reading* here means not the mere matching of marks and sounds but intelligent reading for meaning. Contrary to the presuppositions of much elementary teaching, this great step into use of notation is far more easily and securely taken with strictly factual statements *suitably sequenced* than through "Jump, Jerry, jump!" "Oh what fun!" and the like. By suitable design the step of seeing how a notation (writing, print, figures, diagrams, schematic depictions) works can be immensely simplified—in comparison with any of the widely current prescriptions for beginning reading. The main recommendations of this simplification can be tabulated:

1. Use at first a minimum number of highly distinguishable letters. Seven: a h i m n s t have proved a satisfactory beginning set.

2. Add further letters slowly and only as management of those in use is secure.

3. Use clear unambiguous factual sentences stating facts immediately and perceptually verifiable by the learner. Schematic nondistractive depictions showing clearly what the sentences are saying are the most convenient means.

4. Keep the syntactic form of the sentences used constant throughout the early stages.

5. Since language works through opposition, use opposition in designing the sequences through which to build up the learner's power of seeing which changes in the words correspond to which changes in the meanings of the sentences. For example, *here* is meaningless apart from its opposition to *there*.

It will be seen that an introduction to reading following this prescription lends itself very easily to computer handling. It has been field tested via film strip and film and revised repeatedly. A singular absence of spelling troubles later is a marked characteristic of those who enter reading through this sequence.

The heart of this design is intelligibility. The nature of the task the learner is invited to attempt must be made fully apparent. Beginners in reading commonly fail because they do not discover how the notation works or what they should look for. A mode of presentation designed to help them to see for themselves what is happening and to check for themselves why they may make mistakes, what went wrong and how to make it go right is for many reasons preferable to any arrangement that relies on mere repetition and external reinforcement. Design is engaged not only with the structure of the materials but with the structuring of the activities of the investigating mind of the learner. It can order these by arranging the oppositions displayed in its sequences so that *they* show the learner what he has to take in. When these indications are confirmed, and rewarded by success, the learner has divined three things: how the game goes, what he has to do, and how the teaching mind is playing it. The differences between this and the lucky guess merely confirmed by authority are what the true designer must keep his eye on.

We can relabel these three things as the structure of the world, the structure of inquiry, and the structure of instruction. These labels may help elucidate for us how the exploration of things differs from other ways of being taught about them. This triple concern puts the learner into a cooperative and creative contact with what is being studied, with his own endeavors, and with the presentation offered to him. While trying to form his own ideas, he is also attempting to penetrate the veil and to participate in the thinking of others.

We are guilty of lumping together various and often antagonistic processes under the master term "learning." The chapters that follow offer a variety of divergent views about this prodigious undertaking.

Not all human beings, doubtless, can learn well through inquiry. For those who can, to make them learn in other ways what then will be only nominally "the same things" may be a grave disservice. But there are useful provinces of knowledge which are best entered by different ways. No one could think out *Materia Medica*. And at the other extreme, should anyone end a poem by induction from how other poems have ended?

Several of my fellow contributors eloquently regret that we have as yet no adequate theories upon which programming might be based. Perhaps we will do better without them, remaining the more alert to the *what else* that may be relevant. To be baffled over a choice is rather a good position for a programmer to find himself in. Writing a good program is strangely like writing a live poem. Every possible path seems to be precluded. You have no way on, then, suddenly and unexpectedly, you have it. What you have done so far tells you what you must do. The *design* is completing itself.

This essay has been pleading for intelligibility in what is offered to the student, above all in the earliest phases: intelligibility as to the character of the task and what will fulfill it. We must however recognize an irreconcilable: a problem must be a problem, yet something you need to understand before you can solve it. A poem of my own may well be addressed to programmers:

> Then be you not neglectful
> Of incompatibility;
> We ARE because we went to school
> To views we could not see.[3]

This book is confined to *The Computer in American Education:* a large enough assignment. But most of the rest of the planet is doomed to suffer far more than we from the shortage of teachers and excess of pupils. It would be lunacy to suggest computer instruction for Africa or India or China. But here perhaps can be found America's essential pioneering role. The computer is beyond the economic means and the technological know-how of the developing countries. Nonetheless, computer-borne instruction can produce programs of high general efficiency to be distributed by films, television, texts, hand-operated phonographs, etc., at costs practicable even for impoverished regions.

---

[3] From "Complementary Complementarities" in *The Screens*, New York: Harcourt, Brace, 1960. See also the Appendix: "The Future of Poetry," in the same volume.

One or two well-designed computer-aided inquiries into an introduction to English could produce programs for inexpensive distribution which would redeem many gallant but at present fruitless efforts.

We can at least be sure, as several of the contributors to this book remark, that the computer requires of those who serve it a deep consideration of what they are doing—a consideration that may be worth much more than the machines. Herein is a fountain of hope. The programmer, willy-nilly, is in the role of one of Plato's guardians sent back down into the cave to serve its inmates and "get used again to seeing in the dark." In thinking of the programmer and the instructor, we may keep in mind a sentence from Alexander Dumas' *The Count of Monte Cristo* in which the hero is approaching another sort of treasure: "He then began to climb down into the cave with a smile of doubt on his lips, murmuring that ultimate word of human wisdom: 'Perhaps.' "

I. A. Richards
Professor Emeritus
Harvard University

contents

part 1
Individualized Instruction and Social Goals

Have we dealt adequately with the impact of computers on society? Once they change life, then curriculum must change. We are assuming that much of what now exists in education will remain the same after we have started using computers. But as soon as we use the computer, in a sense life itself will change.

chapter 1

Cybernation and Changing Goals in Education

Donald N. Michael

Cybernation has an impact on the social context, and hence on the goals, of education; by the same token, a changing social context will affect the impact of cybernation. The interactions between cybernation and changing goals are so many that only a few important issues can be mentioned here. In particular, I shall not comment on plausible trends in other parts of the world, although what happens here may very well be determined by what happens there far more than by the efforts of educators and computer experts combined.

Both educators concerned with "education for what" and computer people concerned with facilitating education need to be future oriented; for both are engaged in a struggle to make the best use of what lead time there is to prepare for the use of computers on a wide front in education. This paper, therefore, will look at some of the important aspects of the social context with which both educators and computer people will need to deal, and will mention some of the issues that merit attention in the application of computers to the fulfillment of American

3

educational goals—especially if these goals are changing. We are referring to education in relation to both young people and adults, including older adults, who present different problems, different opportunities, and perhaps different goals in education. Keep in mind, too, that the educational environment will expand beyond the physical confines of the school, partially as a result of computer capability. Much of this discussion, of course, is highly speculative.

First, let us look at population characteristics over the next decade or two, since today's children and today's adults will be trying to cope with many social transitions during that period, and in the process of coping will have to be educated and reeducated not only for work but also for leisure and for new perspectives. We are told that by 1975 the population of this country will be about 235 million; and by 1980 it will be about 250 million. By 1975 those who are 25 or younger will represent about 50 per cent of our population, and the proportion who are over 65 will have increased very substantially—by about 20 per cent.

This means, among other things, that we shall have a population not only of unprecedented size, making radically new demands on our social and material technological capabilities, but one also more polarized than now in terms of age and hence in terms of values brought to the educational experience. Education will have to enhance or modify the values of both young and old, which, as they reflect social needs and aspirations, are not necessarily compatible.

The second contextual factor is that of the increasingly urbanized condition in which our population will live. We are familiar with the growth of the megalopolitan areas on the East and West coasts; there is one growing in the Middle West as well. The result will be a greatly enlarged population living in an interactive environment without precedent, where cities are no longer isolated entities working out their problems separately, but instead must work together as parts of regions, or at least of very large urban systems.

The third contextual factor has to do with the increasing role of government. There seems to be no extant social invention, other than that of large-scale government, to deal with the enormous scope and complexity of the issues that society faces and to do so in the kind of long-range system-planning context that is required if we are going to take advantage of our opportunities and minimize our problems. The size of the population and the growth of megalopoli that ignore state boundaries seem to demand increasing federal involvement, a much larger federal contribution to the direction of the society. Certainly we shall also have experiments with new forms of local governments: city governments as we have known them will be less and less effective and gradually will die hard.

Another factor that is extraordinarily and radically important to this set of relationships will be the increasing effectiveness and utilization of what we can call social engineering: the systematic application of knowledge in economics and social and behavioral sciences to the design, planning, and manipulation of the society and its parts in order to attain efficiently specified goals. The stimulus is there, especially with the development of such nationwide activities as the poverty program, the extended education legislation, and—while we don't talk about it —the area of counterinsurgency. In all these instances we must be able to plan exceedingly complex programs far enough in advance to phase and operate them effectively. Here the computer provides an unprecedentedly powerful tool for better understanding men and their institutions, and hence for planning and for implementing these plans. For the computer provides us with the capability of simulating very complex models of human and institutional behavior with adequate real-time data-processing capabilities to test the models against society as it is today, not as it was five or ten years ago. In particular the computer provides the technology for storing and processing the data required to do longitudinal studies. Such studies are crucial for developing the needed understanding of social processes and social change. For the most part these studies remain to be done.

An awareness of these research areas is growing, and inevitably new knowledge will be applied increasingly by the government and others to the needs of such a large population living in such a complicated society. Increased rationalization of programs and planning, as practiced in the Defense Department, is beginning to be applied to the education and the poverty programs. Obviously this increased rationalization of social processes and of the means for planning and implementing them depends on the existence of the computer—not only because the computer makes possible the simulation of alternative policies and programs, but also because it allows us for the first time to encompass significant aspects of the environment. We might doubt, for example, whether our exciting plans for nationwide revisions in education could possibly be carried through if the high-speed data-processing capacity of the computer did not provide us with the understanding of what is happening in time to take advantage of it as it happens. National planning—long lead-time planning—clearly requires the existence of the computer, and will grow from that very existence.

One way to represent this societal context is to state that it is of unprecedented complexity, and that to deal with this complexity we will have available to us through cybernation and other technologies an unprecedented capacity for doing enormous good to ourselves, or enormous evil. With this background in mind, let us turn to some specific issues which relate cybernation to the changing goals of education.*

We are going to need more planners who are able to use these technologies and can grasp larger social issues and work with them in a broader context. There is a real question about how to provide the education for this kind of role. It will take more than knowledge of computer techniques and the behavioral sciences to do this job both efficiently and humanely. For increased rationalization also means increased "guidance" or "manipulation" of various segments of society. The technology for controlling others exists and it will be used, given the persistence of power-seeking motives. Furthermore we will need to use it, since the necessary social changes cannot come about if the affected people do not understand and desire them. Thus the pressures, the good moral and ethical reasons, for using attitude- and behavior-changing techniques will increase; the potency of the technology for doing so also will increase; and, of course, there will be a mounting danger to the democratic tradition and the Judeo-Christian tradition on which it is founded—unless we learn how to educate to protect them. We shall return to this point later.

Another question, in addition to that of educating leaders, arises: how do we educate "run-of-the-mill" citizens for membership in a democratic society, given the enormous complexity of social issues and the increasing abstruseness of the techniques for dealing with them? What, indeed, are the appropriate political roles for citizens in such a society? How, for example, do we educate to make people comfortable with, sensitive to, and aware of complexities? How do we teach people to understand their relationship to long-range planning? Our popular mythology describes a national tradition of short-range or last-minute planning at best. And how do we teach people to be comfortable with, indeed to embrace, change and the process of change? Should we educate for this? We shall probably have to. But how?

The need for educating to embrace change is not limited to young-

* In the educational system, whether computers are used or not, we are programming people—both by the choice of curriculum content and by the methods of instruction. A certain amount of factual information and certain habit patterns are being programmed into the heads of students. Their concept of how to study, how to learn, comes by and large from their school experience. If we program the study habit of learning things by pushing buttons, what will be the ultimate effect on the student?

sters, but includes the teachers of youngsters as well. Education for tomorrow's world will involve more than programming students by a computer; it will equally involve the ways in which we program formal teachers and administrators and parents to *respond* to the education their students and children get for this kind of world. To the extent we succeed with the youngsters but not with the parents, we will have an interesting and, probably, a very serious consequence: an increasing separation of the young from their parents, a kind of parallel to the difficult relationship of immigrants to their children in earlier years in this country. Perhaps it will be a more drastic one; certainly it will have psychological repercussions, probably producing in the children both guilt and hostility (arising from their rejection of their parents' views and values and life styles) and the kind of vitality or drive that often goes with these neuroses, or which has done so in the United States in the past. Those planning curricula for the young, I think, should not overlook this problem of producing too great a psychological gap between the young and their parents.†

Let us consider some implications of cybernation for work in this society—aside from the question of unemployment—and the consequent implications for changing educational goals. Many employed persons will be changing what they do two or three times during their lives as a result of job displacements and job transformations produced by cybernation. The question becomes: who are they in relation to what they do? Given a career or a type of job that has defined my identity, what happens to the definition of who I am when the type of job changes? Work in our society means more than income; it has provided psychological meaning for generations of people who have defined themselves and have been defined by their work; and it is the basis for the "Protestant ethic" regarding the sinfulness of nonwork. These psychological and theological definitions of self hold not only for young people; traditional values about work are reflected by the bulk of the teachers in primary and secondary schools. To the extent that work changes its

---

† We need to make continued philosophic assessments, to experiment, to examine and reexamine goals, to pose new problems, dealing with the far-out ideas of today that may become the realities of tomorrow. We must design specific activities to get the school practitioners of today to begin thinking more imaginatively, more effectively, about what is going on in the world around them. We do not have to look very far to find what have been called "yesterday's people": people who increasingly are unable to function economically in today's society, who simply cannot make a decent living. There will be a psychological and intellectual gap between child and parent, but the children are going to be yesterday's people, too, unless we educators do something about it.

meaning in the years ahead, deep questions will be raised about the appropriate, the "right," education needed to provide a redefinition of the relation of self to work. This is a problem already for older people forced or "encouraged" to retire before they are ready, often as a result of cybernation's impact. It does not follow, of course, that the approach appropriate for giving theological, ethical, and psychological self-definition to the early retired will be applicable to the young.‡

Of great importance in connection with work is the fact that some of the most interesting jobs increasingly will be human oriented. These are not sales jobs, but rather the kind of subprofessional occupations that involve real—not pseudo—rapport between people; jobs that we either cannot or do not want to do by machine: teachers' aides, clergymen's aides, welfare aides, mothers' helpers, and so on. How do we educate for the kinds of roles appropriate for such jobs? How do we educate people to be nonexploitive and nonmanipulative in their relations with others? How do we educate for rapport and empathy? And what is the relationship between educating for those human-related aspects of the future work situation and the tendency increasingly to expose people at all ages—but particularly young people—to a machine-educative environment? I believe in and support the computer and the programmed environment, but a real question must be raised: what will be the effective means—in a computer-valuing environment—for teaching these other "human" characteristics that will be so important? § Part of the poignancy of this problem is that many teachers, it seems clear, are deficient in these characteristics as well. Their past tradition has directed them to be teaching machines for intellectual skills and for work; not for education, not for emotional openness, not for tolerance of ambiguity and cultural differences, and not for other characteristics needed for social-aide roles.

Because cybernation will radically change the work-force composition and the purpose of work, education not only must assume the task of altering its goals and its techniques for dealing with work but also it must develop a radically different capability to educate for leisure. To

‡ What will happen to the values of self-organization, self-actualization, the child's perception of himself, beyond reinforcement of a certain kind of learning?

§ I am concerned with the problem of societal values of children. A child or an adult at any moment is functioning as an individual and as a member of the group. When we work toward computer-aided individualized instruction, we tend perhaps to overlook the danger of removing the learner from the social context, and in doing so make it more difficult for him to behave in this social context. What kinds of problems can the social studies teacher define and help children work through in terms of value systems that grow out of the presence of computers?

the extent to which cybernation provides more productivity, it provides the opportunity for more leisure. The world's work, of course, is never done; there is plenty to do to keep everybody busy twenty-four hours a day. But people have chosen to take some of the increased productivity in increased leisure; and there is every evidence that they will choose to do so more and more as the productivity of society grows—in significant part as the result of cybernation.

How do we invent—and invent is probably the right word—adequate life styles for increased leisure time, and how do we teach them? Some people will say, "If I had leisure no one would have to invent a life style for *me!*" Generally these are not the people I am talking about: they tend to be the overworked professionals, and top-flight professionals will be scarce and overworked for a long time to come. For the rest we have to invent these leisure roles, and then to invent educative means for inculcating them in both the younger and the older people who will compose most of the working population. There is no evidence that masses of people can suddenly learn "leisure" at the age of 50, or even at 20. And we find little comfort in the historical "precedents" sometimes put forward to suggest no serious issue here. Investigation reveals no historical models adequate for a 250-million-person, highly technologized society trying to spend its leisure time meaningfully—not necessarily productively or creatively, but self-fulfillingly. Here is an enormous challenge: how to inculcate the cultivation of self. And can we operate to this end within a school system which, for the most part, is still premised on education for work and administered with a beady eye on efficiency?

To summarize, it seems to me that the ultimate challenge for educators trying to establish and implement goals for living meaningfully in a cybernated society is twofold: (1) that we be able to produce more intellectually and emotionally competent people, and (2) that we be able to produce in numbers and in quality, as never before, *wise* people. Now, in some important sense, wisdom is a function of trained intelligence, but wisdom implies more than this. We are going to need wise citizens if they are to have responsibility for the direction of tomorrow's world and if they are going to prepare themselves and their children for it. But in particular cybernation puts enormous burdens on the leadership of society, for the efficient and humane use of cybernation will require a much larger number of people displaying a far higher level of wisdom than is found in the leaders of our society, or indeed in those of previous societies.

It will be increasingly difficult for leaders to maintain the balance between the individual and the mass as society becomes larger and aggregate solutions become more sophisticated or more necessary. This is probably true even for the process of trying to determine how to "individualize" instruction. Individualized instruction for individualized or aggregate ends? The pressures arise partly because the computer provides special techniques for dealing with the mass. The pressure also exists because there will be political demands to deal with the mass. Our very ability to manipulate a large society is provided by the computer, in part directly through information on what is happening to the society, and in part through the knowledge it has previously helped produce about how society behaves. There will be pressure on leadership to deal with the mass rather than the individual because there will be a tendency to value most highly those things the computer can define, measure, and otherwise handle. In this society, science and technology are our faith and, as all true believers, we will emphasize and cling to what our faith purports to answer even if it falters in doing so.

We need what the computer can do, but equally or more so we need a broader perspective. We need people who understand the human predicament beyond that which can be encompassed by programmed instruction and computerized education. We certainly do not know what wisdom is or how to produce it. Certainly we do not know what the relation of live teachers—to say nothing of computer teachers— might be to the production of wisdom. But understanding this blessed state of mind, cultivating it, and providing the context which allows it to operate will become an increasingly crucial task for educators. For, among all these speculations, one thing is clear: new curricula, new administrative methods, and computer technology will give more men than ever before greater power than ever before to create or to destroy themselves as bearers of the Judeo-Christian tradition and as practitioners of the democratic process.

chapter 2

On Using Computers to Individualize Instruction

Patrick Suppes

The theme of individualizing instruction is a very old one in education, and the supporting psychological documentation of significant individual differences in initial abilities, in rates of learning, and even in general approaches to learning, is by now overwhelming. Yet it is fair to say that for simple reasons of economics we have not been able to individualize instruction to any very deep extent at the elementary, secondary, or college level. Costs for providing this sort of instruction are simply too great for a society like ours, committed as it is to universal education at all but the highest levels. Administrators and teachers continue to struggle with the problems of meeting every child's educational needs. In the elementary school serious attempts are made at grouping within the classroom for important subjects like reading, and recently the ungraded elementary school has begun to attract considerable attention. Without question the main intellectual justification of the ungraded classroom is the opportunity it provides for a greater degree of individualized instruction. To some extent the introduction of team teaching

11

has had the same sort of motivation, although in this case another aim has been to provide better qualified teachers by appropriate pairing in skills and training.

Efforts like the development of ungraded elementary schools undoubtedly will continue, and will be important in the future as we make further attempts to tailor education to the individual child. Other solutions are clearly needed, however, if we are to approach anything like a tutorial mode of individualized instruction. It now seems that the burgeoning technology of computers may offer a real avenue of approach to providing the kind of instruction we want.

The application of computers in school instructional programs has barely begun and is not yet well understood, but some examples will be sketched in sufficient detail to give the reader a feeling for the real prospects and concrete problems of this sort of instruction. Since my own efforts have been devoted mainly to the elementary-school mathematics curriculum, my examples will be drawn primarily from this part of the curriculum. One or two other specific possibilities, such as foreign-language teaching at the high-school and college levels, will be mentioned.

COMPUTER SYSTEMS

THE "LOOK" OF COMPUTER-CONTROLLED TEACHING DEVICES

There are three levels at which computers may be used to individualize instruction, but perhaps it will be helpful to describe first the kinds of devices or terminals that may be attached to the computer for students to use. Of primary importance is a visual-display device on which the student may look at messages brought up from computer memory. A device that is now becoming familiar is the cathode-ray tube (CRT), which looks very much like a small television screen, and on which alphanumeric character messages may be generated directly by the computer. Attached to the CRT is a standard keyboard that the student may use to respond to the instructional program. In some environments the student will also have a light pen that he may use to point to correct responses on the screen of the CRT. A device such as a light pen is particularly important for young students in the elementary school. Communication with students through appropriate audio devices is desirable at all levels, though again it is especially needed with younger children. With the more developed programs, prerecorded messages are available fairly rapidly at appropriate points. Additional visual-display devices are also important; for example, displays of photographs or more complex line drawings than are easily presented on a CRT are useful at almost all levels of instruction. Since the CRT equipment will make no appreciable noise while in operation, the devices described here can be placed in an ordinary classroom if the student uses earphones. If the CRT is replaced by a typewriter or teletype, then some sort of acoustical isolation is necessary for ordinary classroom operation. A variety of configurations seems practical, ranging from a single CRT in a classroom shared by many students during the day, to a classroom containing a large number of CRT's. In the latter configuration each child would spend at least an hour a day on the CRT, perhaps working in thirty-minute sessions, once in the morning and once in the afternoon; but it should be emphasized that he would spend most of the time in his regular classroom. Again I have in mind the elementary school; the appropriate change in environment required for college applications should be obvious.

There is already a good deal of evidence that students at all age levels gradually come to feel as much at home with the sort of terminal equipment described here as they do with an ordinary television set. Of course, it is understood that young children in the elementary school are not expected to input long messages on the keyboard. For most exercises a few digits corresponding to numerical answers, or a single word, would be the most required. Longer responses are appropriate for older students; we shall return later to the rather complex problems of evaluating constructed responses of any substantial length.

In current work at Stanford University on computer-assisted instruction, there are three levels of interaction between student and computer program. A brief description of each level will be given, although it must be emphasized that the third and deepest level is still mostly beyond us from a technical standpoint. For now, it represents an ideal to be attained in years to come. Each of these levels will be referred to as a *system*, in conformity with rather widespread computer usage. The point is that in each case a computer system is built up to perform the required level of instruction.

DRILL-AND-PRACTICE SYSTEMS

This level of interaction is merely supplementary to the regular curriculum taught by a teacher. In the case of elementary-school mathematics there is abundant evidence from both pedagogical and psychological studies that students need a great deal of practice in the algorithmic skills of arithmetic before a reasonable level of mastery is obtained. They need corresponding practice in the standard applications of arithmetic and, more generally, in developing what is sometimes called a good "number sense." The point of a computer system at this level is to provide a simple, straightforward, and *individualized* approach. It is intended to relieve the teacher of a considerable burden and at the same time take a substantial step toward providing practice work at a level appropriate to each student.

For the minimal drill-and-practice system we can forego the audio component of the total system described earlier, as well as the light pen. We can use a CRT with keyboard, or a typewriter under computer control with keyboard. The CRT makes it possible to display multistep algorithms like that of long division in a more direct fashion than the typewriter allows. Even with the CRT and keyboard, we might make the response of traditional education and give elementary-school students a standard set of exercises that will be the same for all, with the familiar ring of drill and more drill. But the most important difference from traditional methods is that we are not committed to giving each child the same problems, as we would be if textbooks or materials prepared at the school were used. It is a straightforward matter of computer programming to offer exercises of various degrees of difficulty, and to select each student's level according to his past performance. In a program we are now running in the upper-elementary grades at Stanford, there are five levels of difficulty at each grade level and on each concept in elementary-school mathematics. For instance, five different exercises illustrating the fact that subtraction is not commutative might be given to different students on the basis of their past performance, at the same point in the school year. Typical of such exercises, which also provide additional practice in the algorithm of subtraction, are the following:

A. $4 - 2 = 2 - \rule{2cm}{0.4pt}$.
B. $16 - 12 = 12 - \rule{2cm}{0.4pt}$.
C. $34 - 25 = 25 - \rule{2cm}{0.4pt}$.
D. $63 - 45 = 45 - \rule{2cm}{0.4pt}$.
E. $123 - 75 = 75 - \rule{2cm}{0.4pt}$.

A moment's inspection shows that the five exercises all exemplify the same general concept and yet vary considerably in levels of difficulty, particularly in terms of computational skill.

To take another example, a typical three-day block of problems on the addition of fractions would vary in the following way. Students at level A get problems that involve only fractions having the same denominators. Levels B and C, on the first two days, also have only problems in which the denominators are the same. On the third day the fractions have denominators that differ by a factor of 2. At level D the problems have denominators that differ by a factor of 2 on the first day, and at level E the denominators differ by a factor of 3, 4, 5, or 6.

At the present time we are moving the students up and down the levels of difficulty on the basis of the previous day's performance. If more than 80 per cent of the exercises are correct, the student moves up one level, unless he is already at the top level. If less than 60 per cent of the exercises are correct, the student moves down a level, unless he is already at the bottom. If his percentage of correct answers falls between 60 per cent and 80 per cent he stays at the same level. It should be emphasized that the selection of exactly five levels and of the percentages 60 and 80 has no firm theoretical basis but is based on practical-pedagogical judgments. As systematic data are accumulated, we expect to modify our choices in the light of experience. The important point for the present is that we are operating a highly individualized program of instruction, which even at the level of drill and practice depends on the availability of computer-based terminals. In principle the work we are doing could be done, of course, without a computer, but only with a very substantial addition to the teaching staff. It would hardly be possible in practice. Obviously this is true of almost everything that we ask of computers, not only in education but in industry and government as well. The operations carried out by the computer could always in principle be carried out by hand, given enough time and personnel. In the drill-and-practice exercises we are discussing, the computer can be used to analyze and collect data in a fashion that would be extremely difficult for a teacher. Above all the computer can systematically make an item analysis as well as present a daily written record on each student. The particular significance of the item analysis is that it can be used to refine the selection of items for the different levels of difficulty, and can give the teacher information on the kinds of concepts that are most difficult for her students.

There are also deeper levels at which drill systems can operate. I have described the preparation of five levels of exercises, which are prepared in advance of any use by the student. It is also possible to write programs with a more complex structure in which the individual items presented are contingent upon previous student performance. That is, items in each category are selected on the basis of a more detailed use of a student's past history than the one just described. For example, a student may be given more problems that emphasize the types that he has found most difficult over the past week or two.

TUTORIAL SYSTEMS

In systems of this type, in contrast to the drill-and-practice systems, the aim is to take over the main responsibility for developing skill in the use of a given concept. In the teaching of elementary Russian at the college level, for instance, it could be the responsibility of a tutorial system to offer a complete body of curriculum material on phoneme discrimination during the initial hours of the course. It is also easy to select an example from the initial lessons in arithmetic in the first grade. It is a familiar experience of many teachers that children entering the first grade cannot properly use the words "top," "bottom," "left," "right," and so forth. In order to give instructions it is highly desirable that the meaning of these words be clear to the children and that they be able to respond in unequivocal fashion to instructions using them. Here is the sequence of concepts we have used at Stanford in the first section of first-grade arithmetic:

1. Using the light pen—the child uses the light pen to point to the picture of a familiar object shown on the CRT.
2. Using a box to respond—the child touches the light pen to a small square box shown on the screen next to a figure.
3. Auditory introduction of the words "first" and "last"—the computer speaks to the child.
4. Auditory introduction of "top" and "bottom"—the kind of instruction given to familiarize the child with the use of these words is of the following sort: "Put your light pen on the toy truck shown at the *top* of the display."
5. Introduction of the word "middle" in the sense of vertical position.
6. Introduction of "left" and "right" in selecting one of two things.
7. Introduction of "left" and "right" in selecting among three things.
8. Introduction of "middle" in a horizontal sense.
9. Introduction of "left" and "right" in selecting among a row of things shown.
10. Introduction of "between" in selecting among several things—for example, "Pick the chair that is shown *between* two tables."

Space does not permit a description of the details of the tutorial program used to introduce these various concepts; but this concrete example may demonstrate that by using the auditory capacity as well as the light pen attached to the CRT, it is possible to approximate the interaction a tutor would have with a student. Above all it is possible to analyze each child's comprehension in greater depth and detail than is usually possible for a teacher of thirty students in a first-grade classroom.

It should also be apparent that in the tutorial system we may individualize instruction for the entering first-grade child. The bright, organized child who has been going to kindergarten and nursery school for three years before entering the first grade, and who has a large speaking vocabulary, could easily go through the concepts I have listed in a thirty-minute session. The culturally deprived child who did not attend kindergarten may take as many as four or five sessions to get through these concepts. These slower children may also be handicapped by an inadequate vocabulary in standard middle-class English, since their speaking experience may have been mainly with a dialect. These children often will require several different approaches before the concepts are thoroughly mastered. The important point is that in the tutorial program every effort is made to avoid an initial experience of failure for the culturally deprived child. The program also has enough flexibility to avoid boring the bright child with endlessly repetitive exercises that he fully understands. The child progresses through each concept in the sequence listed as he meets a criterion of performance for each. The child who makes no errors—that is, who fully understands the concepts to begin with—will meet each criterion very rapidly and move through the entire sequence in a single session.

In view of the kind of examples presented, the reader may feel that the instructional mode in a tutorial system will not permit freely constructed responses on the part of the student. Without entering into details here, a brief discussion of our program in mathematical logic will show that such responses are possible. This is one of our best-developed programs. The student is permitted to make any valid inference, and the main function of the tutorial program is to assess the validity of the inference he makes. The relative wisdom of the step taken by the student is not indicated until he has at least made a serious effort to find the correct proof of a theorem. As is usual in proofs of mathematical theorems, different students will find different proofs, and the computer program will accept any proof that is valid. When students do not succeed in finding a proof, the program gives them hints.

Concerning the future prospects for tutorial systems, it should be evident from the sorts of examples stated that the skill subjects such as reading, mathematics, and elementary foreign languages can be handled most easily and are best understood as taught in this environment. Tutorial systems can be used to carry the main burden of teaching skill subjects. Widespread application would lead to a radical revision of the organization of teaching, because a rather large part of all instruction is at the elementary-skill level. For this reason it is common to ask what will be the teacher's task if these elementary skills are taught in a tutorial fashion by computer-based terminals. The most important point to be made in this connection is that no tutorial program for computers in the near future will be adequate to handle every type of problem that arises in students' learning. It will be the teacher's responsibility to move to the much more challenging and important task of troubleshooting, of helping those children who are not proceeding successfully through the tutorial program and who need some sort of special attention. At Stanford University the tutorial programs have what is referred to as a teacher-call. When a student has run through all the branches of the concept, and has not yet met a satisfactory performance criterion, there is a teacher-call at a proctor station, and a teacher comes to give individualized instruction as extensively as needed.

DIALOGUE SYSTEMS

What we envisage as dialogue systems are computer programs and appropriate terminal equipment able to conduct a genuine dialogue between the student and the program. Such dialogue systems exist now only as elementary prototypes, and successful developments in any depth demand the solution of some relatively difficult technical problems.

Two central problems may be described by beginning at the college level and moving down to the elementary-school level. Suppose that in a program on American history, the student types in the question "Why did Booth kill Lincoln?" or a more complicated question such as "What was the role of the railroad in the economic development of the Mississippi Basin in the nineteenth century?" It is a very difficult problem to write programs that will recognize and provide answers to freely constructed questions of such generality and complexity. The situation is by no means hopeless, however. In curriculum areas that have been taught for a considerable time and that have a reasonably sharp focus of subject matter, it is possible to provide a fairly thorough analysis of the types of questions that will be asked. In these subject areas we can make considerable progress toward the recognition of the question by the computer program. The central intellectual problem at the moment is not that of writing information to give an answer, that is, of having in storage information that will give an answer to any question. Rather it is to recognize from the standpoint of the program precisely what question has been asked.

The second sort of problem arises in working with elementary school children for whom it is essential that we be able to recognize their spoken language. It is certainly not reasonable to expect a child in the first year of schooling to be able to input a question on a typewriter. He can ask or answer a question in a fairly complex way, however, if his speech can be recognized by a computer program. The problem of speech recognition simply adds another dimension to the problem of recognition of sentence meaning. There is reason to hope that within the next five or six years much progress will be made in the area of speech recognition. If the difficulties can be overcome, then in many respects the problem of the elementary school is easier than that of higher grades, for the types of questions and answers that occur are considerably simpler than at the secondary or college level.

PROBLEMS

Whether the computer system we are using to individualize instruction is a fairly thin drill-and-practice system or a very rich dialogue system, the kinds of problems that arise in designing curriculum materials and in organizing and using the system are very similar. In this brief survey emphasis is placed on behavioral rather than technological problems. Until we know how to settle the kinds of questions I shall raise, it will be unclear precisely what technological requirements must be met. To some extent the listing of behavioral problems is grouped around the classical concepts of stimulus, response, and reinforcement, but the classical formulation of these concepts certainly is not adequate to the problems we encounter in individualizing instruction.

STIMULUS SEQUENCE

Perhaps the first problem we encounter is the gross one of how we should think about organizing the curriculum materials. In what order should the ideas in elementary mathematics be presented to students? What mix of phonics and look-and-say is appropriate for the beginning stages of reading? Should phoneme discrimination be taught before word recognition or phoneme production in foreign languages? These are the kinds of difficult and perplexing questions that arise, even in the very early stages of preparation to teach mathematics, reading, or foreign languages. What is to be emphasized is that we are very far from a detailed scientific answer to any of these questions. Individualized instruction in a computer environment must proceed for some time on the same basis of practical judgment and pedagogical intuition that we use in arranging curriculum materials for ordinary courses in ordinary classroom settings. We have the hope of developing a more scientific and therefore a deeper understanding of these matters, but we are still far from having that understanding. The magnitude of the problem of stimulus or curriculum sequencing is difficult to overestimate. It is easy, for example, to lay out experiments that would need all the children in the world as subjects, in order for us to decide how to teach mathematics in the first grade. This problem of sequencing, magnified once again by relative priorities for different subject matters, leads directly into a combinatorial jungle that even large school populations and the power of the computer are not adequate to touch. It is a straightforward matter to show that the number of possible sequences of concepts and subject matter just in the elementary-school curriculum is in excess of 10^{100}, which is larger than even generous estimates of the number of elementary particles in the universe.

The only sensible hope for emerging from this combinatorial jungle would seem to lie in the development of an adequate body of fundamental theory about the learning and retention capacities of students. The history of science in many of its domains (particularly astronomy) is testimony to the importance of having large bodies of dependable data for theories to describe and explain. It is to be hoped that as systematic bodies of data become available from computer systems of instruction they will have a measurable impact on the development of learning theory. At the present time extrapolations from the kinds of experimental studies done to support fundamental learning theory and the central problems of subject-matter learning are tenuous, and existing theory inadequate for the complex problems of learning that arise in the context of the curriculum.

RESPONSE MODES

We do not yet know how critical it is to have various response modes available for instructional programs. The problem of interpreting complex constructed responses has already been mentioned; how essential such responses are to the learning of most elementary subjects is not fully known. A problem at least as difficult is to organize computer programs in such a fashion that the responses of the student are used in an insightful and informative way, both in telling him things and in deciding what he should be exposed to next. One of the most difficult tasks is to know how to make use of unexpected responses as a good tutor would. For the immediate future, perhaps the best use that can be made of unanticipated responses will be to record them for off-line analysis by those who must revise and improve the curriculum materials.

Again the problems we face are not easily overestimated, if we look ahead to the full task we would like the computer system to undertake. Beyond question one of the most tedious and unrewarding aspects of teaching English, either at the secondary or college-freshman level, is the thankless task of marking student papers. It is hard to think of a teacher task that one would rather turn over to a computer, particularly for routine mechanical errors. Unfortunately, apart from a check of spelling, it is still extremely difficult, and from a practical standpoint impossible, to give such tasks to any computer system now available.

REINFORCEMENT SCHEDULES

The possible types of reinforcements are a source of many open problems in designing curriculum for computer systems. A wide variety of alternatives are available to us. A difficulty is the lack of adequate theory to inform us on the best procedure to follow. There is conflicting evidence as to whether or not students should be corrected immediately each time they make an error. It is not clear to what extent students should be forced to seek the right answer, and indeed whether this search should take place more in what has come to be called a discovery or inductive mode, as opposed to more classical modes of instruction which consist of giving a rule followed by examples and then exercises or problems that exemplify the rule. A particularly troublesome issue that has come to the fore in recent research is the question whether different kinds of reinforcements and different sorts of reinforcement schedules should be given to children with different basic personalities. So far as we know, no large-scale curriculum efforts that build in variables of this sort have yet been made in this country. It would be very difficult to think about how to write two different elementary-school mathematics curricula with this kind of variable in mind—although some of my colleagues are more sanguine about it.

COGNITIVE STYLES

Closely related to the last point about personality differences is the body of evidence bearing on whether children have fundamentally different cognitive styles—for example, are either impulsive or reflective in their approach to problems. Perhaps the primary difficulty with the research on cognitive styles, as it relates to the construction of curriculum for computer systems, is that the research is primarily at an empirical level. The reach of theory is as yet very short, and it is not at all clear how the empirical demonstration of different cognitive styles can help us to design highly individualized curriculum materials adapted to these different styles. An even more fundamental question of educational philosophy asks how much the society wants to accentuate these differences in style by catering to them with individualized techniques of teaching. I do not mean to suggest that a curriculum design using information about these differing styles would necessarily cater to them, but this is one direction in which it is easy for curriculum to move, once such problems are brought to the surface. One may be reminded, in this connection, of the kinds of curricula that have been given children with special talents in our society for many years—for example, children with exceptional musical talent.

PAST PERFORMANCE

In the near future the use of computer systems to individualize instruction will surely encounter a more pressing problem than those of personality differences or cognitive styles: the problem of making effective use of information about the recent performance of the student. In standard classroom teaching it is impossible to use in any sensitive way the different achievement records of the students in the class. Partly because of the requirements of group teaching, we have very little experience in such matters. A gifted tutor will remember and use many facts about the past performance of his pupil, but scientific studies of how this should be done are as yet in their infancy. Practical decisions about the amount of review work needed, the time needed for the introduction of new concepts, and so forth, which vary widely from student to student, must ultimately be much influenced by the student's past performance.

DATA LOGISTICS

When students are set to work on an individualized basis, the problem of keeping records of work accomplished is enormously complex, particularly when it is intended that those records will be used to make decisions about the next stage of instruction. We have found at Stanford, in planning for the processing of 5000 students per day through a large computer system, that one of the most difficult decisions is that of selecting the small total amount of information it is possible to keep permanently. It is very easy to give teachers, administrators, and curriculum writers such an overwhelming amount of information that there is little chance of their absorbing and using it effectively. In terms of the variety of summary statistics one may easily obtain in a computer system from a day's work with students, it is not at all difficult to have the data output run to a thousand pages when 5000 students are being processed. The problem is to reduce the number of pages of data output from 1000 to something more like 25 or 30. The most essential problem in making this reduction is that we do not yet have well-defined fundamental theoretical ideas that can provide guidelines for making the reduction. Present decisions about what reductions to make are based primarily on general pedagogical intuitions and the scientific traditions of quantitative data analysis in experimental psychology. Neither of these guidelines is very effective.

It is easy enough to talk about individualizing instruction in the schools. This brief list of problems should convey how complex is the task of actually implementing such instruction by use of computer systems. Above all it is important to realize that the problems are not simply the technological ones of having computers available and adequate computer programs for preparing and presenting curriculum materials. Any deep and creative use of computer systems for individualizing instruction faces major theoretical questions still unanswered. From a scientific standpoint the search for the answers to these questions is the most exciting aspect of the whole venture.

CONCLUSION

Computers do not offer a panacea for the many problems of instruction we face in our schools. As with any new technology with a potentiality for solving old problems, the initial development and implementation create nearly as many problems as are solved. The road that lies ahead is tortuous and bumpy, but the signs point upward toward the heights of educational excellence. Many of those most concerned with the preservation of humanistic or individualistic traditions view the increasing importance of computer technology in our society as a threat to those traditions. If such critics understood better the scientific world in which we live, they would realize that this technology offers a possibility of individual fulfillment in education hardly conceivable fifty years ago. It is not too much to claim that for the first time since public education for everyone became a major goal of our society, individualized instruction at a genuinely deep level is now a feasible goal.

chapter 3
Sustaining Individualized Instruction through Flexible Administration
Robert H. Anderson

THE EDUCATIONAL REFORM MOVEMENT

For the past ten years we have been caught up in the heady excitement of a major educational reform movement, involving unprecedented departures from established practices and enjoying levels of financial support and public interest without parallel in history. Both in its massive scope and in the quality of changes taking place, this reform movement is almost certainly the greatest upheaval in our educational system in more than a century.

At the very heart of all these changes are the numerous national curriculum projects, some of these sparked primarily by scholars in the academic disciplines. The very participation of these scholars in the reform movement is one of the most welcome and remarkable developments of all. What these men and their educationist partners are striving to accomplish is, on the whole, less a redefinition of the goals or purposes of education (though some new directions are being charted) than

25

the development of new ways for achieving long-established ends and objectives. What is new about the "new math," for example, is not only the nature of the mathematics being taught but particularly the way teachers now go about teaching it.

Under the rubric of curriculum reform, too, fall all of the exciting and important projects focusing on the educational development of preschool children, culturally disadvantaged youngsters, alienated youth, and the academically talented. All these activities influencing the curriculum, with attendant reexamination of instructional methodologies, constitute far and away the most important dimension of American school reform today.

The emphasis of this chapter on effective and flexible administration therefore needs at the outset to be placed within the larger context of overall program improvement, and such enthusiasm as may be shown for various administrative and organizational procedures derives primarily from the hope that these will make it all the more possible for better teaching and learning to take place.

In addition to major reforms of the curriculum itself, there are roughly six other kinds of proposals for the promotion of more effective teaching and learning:

1. Different approaches to the recruitment, preparation, and in-service professionalization of teachers.

2. New patterns for the utilization and assignment of both professional and nonprofessional workers in the schools.

3. Various patterns of school unit organization, departures from conventional graded organization, flexible schemes of pupil grouping and scheduling, and related arrangements designed to build more flexibility into the total school structure.

4. Greater and more skillful use of electronic and mechanical contrivances such as television, audiovisual aids of all sorts, autoinstructional devices and teaching machines for programmed materials, computers and data-processing equipment.

5. Innovations in the design and the construction of school buildings and equipment.

6. Cooperative approaches to educational research and development, through partnerships that bring together school systems within a region, school systems and universities or state agencies, and other organizations concerned with education.

It can be seen that all of these categories relate to each other in significant ways, and it is possible to argue that any one of them (e.g., the computer) is essential to the success of all the others. It can also be seen that all of them have important meaning for the work of the school administrator, and all of them in some way depend on the skill and the efficiency with which administrators perform their functions as managers and facilitators of the educational enterprise.

At the risk of oversimplification, let us therefore define educational administration as comprising an array of activities and services whose ultimate purpose is to facilitate teaching and learning within the schools. Let us further define the mission of the elementary and secondary schools as the provision of opportunities for each child to acquire the information, skills, attitudes, and other intellectual equipment he needs in order to realize his innate potential for academic, social, vocational, and civic accomplishment.

It is not necessary in this discussion to claim that the schools have the sole responsibility for achieving these worthy purposes, and perhaps at the outset we should stress that one important function of administration is to maintain appropriate lines of communication with other institutions and agencies whose programs also contribute to the development of children's powers, particularly their intellectual powers.

The singular importance attached by Americans to universal high-quality public education, at least as a national aspiration, is unfortunately not matched either by appropriate levels of financial support or by well-conceived policies to facilitate the achievement of truly excellent programs. Without discounting the many accomplishments of the schools or the talents of many teachers and administrators, we are obliged to conclude from much evidence that the schools are not achieving their lofty mission. That is, there is still too large a gap between what the schools could be accomplishing, given knowledge already available (e.g., from the curriculum projects already noted), and what they are actually doing. And, to leap over complicated analyses of why this is so and what needs to be done, we may rightly conclude that one urgent need is greater flexibility in both the governing policies and the administrative and pedagogical machinery through which the goal is being pursued.

It is also necessary for us to leap over a great mass of evidence concerning the full extent of human diversity. Granted that man shares a fantastic array of talents, needs, and predispositions with all his fellows, we now realize as never before how remarkably unique each separate individual really is. If only all this information were properly classified and examined, and if only theories to guide us in the application of such information were well enough developed, as eventually they may be (with the help of computers, to be sure!), educators would have available to them an overpowering but exciting view of the complex and diverse population they serve.

Already it seems reasonable to claim that we have at our command the most complete and the most valid definition of the human creature in all of earth's long history; and for the educator (as, indeed, for all others who serve mankind) this is therefore an age in which more appropriate and effective technologies can be developed than ever before. Obviously future scholars will come far closer to the truth about how man learns and develops, but in our time there is at least the exciting and tantalizing scent of such truth in the air. There is also the sobering realization of many ethical issues that will confront educators as their powers and influence increase.

Stimulated both by the clues of new knowledge and the embarrassment of old mythologies, half-truths, and untruths that still haunt twentieth-century education, school administrators and their allies are obliged to join and extend the educational reform movement in every possible way.

SCHOOL ADMINISTRATION TODAY

Among the characteristics of school systems today are that:

1. They are fewer in number, and larger and more complex as organizations.

2. They are caught between the society's growing aspirations on the one hand, and the inability or unwillingness of the society to allocate its financial resources for needed school programs on the other.

3. They serve as a battleground for some of the nation's most vexing problems—for example, cultural deprivation, inequities of opportunity, the church-state issues, local versus federal control, the meaning and the mission of democracy, and controversy between such interest groups as labor and management.

4. They represent in every community one of the most costly enterprises and one of the enterprises most vulnerable to public inspection and complaint.

For these and related reasons, it is extremely important for the administrators of school systems to press forward on at least four fronts:

1. Assisting the citizenry to relate both its present and its future welfare to its organized system of education and to develop the broad policies whereby that system can flourish in the community interest.

2. Providing leadership in the establishment of school procedures and programs through which the community's policies can be implemented.

3. Managing and maintaining the educational enterprise, obtaining and allocating resources, providing and supervising personnel, extending curriculum development, evaluating results, and coordinating both internal operations and external relationships (e.g., with the colleges).

4. Helping the school system to refresh itself through the generation of new ideas and arrangements, collaboration with other systems and agencies in research and development, and lively interaction with other sources of knowledge and invention.

All of these functions depend, of course, on the existence of theories to guide practice and on the ready availability of great masses of data that help to confirm these theories. At the community level one needs a complete picture of the community's resources and of the relationship of resources to aspirations. One needs to know what values are held by which groups of persons, how the power structure operates both overtly and covertly, how voter behavior is influenced by these and other forces, how various school policies and procedures are accepted by the people they affect, and how effective in fact these policies are. One needs more information about alternatives when decisions are to be made, and the means for predicting the consequences of each possible action.

Internally, school administration focused on the implementation of a master plan requires equally great masses of data concerning the tasks to be performed and the optimum means of performing them. In the fields of personnel administration, of business management, of planning and development, of articulating the various subunits of the school system, and of assessing and interpreting results, it can be seen that *access to information is literally the foundation of the administrator's work.*

Let us select one example, that of school plant planning and maintenance. Typically today school maintenance is still only a primitive science and the various subfunctions of maintenance scheduling, supplies selection and control, personnel training and supervision, and maintenance accounting are usually conducted less efficiently and skillfully than is possible. Furthermore, most school buildings now in use are functionally obsolete in significant ways because neither their original design nor efforts at modernization and renovation have rendered them as flexible and useful as modern programs require. Even in 1965–66, despite overwhelming evidence favoring flexible grouping patterns and other departures from "egg-crate" school designs, billions of American tax dollars were being wasted on new but inflexible structures destined to be obsolete before they were dedicated. Equally shocking is that school planners almost never base their school-construction schedules on adequate demographic data, on hypotheses about the fluid uses of school facilities across neighborhood lines, on long-range studies of the ways computer-based audiovisual programs may influence space requirements, or on studies of community change as they may influence the design and the functions of schools. On the contrary, most school buildings are planned (if that is indeed the correct word) in an atmosphere of crisis and on the basis of only a fraction of the information that bears on the problem.

Inasmuch as the example of school planning is closely related to another important area in which planning must be done, namely the organizational structure within which the schools shall operate, this discussion should lead us to an examination of the several forms available. In preparation for that topic, on the assumption that our commitment is to the well-being of each unique individual, let us review for a moment what is meant by individualized instruction.

INDIVIDUALIZED INSTRUCTION

"Individualization of instruction" is a phrase with many meanings, and it serves as the cornerstone of such organizational arrangements as the nongraded school and cooperative-teaching plans. Virtually all discussions of curriculum development, teacher-pupil relationships, the size and function of each school unit, class and group size, and educational technologies are geared predominantly to the notion of serving individual pupil needs. Almost all innovations in education for the past ten or more years, even those involving large-group instruction, have been advocated primarily because they have allegedly made individualized programs easier to achieve.

Individualized instruction does not necessarily mean that each youngster is confined to activities in relative isolation or in a very small group. The teaching machine and an increasing variety of audiovisual devices, whether or not computer based, have led of course to greatly increased use of lessons to which the learner responds in isolation from other learners. Correspondingly, many schools are striving to increase the use of small working and interacting groups—approximately six youngsters working on a project together, or a dozen engaging in lively discussion—and school planners are being asked to furnish spaces capable of accommodating such activities in reasonable privacy.

But these are not the only ways a school program can be made more relevant and meaningful for individual students. Conventionally sized classes and larger classes can also be highly suited to the interests and the learning characteristics of the various students involved, especially if the teachers have taken pains in advance to assemble a great deal of information about pupil achievement records and pupil needs. That many lessons fail to be relevant to all the participants is due largely to the fact that teachers generally possess neither the tools nor the time for conducting such studies and for the detailed curriculum planning that is required.

We may define "individualized instruction" as requiring school situations in which:

1. Individual pupils interact with programmed materials, work independently in libraries or other school spaces, or otherwise pursue learning tasks by themselves and on their own timetable.

2. Individual pupils receive counseling, tutorial service, or other personalized help from a member of the school staff.

3. Small groups of pupils, presumably very similar to each other in aptitude and achievement history, engage collectively in a task that promises essentially the same educational benefit to each of them.

4. Small groups of pupils, presumably different from each other in aptitude, interests, experience, and other factors, engage collectively in an activity (such as discussion) that promises to benefit each of them uniquely.

5. Groups of pupils attend a lecture or presentation by the teacher, a demonstration, an audiovisual lesson of some sort, or other class activity in which all the youngsters are exposed to a common stimulus but the responses expected of the children either at that moment or in some subsequent activity will vary within a range the teacher has in mind.

Perhaps still other situations can be imagined, but in general these five include the arrangements most commonly found in the schools. Educational planners share the hope that teachers will learn how better to exploit the potential advantages of each arrangement in a balanced program that provides for each its proper place. Almost certainly the computer is slated to make an important contribution to this kind of teacher planning.

FORMS OF SCHOOL ORGANIZATION

Granted that what teachers and pupils do is far more important than the organizational setting within which they do it, it is nevertheless widely accepted in today's educational literature that the administrative and organizational environment of the school has a profound influence on pupil achievement and morale. A great emphasis within the educational reform movement has been on abandonment or modification of the rigidities inherent in the graded school and the self-contained classroom. Experimentation with alternative ways of grouping and deploying pupils within the school at any given moment in time (hence the term "horizontal organization") and of regulating and describing the year-to-year school progress of children (vertical organization) therefore has commanded a great deal of interest and attention.

In brief, the alternative mechanisms of vertical organization are only two: graded structure, in which the school program is rigidly compartmentalized into annual segments of subject matter, and the more flexible though more ambiguous arrangements summarized in the rather awkward term "nongraded organization." The latter is inseparable from the concept of individualized instruction; it implies that progress within the overall school program will be continuous, unbroken, and appropriately paced for each child, regardless of the uniqueness of his needs and capacity for learning. Thus "nongraded organization" is not so much organization, though it does have its own organizational structure and vocabulary, as it is a philosophical point of view about what makes sense given the fact of human diversity.

The alternatives with respect to horizontal organization include:

1. The so-called "self-contained classroom" at the elementary level.

2. Conventional forms of departmentalization as found in most secondary schools and a small proportion of lower schools.

3. Various types of cooperative teaching or "team teaching," both formal and informal, of which a major characteristic is a great deal of coplanning and coinvolvement on the part of the teachers.

Although much has already been written about them, these various organizational forms are still poorly understood even by educational leaders with a special obligation to understand them. For example, a past president of one of the largest and most important national organizations in education, writing about the need for better curriculum patterns, recently made this grossly inaccurate statement: "We really have three kinds of models and not much variation in these: the self-contained classroom model, the departmentalized model, and the nongraded model." Failure in this case to identify the nongraded vertical model as wholly distinct from two horizontal alternatives, with which it might conceivably be combined, results in distorted discussion of the virtues or weaknesses of all three arrangements mentioned.

It seems increasingly urgent that administrators in particular acquire a deeper understanding of these organizational forms and equip themselves and their school systems with knowhow that will enable the superior formats to prevail. There should be no equivocation regarding formats that now seem reasonably well supported by research and experience.

It is my thesis that the literally self-contained classroom no longer makes sense, even for kindergarten and primary children. Most of the advantages long ascribed to this deeply entrenched arrangement have been questioned over the past decade, and many new insights are now available with respect to children's emotional and personal needs, the optimum teacher-pupil relationship, the optimum size of classes and schools, pupil grouping for this purpose and that, and the nature of teaching itself. To me these data suggest that most pupils have need for associations with a larger total number of classmates than can be assigned to a single self-contained classroom, and that they need more variety in the contexts and situations within which they interact with other children. These data also confirm that a greater range and variety of teacher talents are needed in children's school lives. Another conclusion in support of the alternatives to self-contained classrooms is that teachers themselves need more professional interaction with their colleagues.

Even more intense is my conviction that the graded school in all its evil forms and manifestations must be swept away before American educators can ever achieve their most precious goal: that of enabling each child to fulfill his maximum potential in ways and at rates specifically appropriate for him.

My central theses, then, call for more flexible patterns of pupil progression, class and group composition, and staff utilization. The child is best served when he lives in a school dominated psychologically and structurally by certain simple but compelling principles of child development, learning, and motivation.[1] He will be happier and more productive if at each stage he belongs to a basic school family that includes more than the conventional twenty to thirty children with whom he can develop significant affiliations over time, and includes several adults with whom he can establish different appropriate relationships.

Perhaps the best of all possible school worlds for children is one in which they associate alternately with children who are very similar to themselves in some respects and with children who are notably different from themselves in other respects. In keeping with our foregoing arguments, it will also be apparent that in such a school there is need for class and group activities involving a great range of materials and topics, requiring spaces of varying size and versatility, and thus requiring administrative coordination and services greatly exceeding those we are content with today.

CONCLUSIONS

All of the newer organization patterns and ideas described in these paragraphs, whether combined (as I prefer) or separate, depend ultimately on two things: (1) wholehearted acceptance by teachers and administrators; and (2) significant improvement in both the quality and the quantity of curriculum guides and materials geared to the wide range of requirements in every pupil team or group.

Although there is brave talk about spiral curricula, broad-gauged curriculum planning, and flexible instructional materials, the fact is that so far little has been done to make these notions operative. Most teachers have at their command neither the diagnostic instruments nor the instructional resources necessary for a truly individualized program for each child. Given the premise that children will no longer be herded together in permanent packages of twenty to thirty, but will instead move back and forth within a fluid, larger setting that allows for independent study, small-group work of many types, and various larger-class activities, the typical teaching staff is hard-pressed to keep track of each youngster's progress and at the same time to organize the overall program around topics or themes with relevance for everyone. The reporting of pupil progress—another field in which practice lags far behind existing knowledge—looms as a frightening responsibility for the teachers, and a number of related administrative problems are aggravated. As a result the new format does not flourish and teachers tend to shy from the workload that full-scale development seems to require.

[1] As described by John Goodlad in *Saturday Review*, March 20, 1965.

Most if not all of the foregoing problems are solvable through resources and procedures already in existence. Although little direct reference has been made to research, it must be obvious that a vast increase in the range and quantity of data is needed to guide administrators and others in their search for better policies and practices. More useful ways of examining and utilizing these data (for example, computer-based simulation as a way of exploring alternatives and as a means of training) also are urgently needed.

In addition to a better understanding of what is feasible and desirable, educators need greater sophistication in the dynamics of planned change. Notable in the past few years has been the emergence of a significant new literature on innovations and their implementation in the educational setting. Most administrators on the firing line have an urgent need not only for the translation of this literature into operational recommendations, but also for continuing access to the ideas and resources that derive from this field of scholarship. School systems will find it necessary to add to their central office staffs persons having those specialized skills without which administration could remain a crisis oriented, inflexible, and inefficient arm of the school enterprise.

We are concerned about the nature of learning and the learning situation. We begin by asking what makes for effective human learning of given material under given circumstances. When we look toward computer-based instruction as a system that will simulate the effects of teaching, the first task is to define the subject matter. It seems that some aspects of the teaching act can be relegated to the machinery to free teachers for creative interaction. But we cannot develop new types of instructional situations without tying them to the requirements of the curriculum. It is the subject matter that will dictate what we are going to do.

chapter 4
Computer-Based Instruction and Curriculum Reform
Judson T. Shaplin

As a novice with respect to computer technology and to the possibilities of computer-assisted instruction, I approach these topics from my own interest in curriculum reform in the elementary and secondary schools and the reorganization of personnel that is required to accomplish it. The temptation of the novice is to concede all capability to the computer and to assume that all claims for it are justified. As a result of attending the AEDS-Stanford conference, my perspective has changed: it appears that the computer-assisted instruction effort faces all of the same persistent problems that have plagued other curriculum reform movements.

The beginnings of the effort are surrounded by a mystique of expertise and innovative power and by the creation of excessively negative images of present practice as a rationale for innovation—by what might be characterized as the "breakthrough complex." The demands of research and development lead the computer innovators to neglect the need for relating their work to existing practices in the mainstream of

36

American education, particularly recent reform efforts, and to ignore the implications of their work for personnel organization and training, all potent factors in future acceptance patterns. The innovative center is a curriculum and learning "laboratory," and the future problems of implementation and dissemination thus are largely neglected. The nature of the computer shapes the kinds of curriculum elements that can be selected and the processes of teaching that can be employed, raising a central question: "Do we want this type of selection and process to be central to the educational system or supplementary to it?" The innovators seem to assume centrality of function for the computer-assisted elements of instruction.

CURRICULUM REFORM

In this discussion of individualized computer-assisted instruction in relation to other curriculum developments, the primary concern will be with the policy and strategy of curriculum reform. Particularly the focus will be on the institutionalization of curriculum reform as a continuous, built-in process of revision and personnel development, eliminating the need for a major educational revolution every twenty years. Few signs of such institutionalization appear among the major curriculum reform efforts of the last fifteen years. Rather the pattern is typical of the diversity of American education, with competing systems, each of which is altered radically or "watered down" as it diffuses into the local educational systems and as accommodations are made to the prevailing practices of the schools.

The curriculum reforms of recent years, with the Physical Sciences Study Committee as an early and primary model, represent a new kind of organization for curriculum development. Leadership has been vested principally in teams of university subject-content specialists who have high renown in their fields. The programs have been located at universities or, if independent, within the sphere of university influence. Attention has been given to the full range of curriculum materials: curriculum guides and specific lesson plans; textbooks; supplementary reading materials; teachers' guides; and a wide variety of audiovisual materials, including films, film strips, transparencies, etc. Teachers, and occasionally teacher-trainers, are brought into the teams as experimental trials are made in the schools and as the materials are revised on the basis of experience. Often the professional societies of each particular subject field have provided the sponsorship.

The principal avenues of diffusion, apart from the development team and its associated schools, have been commercial publication and federally sponsored summer and academic-year institutes for teachers. Rarely have the projects undertaken to provide advanced training for future personnel to carry on the work. The amount of money available for these reform projects, from both federal sources and private foundations, has been massive compared with earlier efforts, but hardly sufficient for the work that needs to be done.

Meanwhile the massive teacher-training apparatus of the colleges and universities moves onward relatively untouched, with a few notable exceptions. Of the ninety institutions listed by the American Association of Colleges of Teacher Education as producing 400 or more new teachers a year (and some as many as 800, 1400, or 1600), few offer their prospective teachers the opportunity to study and analyze the new curriculum developments; few offer arrangements of content courses designed to facilitate understanding of curriculum developments; and only a minority offer practice teaching in situations where curriculum reforms are being implemented. It is rare indeed in the usual teacher-training program for the content specialists, curriculum specialists, field supervisors, and cooperating teachers in the schools to share common perspectives and ideologies about teaching. In only a few centers have advanced degree programs been provided which offer the combined elements of subject content, curriculum research and development, and field supervision and implementation. The shortage of such specialists has been one of the most persistent and tragic of the personnel shortages in American education for many years.*

At the Graduate Institute of Education at Washington University, we have been attempting to bridge the gap between curriculum analysis and practice in the schools, with particular reference to the social studies. Three years ago we started close to zero, with little or no relationship to national social-studies curriculum developments, and with routine instructional and practice arrangements. The first year was devoted to initial staff development and planning, including the preparation of grant requests. The second year was devoted to the development of new

---

* Suppose we want to have all the teacher-training institutions make sure that every teacher going out from an undergraduate curriculum has the ability to program instruction. Where are the teachers for that effort going to come from? Suppose we decide that more time ought to be spent on mathematical models for master schedule development. Where do the instructors come from? A good graduate program designed to produce them might be part of the industrial engineering department or the college of business administration. It would take a fairly large college of education with a rather unusual orientation to support this kind of staff.

curriculum courses for prospective elementary and secondary teachers, the systematic collection and analysis of plans and materials of some thirty-five national curriculum efforts, the development of close relationships with some of the most promising social-studies teachers in the area and the recruitment among them of members for a curriculum team. The improvement of practice-teaching arrangements with the schools and the sponsorship of a special summer seminar in curriculum analysis for experienced teachers of the area were also tasks of the second year.

The third year, with an augmented staff, saw the following activities:

1. Continuation of the curriculum center and its opening for use by school personnel as a study center.

2. The design and approval of a new master's level teacher-preparation program and of a doctoral social-studies curriculum research and development program, the successful application for federal fellowships for these and other programs, and the recruitment of students into the programs for the coming year.

3. The design and presentation of major grant applications to continue the work.

4. The design and initiation of a new elementary-school social-studies curriculum project based on concepts of political socialization, including first field trials in an urban school where arrangements had been made to conduct the experimental work.

5. A summer institute for St. Louis area elementary-school teachers of the disadvantaged in which experimental teaching of the new materials constituted a significant part of the training.

6. The holding of two metropolitan-area working conferences for school and university personnel to analyze significant social-studies curriculum projects.

During the fourth and current year, in addition to continuation of the activities just described, the following two elements will be added: the development of a field implementation center in one school system with six other school systems related to it, and the joint school-university implementation of a junior-high-school curriculum project. The approximate costs of this program, always operating on a marginal and risk basis, have been $3000 for the first year, $25,000 for the second year, $50,000 for the third year, and $90,000 to $120,000 for the current year depending on the success of grant applications.

In addition, of course, have been other expenses carried directly by the students, teachers, and school systems involved. These figures will illustrate the amount of financing necessary for a small regional effort to initiate curriculum development, disseminate and implement national efforts, improve teacher training, and provide advanced training in the context of school-university cooperation.

To my knowledge the only project in computer-assisted instruction that approaches other national curriculum-reform efforts in scale and scope of objectives is the work of the group at Stanford University, under Professors Suppes and Atkinson, in developing a computer program for teaching reading, mathematics, and logic at the elementary-school level. All the other instructional programs seem to be directed toward rather specialized problems of university training, such as graduate language or statistical requirements, far removed from central curriculum problems of the elementary and secondary schools. It would seem, therefore, that the "revolution" of computer-assisted instruction is just beginning.

A brief observation of the Stanford group also reveals the large cost of computer-assisted instruction as compared with other types of curriculum reform. In addition to the financing of the team assembled for writing the program, there is the cost of the computer equipment and the salaries of the many technicians required to keep this equipment operating and to advise on computer programming. It would appear that only a few of the major curriculum groups have had comparable access to funds. Yet the actual approach is applicable to only a small fraction of the total elementary-school curriculum. It is clear that the extension of research and development in computer-assisted instruction to other significant areas of the elementary and secondary school will require an enormous infusion of funds at a level only possible from federal sources. The scale of operations suggests that if significant advances are to be made quickly, then regional or national research and development laboratories with this focus alone will need to be established and sustained over a period of years. This view raises a series of important questions. How many such centers can we afford? Should there perhaps be monolithic, single efforts at development by subject fields, or can we continue the typical American pattern of multiple, competing centers? And what will be the role of private enterprise during this development period, particularly the new electronic-publishing complexes now being formed?

The team assembled by Professors Suppes and Atkinson is unusual in the curriculum field. It is a vital, highly motivated group of young people coming from the diverse fields of mathematics, mathematical statistics, psychology, and computer technology. The team is short, however, of high-level talent in the curriculum fields in which it is working. The laboratory is a training center with bright students from many programs, master's and doctoral, involved directly in the work. Direct connections with the regular departments of elementary-school curriculum and teacher training are not so apparent, nor are connections with other national efforts in elementary mathematics and reading. The focus is on the development work and not on the training of elementary-school mathematics and reading specialists. These statements are not made negatively, but merely to show that the pattern of the Stanford experiment is not directed toward long-term institutionalization of personnel training, nor toward curriculum development in its broader sense of dealing with the full range of programs required by the schools.

THE PROCESS OF TEACHING

All of the recent curriculum-reform groups have been concerned with the process of teaching as well as with the selection and ordering of content. In fact, a new "psychology of teaching" has emerged, as yet not fully rationalized in the parent discipline, based on such notions as the "discovery method," "inductive teaching," and "critical thinking," to mention a few. A variety of specific techniques of teaching and of aids to teaching have been built into the new curriculum products. In general this has been a boon to teacher-training programs where there is often a lack of coordination between courses in educational psychology, curriculum, principles or process of teaching, and applied classroom teaching.

In this area the possible contributions of computer-assisted instruction are clear and direct. The stress is on individual student progress, in logical, sequential steps, and on immediate reinforcement of learning. The direct lineage from the programmed-instruction movement and the reinforcement theory of learning is immediately apparent, with the computer program replacing the programmed text or teaching-machine program. In fact, the computer replaces the earlier concept of the teaching machine, providing infinitely more complex and promising possibilities.

But this approach is also highly selective. The stress is on encoding and decoding processes in sequential order. Much of the present curriculum is not amenable to such treatment; in fact, it is difficult to think of large segments of the elementary-school curriculum, other than in the areas of reading and arithmetic, which are subject to such an analysis except in a fragmentary way. Our present activity orientation in elementary science can hardly be programmed by computer. Neither are the oral language-development aspects of the language-arts programs, on which reading is so dependent, susceptible to computer treatment, since the handling of verbal responses is not yet within computer capacity. Activities in music and art provide further examples. Much of school learning is topical rather than progressive or sequential in nature, and individualized learning in such cases may be inefficient and uneconomical. Also we have long held goals of group learning, either for the social purpose of understanding how other people think and feel, or for the development of individual communication capacities with the group. The burden of proof is on the proponents of computer-assisted instruction to provide criteria of appropriateness in applying their methods as opposed to those of other types of instruction. Certain earlier protagonists of programmed instruction used to claim: "Tell me what your objectives are, and I will help you write a program." There is no need to follow that path again.

If some elements of a curriculum in a given subject are chosen for computer-assisted instruction, then the teaching of the remaining elements requires a change as well, adapted to the computer phase. Further, the amount of time that each pupil spends at a computer call station will be limited, and activities initiated by computer will need to have follow-up activities and materials away from the computer, either on an individual basis or in groupings by rate of progress. And, finally, there is the danger of unbalancing or distorting the instructional program by emphasizing the innovating elements and relegating other elements to a residual status or pushing them out altogether. All these factors need to be considered fully by curriculum-reform groups using computer technology.† The receiving schools will need a complete program in the given area, including the computer program, supplementary materials and audiovisual aids, revised programs and materials for noncomputer elements, textbooks, teachers' manuals, and recommended schedules and implementation plans.

† One problem for which there is concern is that of providing the potential user with the means to determine the applicability of a particular computer-based curriculum to his total instructional program. Often unstated assumptions embedded within a program may be at variance with the aims of the user. A reading program, for example, may contain material which, although adequate in terms of reading level or vocabulary, may express a value system contrary to that considered desirable by the user.

REORGANIZATION OF PERSONNEL

The introduction of computer-assisted instruction into the schools obviously has important implications for the type of school personnel needed and the way in which the school is to be organized. It is difficult to make predictions when we do not yet know how much of the school program will be handled by computers. If each child spends as much as an hour a day (in several short sessions) of a six-hour day, a minimum of 100 computer call stations will be required in a 600-pupil school. Will there be a central call-station area to which pupils are scheduled from peripheral classrooms, or will there be call-station areas adjacent to each classroom? The scheduling and movement of pupils will be complicated, since they must be drawn from and return to some type of activity.

Teacher roles probably will tend to become more specialized in such a program. Individualized progress by pupils places a heavier demand for knowledge and flexibility on the teacher, and the computer programs will require a more technical knowledge of the subject in order for the teacher to be able to assist the pupils and carry on with supplemental materials. In turn, teachers of noncomputer elements will have to be specialists in those areas. This will probably lead to complicated patterns of team organization and complex scheduling of both pupils and teachers and will require retraining of supervisors and principals to handle the new arrangements. Plans for training personnel and for suitable organizational patterns need to be developed well in advance of any program of dissemination.‡

We can sympathize with the investigator who says: "This is a learning laboratory. We don't have enough time as it is to carry out experiments on how children learn through computer programs, much less the time to worry about the total curriculum, the training of personnel, and school organization plans." The demands of the work are clear. Future success in dissemination and implementation of the programs in the schools, however, will depend substantially on the degree to which the issues raised here are met.

‡ First we are faced with the problem of training the professor of education to have a new orientation. It is a bootstrap operation: we want to train both the professors of education and the teachers. To do it, we need a concentrated college-level effort and an environment in which the teachers will feel comfortable.

*The educators came to the computer engineers and talked about
flexible scheduling and new methods of nongraded instruction. They
said, "This is what we would like to do to educate students better
Can you do it for us?" But now how do we take these computer-
supported systems, house them in a building, and get the staff to do
the teaching? What about putting all this into 25,000 school districts?*

chapter 5
Systems Planning for Implementation of Change
C. West Churchman

During 1965 I attended several conferences on the introduction of
operations research and computer technology in a variety of areas:
health, law, information processing, industry, space sciences programs,
defense, and so on. In every one of those conferences, many of the same
remarks were made. The constant theme that we are not getting ahead
fast enough often was countered by the theme that, after all, we have
not been doing it very long. There was the cry that implementation is
the most pressing and the most difficult problem, the one about which
we know the least.

In operations research there is much speculation about the total
amount of effort that the researcher spends in three areas: (1) the area
of technology, which here involves the application of computer know-
how to the educational system; (2) the area of problem formulation
and data gathering; and (3) the area of implementation and evaluation. If percentage figures were assigned to the amount of time researchers spend on these, it would turn out that about 1 per cent of the time

44

is spent on technology, perhaps 20 percent on formulation and information gathering, and the rest on implementation and evaluation. The difficulties of implementing certain technological innovations may be well beyond the intellectual capabilities of the human race today.

If we are to worry about the technology of flexible school systems, individualized computer-based education, and so on, the worry should focus on whether there has been sufficient exploration of alternatives. There is often considerable danger of excessive enthusiasm about one technological plan because we know so much more about one plan than about others that may be cheaper and far more feasible. In this stage of the technology of systems design, when we try to review alternative techniques, we constantly encounter the question: what is the system trying to accomplish? The question often forces us to abandon a whole line of attack because we come to realize that we have been concentrating on an alternative that has led us to believe in the existence of certain objectives. In other words, the objectives have been defined by the technique.* Of course, there is always an interplay between alternative strategies and goals, but it is important to begin by establishing objectives.

It is well worth looking, for example, at the teaching of grammar in terms of teaching students to teach, as well as teaching them to learn materials. A great deal might be done with computer-based instruction in getting students really interested in teaching not only themselves but also other students. If that avenue of attack is sensible, it opens up a new set of alternative designs in computer-based instruction.†

In the area of problem formulation and information gathering, we are entering an era of technological change in which the Congress and managers at all levels—federal, state, local; presidents of universities and school principals—will not only have the right to ask for cost effectiveness analysis but will have techniques for raising their questions in

---

* We are in danger of becoming so intrigued with the idea of computer-based instruction that we set as our goal the teaching of something with a computer, whether or not that is the best way to teach it. If we are able to devise a program that works for the computer, we are happy. But we do not want to find ourselves looking for computer applications just for the sake of it, or because everyone else is doing it. We must seek alternatives and do more in the way of cost-effectiveness studies.

† One important factor is to reward achievement—particularly for the students who might be called sit-ins: the ones who have not dropped out but are no more than physically there every day. As part of an effort to provide learning environments in which they can succeed, we have a program of cadet teaching. Some not very good students can help younger ones to read or spell. What is important is to help these students develop an individual sense of dignity and worth.

more specific form. Individualized instruction is a good idea. It may well do all kinds of things much more effectively than the standardized classroom policy now operating in so many of our schools. But administrators and those concerned with funds are correct in asking whether a particular implementation might mean the sacrifice of some other important social values.‡ It is time to begin talking about how to measure the cost as well as the effectiveness of the new systems being proposed. In both of these contexts we must think of alternative strategies and ways of determining what information is relevant. Many of our studies have waited too long to raise these basic questions—often much too long to do an effective job.§

What about implementation? This is probably the most pressing problem we face as a society today. The idea of an interrelationship between the real world and the research laboratory is excellent. The School of Business Administration of the University of California at Berkeley attempts to send the researchers and the students out to do jobs in industrial firms, government agencies, and the like. In the meantime, basic research is going on in the laboratory. That kind of connection is absolutely essential. It is also essential to understand the problems of the real-life organization, many of which go beyond research questions.

Several kinds of resistance that are not well understood are likely to occur. They may be called stubborn, ignorant resistances on the part of managers, but their psychological roots are deep. A fundamental suspicion exists about computer technology and mathematical technology applied to management. In some sense the suspicion is justified because the technology has many implications that are not well understood, and can only begin to be understood in the context of the much larger system in which technological advances are imbedded.

There is no centralized decision maker in the educational system, nor should there be one; the idea of a central decision-making agency is a myth. In an experiment at Berkeley in which subjects tried to per-

---

‡ Educators must consider the applications of computers to their world with the purpose of setting up a structure for decision making, so that they can tell the computer manufacturer, "This is the way we want to do it, for these reasons. . . ." So far we in education have been reluctant to do this.

§ We need systems analysis and a cost analysis of what computer-assisted instruction is. What are the real costs involved? At this point terminals seem much more costly than computers, and the real problems are with terminal and communication systems. Even with time sharing, the big cost is not 2000 pupils sharing a computer, but $5000 a student station, or whatever the cost is. Before we can implement, we need a better idea of such costs.

form a task, decision making was found to be so dispersed that it was impossible to introduce any very logical kind of technical progress. The individuals involved were told to maximize profit. After they became accustomed to the roles assigned to them, one member of the group tried to implement a solution. He knew the answer because he was one of the stooges that psychologists like to introduce into situations of this kind. His job actually was to try to introduce computerized technology into the activities of this organization. It took only about two hours for the experimenters to get the decision making so sifted into the organization that it could not make progress.

I do not mean to be discouraging about implementation, but it is important that we discuss as much as possible the realities of the im-plementation phase.

Regarding the evaluation of individualized instruction, a good prin-ciple in system design is to ask where the particular system under study is imbedded and what effect an improvement of that segment of the system will have on the rest. The freeways are a good example. They were marvelous inventions for moving people quickly from place to place; they were hopelessly bad in their initial phase when they dumped people out into the larger system. What they did was simply to create enormous traffic jams at the points of interaction with the larger system.

Similarly, in education many of the students who are going through grammar-school and high-school individualized instruction will be dumped into the freshman and sophomore years of our universities. It does not take much research to establish that individualized instruction does not occur in those years. It may be that people in higher education should apply themselves to changing this situation. But meanwhile some attention should be given to the problems of the student who emerges from individualized instruction into further conventional edu-cation and a subsequent career.||

Finally, it should be noted that there is a difference between the statement of objectives and the statement of tasks. Over and over again, people working in system design observe that the inhabitants of systems like to state objectives but that there is a vast distance between objec-tives and tasks. Eventually system objectives have to be specified in

|| What is the effect on later educational procedures of having computer-assisted instruction in the primary grades? Are we changing students so much that we raise a whole host of problems about how to handle them in fourth, fifth, sixth grade? This can ripple into a big wave of reconstruction right through to college. We can-not start something that has any revolutionary impact anywhere in the system with-out affecting the whole.

operational and specific terms. In discussing educational reform, for instance, someone will say that it is important that the students know how to communicate, to write good English. This is translated into the task of teaching good English, which becomes English I, which is given to all freshman students. It is an easy transfer from the obvious objective to the rather less than obvious statement of task, and this applies in any area of education. We have to begin to learn how to make that transition from the general objective to the specific task statement. One of the most encouraging things about attempts at individualizing instruction is that in this area we may be able to make the translation in a far more specific way than ever before. We will be forced into saying a great deal more and making far better judgments about the objectives of our educational system and about the differences between general and specific education.⟨

⟨ Two broad kinds of questions constantly plague us in evaluation. One is the problem of determining whether one or another educational innovation, one or another instructional package, one or another system is superior. The other is the problem of whether, within a particular system or method, we actually accomplish what we say we are accomplishing, and how well we do it.

part 2
Computers in Instruction and Research

When we talk about individualizing instruction, we are talking about the interaction between a child, some material, a teacher, and a facility at a given second. This is the smallest unit, and a series of these with a number of children in corresponding circumstances pose the scheduling problem. We must think of the schedule as something derived not for administrative purposes but for learning purposes on the part of the youngster, keeping in mind his interactions with the material, the teacher, and the facility.

chapter 6

Computer-Built Schedules and Educational Innovation
Dwight W. Allen

The traditional arrangement of the teaching day has long frustrated even the most daring of educators. It would be interesting to know how many worthwhile ideas for innovation have withered because they "can't be scheduled."

As schools become larger, manual scheduling becomes an increasingly formidable task, even for routine instructional programs. Imagine the difficulties inherent in individualizing instruction: the possible combinations of staff, facilities required, sequence and length of instructional sessions, variations in the grouping of students, and size of the instruction groups would be overwhelming. Examination of the possible combinations for simple instructional systems would take years even for the most sophisticated computer system now available.

Although computers have proved useful for data processing in the schools, most people discounted the feasibility of programming the intricacies of a master schedule even as recently as five years ago. It was assumed that the assembly of a master schedule, to include all the vari-

51

ables and the staff decisions, was too complex and subtle a problem. Nevertheless a few experimenters believed that master scheduling could be organized by a computer.

Two groups succeeded in devising scheduling systems that were used for the first time during the 1964–65 school year: the Stanford group, Robert V. Oakford, Robert N. Bush, and Dwight W. Allen, which developed the Stanford School-Scheduling System (SSSS), and the M.I.T. group, under Robert Holz, which produced the Generalized Academic Simulation Program (GASP). Both of these programs generate master schedules that allow, and even encourage, curricular innovation. And the freedom to schedule alternatives asks the educator to reexamine his school's objectives, the goals of individual courses, and the overall organization of his instructional program. Therefore the real mission of these computer systems is not just to weave the curriculum, staff, students, and facilities into a whole, but to challenge old patterns and methods by providing alternatives that can range over a far greater curricular, methodological, and administrative spectrum. And finally the construction of such schedules offers the benefit of straightforward and less complicated data-processing procedures related to the school schedule.*

STUDENT-ASSIGNMENT PROGRAMS

Data processing, which now serves many educational functions, entered educational institutions unobtrusively as an adjunct to the business offices of school districts, saving clerical manhours and putting payrolls on time. After a while educators saw that a computer-based student-record system would not only lessen the teachers' nonprofessional tasks, but could also provide easier retrieval of the information needed for decisions concerning the program of instruction. In many school districts the familiar report card was replaced by the computer print-out sheet. Test scores, attendance data, health records, and other information about individual students was transferred to tapes for storage. Such developments made information available so that school schedules could

---

* The computer should be used to generate schedules that are more flexible, what we might call variable-course structures. It is not necessary to teach physics the same way we teach chemistry, and art may be taught in a different manner altogether. But even in a conventional school program, to schedule by hand a school that has 800 students can take 5000 manhours. Few administrators are interested in investing that amount of time for the rewards that are gained.

eventually be influenced and changed. The California Department of Education, through the efforts of Dr. Alvin Grossman, has pioneered the application of data processing in education, and the University of Iowa developed an electronic system for student records which has been adopted for use throughout the state.

School counselors, as they became more familiar with possibilities for data processing, sought a system that would relieve them of the tedious job of placing students in the master schedule. To meet this problem, a variety of student-assignment programs were developed. These programs assign students to previously developed master schedules, and are distinct from master-schedule-construction programs (such as GASP and SSSS) which build the master schedule in addition to assigning students within it.

There are a number of good commercial student-assignment programs now in use (many of them improperly called school-scheduling programs). IBM presently has five student-assignment programs available; two for the 1440, "CLASS" for the 7040, "STUDENT" for the 1620, a modification of the "GASP" for the 7090. One part of Stanford's scheduling system, called SAP, can be used for student assignment. Although programs are extensively in use throughout the United States, the number is unknown. McDonnell Automation Center of St. Louis has worked with over fifty schools accommodating approximately 100,000 secondary-school students. Memphis School District used the IBM "STUDENT" program for the 1620 to assign 40,000 secondary-school students into classes. Service Bureau Corporation's student-assignment program is in nationwide use. The University of Iowa used "UPDATE," a revision of IBM "CLASS," to carry 50,000 students. Purdue University's assignment program is being used partially or totally by the universities of Illinois, Massachusetts, South Carolina, and Seattle. New England Educational Data Systems (NEEDS), a cooperative research and development organization, uses its program to serve fifty-two secondary schools.

NEW DEVELOPMENTS IN MASTER SCHEDULING

Most student-assignment programs, in addition to placing students, provide services that facilitate the manual construction of the master schedule. These include course tallies by sex and grade level, a course-conflict matrix, and class lists for courses with subminimal enrollments. These programs have proved satisfactory; the schedule is still built, however, within the limitation of conventional time patterns, since the main purpose was to speed up current practices, not to develop new programs.

In the early 1950's educators began to question seriously the use of time in the curriculum. The need for assistance in the problems of scheduling large groups, small groups, laboratory, and individual study was acute. Educational theory was far ahead of administrative procedure. A number of alternatives were made routinely possible only through the use of computer scheduling: for example, large and small classes, long and short classes, modular curriculum units, new combinations of staff, more intense use of facilities, the addition of independent study periods, nonstandard courses (longer or shorter than a standard semester, with more or less than the now-standard five hours a week of instruction), a wider variation in the number of classes each student can take, and so forth.

Two separate projects were begun which used the computer to solve the problem of generating school schedules. M.I.T.'s Generalized Academic Simulation Program is based on a pragmatic solution. This means that the generation of the schedule is derived from successive computer runs, each run being updated or revised through human analysis of the previous run. This process is repeated (ten to twenty times) until a satisfactory schedule is created.† The Stanford School Scheduling System is based on Oakford's algorithmic solution, allowing for more preprogrammed decision making in the computer system. Scheduling effectiveness is here a function of the system's algorithms. It assumes that the components of the scheduling problem can be accurately and sequentially defined in sufficient detail to program the computer. This assumption has been satisfactorily validated in field trials. Acceptable schedules are usually obtained in three or fewer computer runs. Although the algorithmic solution is somewhat more sophisticated than the

---

† When we schedule courses, we take basic subjects first and electives last, trying to take care of as many students as possible. When our solution satisfies 99 per cent, we know we have done almost as well as is possible to do. When the solution we arrive at satisfies 91 percent of the course requests, virtually every student in the school has to change his schedule or course requests in some way. Then we do not know whether we have done almost as well as we could or not. It may be that if we come out with 91 per cent, 100 per cent is not possible. But one problem about using heuristic methods is that we do not know what the trade-offs are. The number of course requests satisfied may be too low; the principal will say, "I can't live with this schedule." Then the school consultants start looking for ways to modify course structures, increase the amount of independent study, and so on, to loosen up the scheduling problem and satisfy a larger percentage of course requests. When the chips are down, these course requests are what must be satisfied.

pragmatic approach, the basic requirements of the two systems are comparable. The algorithmic solution, however, can service more schools at less cost. Theoretically, as algorithms are improved, the efficiency of SSSS should improve.

Both GASP and SSSS have been used in recent years, and both have been refined. In the spring and summer of 1965, GASP was used to schedule twenty-five high schools. Nine in the New England states used the 7094 at M.I.T., ten used the 7094 system at the University of Chicago, one Memphis high school used the 7090 at the University of Georgia, one high school in Spokane, Washington, used the 7090 at Washington State University, and McDonnell Automation Center (of St. Louis and Denver) used their adaptation of GASP to schedule three Colorado high schools. The University of Indiana used its own version to schedule several Indiana schools. In addition, GASP has been used as a research tool to study school facility needs.

Thirty-three schedules now in use were constructed at the Stanford Computer Center using SSSS. Twenty-six of these schedules, involving approximately 25,000 students, were used for a complex modular design or flexible schedule. Eleven of the schools were in California, six in Oregon, four in Nevada, four in Colorado, two in Arizona, and one each in Utah, Michigan, Iowa, Arkansas, and Pennsylvania, as well as Yamato High School, an Air Force Dependents school in Tokyo. SSSS was also used for a number of simulation studies to examine the effects of different combinations of resources on scheduling efficiency.

Extensive field tests have been valuable for the development and refinement of master-scheduling efforts. Refinement of the SSSS will illustrate this process. Feedback from real situations is a major source of ideas for adjusting algorithms and streamlining input and output requirements. This feedback further assures that educational needs will be held paramount in the system's refinement. In addition to expanding nearly all of the basic input parameters, several peripheral services have been added to the system. The input parameters for SSSS will presently allow almost any feasible educational design for any high school up to 3500 students (this limit can also be expanded). Success in any computer system depends, however, on valid input; often the more complex the system, the more complex the input and, consequently, the more opportunity for human error. To solve this acute problem with scheduling data, a special auditing program has been written to check and flag over one hundred possible logical and clerical errors. This procedure has proved valuable in assuring valid input data; further, it has saved hundreds of hours of manual analysis and correction searches. Even more important, this data-auditing procedure provides a complete analysis of the input requests, enabling the scheduling consultant to predict major problems and potential success prior to actual generation of the schedule. Thousands of dollars have already been saved by avoiding needless computer runs. Other programs have been developed to fill school needs: one will schedule free student time back with selected teachers for specified periods of time, thus allowing the school administrator to gain different levels of control for selected students and courses; another program is available that will delete dropped students and schedule new students or change student schedules, and so prepare accurate and updated schedules for smoother school openings.

Most of the school principals in the Stanford project have participated in the annual feedback conferences, and have contributed to the refinement efforts for the 1966 model of SSSS. The key to the SSSS refinement process is to maintain a strong commitment toward the educational needs of schools.

Other groups are developing scheduling programs. Memphis city schools have used the 1401 for several years to assist in the construction of schedules for traditional schools. IBM is assisting the Brookhurst Junior High School in Los Angeles to automate its daily scheduling plans. Here the schedule is changed by teacher request each day, and students are rescheduled. System Development Corporation has developed and published a schedule construction manual. For several years Holtzman at the University of Pittsburgh has also been conducting research on the scheduling problem. He reports having used his system to build two successful school schedules in the spring of 1966. Blakesley at Purdue has developed a schedule-building program for universities which has been successfully applied at Purdue, Seattle, and several other major institutions.

WIDER IMPLICATIONS OF COMPUTER TECHNOLOGY

Future opportunities for improvement and development of school-scheduling programs will probably come from two distinct though related areas: theory and technology, and continued pragmatic educational application. Certainly the power potential in the development of new machines with disc storage and random access will increase storage capacity and the speed of processing data. Also, improvements are being made in accessory equipment, such as optical scanners, audio-input systems and telecomputer lines. Concurrent with this improvement in hardware is a phenomenal growth and refinement in machine- and scientific-programming languages. These advances in technology will positively affect school scheduling in at least four ways, by reducing costs, reducing communication errors, increasing capacity to cope with complex variables, and giving easier access to computers, thus allowing more widespread usage. Furthermore, recent work of Robert V. Oakford in the Stanford Study suggests that there may eventually be a mathematical solution for optimum scheduling for a given set of requirements.

Finally, there is the opportunity for educators to use computer-scheduling technology for innovation. One of the most promising approaches is the development of curriculum-simulation studies. Simulation allows the rapid examination of key theoretical and functional questions; therefore it may well be more important than the basic service of real schedule construction.

Engineers have long used the simulated model to test solutions for complex problems. The technical problems encountered in the construction of the Golden Gate Bridge and Grand Coulee Dam have been successfully solved by research models. In the case of San Francisco Bay, tide cycles can be simulated in minutes, data can be collected by automatic measuring devices, observations that would take weeks or years in the real situation can be made in minutes: consequently a wide variety of alternatives can be tested and a valuable resource is being more precisely managed.

Adjustments in curricular cycles in actual schools are painfully slow, made at best in annual or semester intervals. Few mechanical systems are as problematic as our mass-educational process. Not all of its aspects can be simulated, but some can be programmed for simulation models, even now. Modular programs can be tested and interaction effects can be determined in advance of actual field trial. The use of computer-simulated models to solve even a small portion of the complex problems facing educators without direct danger to students, or to professional careers, would be an important contribution. Reduction in the time lag between the invention of new elements in instructional systems and their implementation is an interesting potentiality. A curriculum-simulation study would encompass two basic concepts: first, the opportunity to simulate some specific alternatives related to a local context; and second, the involvement and commitment of a professional staff in developing and pretesting such alternatives.

Curriculum-simulation study techniques allow the local staff to manipulate the variables involved in the design of a school. Curriculum alternatives can be generated for a general revision of the instructional program or for narrowly limited or specialized proposals. Alternatives simulated within the local context allow for extensive preanalysis of needs and costs of facilities. Solutions would be available for major questions: Can the curriculum be expanded? How will suggested changes affect teacher load? How can our present facilities be best used in a particular program? What new facilities will be needed if a new plan is adopted? What will be the cost of an alternative program? What is the best use of a particular combination of available resources? What is the best combination of resources for given program objectives within the limitation of budget, staff, or facility?

If a new curriculum and the changes it entails could be pretested before final commitment by a school, much anxiety and resistance to change might be alleviated. Through computer-simulation experience, research and technology can be focused on a more complete analysis of the implications of innovation; for success or failure in implementing change depends on staff attitudes, commitment, and skill, as well as on technological advances. It is axiomatic that little impact results from a change in structure and the use of time without a simultaneous change in teaching methods and attitudes—and in the content of the curriculum. No organizational change can ever replace the importance of what is taught, but what is taught can be greatly enhanced, limited, or eliminated by organizational demands on the people involved.

Substantial improvement of instruction has already been demonstrated to be possible through computer-built school schedules, but the range of alternatives currently implemented or even suggested is paltry and even irrelevant to the development of computer-created organizational patterns and the evolution of innovations suggested by an intensive program of curriculum simulation.

The result of such effort may be a program of research and development more sensitive to the progress of each individual student. The promise of computer technology is that the automation of planning for instructional systems could lead to the better education of each individual student.

What information can be identified as being helpful and meaningful to a particular pupil? What relevant data, for example, could be fed back to the student on his rate of progress or learning performance in comparison with his peers? What can the computer do to help interpret the broad data for the pupil? What kinds of statements can generate something usable about these data and how can they best be displayed to the child? And, to close the loop, can the computer help us in any way measure what action or reaction comes from the child as a result? Can we feed this back into the system to modify the basic educational program?

chapter 7

Applications of Computer Technology to the Improvement of Learning [1]
Don D. Bushnell

A decade ago a survey of computer applications to curriculum research and applied instructional programs would have produced very little information of importance. Today the on-line use of the computer for teaching mathematics, the sciences, and related subjects is burgeoning at all levels of education: elementary, secondary, and university. More significantly, and only within the past five years, digital computers have become important tools for educational research and development. The computer has facilitated new developments in the following six areas:

1. Simulating learning environments for gaming purposes and for the improvement of educational administration.

2. Automating information-retrieval sources.

[1] This material is a summary of a report prepared for the National Commission on Automation, Technology, and Economic Progress. Washington, D.C., February 1966.

59

3. Assisting in the preparation and evaluation of instructional materials.

4. Integrating instructional media (film, tape, television display, and text) for both group and individual instruction.

5. Applying the power of the computer to massive data collection, controlled observation, and analysis for the study of instructor-learner interactions.

6. Decentralizing the educational system by bringing remote-control educational resources into the home, study carrel, community library, or faculty office.

The challenging reality of individual differences, an exploding curriculum, and the pressure of time and numbers make the uses of modern information-processing technology essential if the goal of education for all Americans is to be achieved. Data problems are woven through the whole fabric of educational processes. *Empirical* data are lacking, however, primarily in the area of instruction. The computer may help to bring the study of this learning process within manageable bounds. Perhaps the day is not too far off when good teaching may become a science as well as an art.

SIMULATION AND GAMING: NEW TOOLS FOR EDUCATION

Computers imitate the real world by processing information as though it were representative of real events. For example, radar operators have been trained in simulated radar centers with no antennas, a computer supplying the input to the instruments. School administrators have been trained by computers that presented them with imaginary though realistic school situations and asked them to solve daily problems of scheduling, budget, allocation of space, modification of curriculum, or public relations (37). Sixth-grade history students have been taught by a computer which presents the student with information related to the economic well-being of an ancient city state for which the student is playing the role of king (115). He is told how much grain has been planted, how many mouths he has to feed, and what the result would be of keeping some proportion of the grain for seed. The student makes certain decisions regarding his city state—often with disastrous results because of the effect of unanticipated natural events cycled in randomly by the computer.

Computer simulation of any system (that is, any ongoing complex of events) has important advantages over observation of the natural events themselves. Time may be speeded up or slowed down. In comparison with traditional instruction through lectures and textbooks, simulation brings a sense of immediacy to the learning task and may be considerably more realistic—thereby challenging the student to participate more actively. The student may learn to deal with systems far more complex than any he could learn to describe accurately in the same amount of time.*

There seem to be no inherent obstacles to the application of computer-simulated instruction to any age group from preschool to senior citizen or to any socioeconomic group from the Harvard Business School graduate student to the Job Corps trainee.

INSTRUCTION OF THE DISADVANTAGED STUDENT

New possibilities for rescuing intellectually and socially underdeveloped persons are evident in artificial instructional environments.

School dropouts are often defeated by traditional educational practices. New learning environments must provide frequent opportunities for success, active and individualized curriculum programs with immediate relevance to the life of the student, and increased peer-group interaction. Gaming techniques offer many of the combinations essential to reaching the disadvantaged student.

The greatest problem is motivation. Nonstudents have given up; they are discouraged or hostile, or simply do not see the immediate relevance of public-school education to the lives they expect to lead. They do not know how to relate to teachers, whom they see as judges who will inevitably "put them down." They seek approval not from adults but from their peers, often from a particular subculture whose values are largely incompatible with success in the larger social and economic world.

---

* To ensure transfer from the training situation to the real-life task requiring the student to perform and use what he has learned, the interface must be designed to approximate the requirements of the real-life task environment. For example, if one is teaching a student to operate a lathe, the visible analogs or controls that the student will be required to manipulate on the lathe probably will be used as an interface device in the training environment. This will ensure transfer of training to the operational task for which the training was designed. The question remains, however, as to how much of the real world one must replicate to ensure good transfer.

Nevertheless these young people have motives. They like the approval of the group, they like to compete in situations where they can win, they like to succeed. They will talk about and participate in things that seem relevant to their own lives. They enjoy being in situations in which discipline does not seem to come from outside or from older authorities or from members of social groups whom they hold suspect. They like to do what they like to do and not what somebody else wants them to do. In truth, most students, urban or suburban, have similar motives. The problem seems to be to set up a learning situation in which these motives can be gratified for the disadvantaged student to the same degree that they are gratified for a National Merit Scholar. We should not be surprised that the situations would have to be quite different for each of the two.

A particular kind of simulation, usually referred to as a game, promises to go a long way toward solving this problem.

In a computer game the student is presented with information about some situation and asked to make decisions. His decisions are fed back into the system and result in a new set of facts, the consequences of his good or bad decisions, about which he must then make new decisions. Certain random natural events can be made to operate in the environment causing the game player to consider a variety of factors in his decision making, as in the Sumerian Game developed by the Board of Cooperative Educational Services (BOCES) in Westchester County, New York (180).

Games offer the following benefits (44) to disadvantaged students:

1. They can be made wholly relevant to the lives of the students as the students see their own lives.

2. They can include competition among teams or between individual player and computer to any desired degree, a condition that tends to increase interest to the point of enthusiasm.

3. They are student-centered and do not involve direction by an authority figure who might be resented. Direction comes from the computer, which is an impersonal machine.

4. The teacher acts as an ally of the student, helping him to play the game so as to have the best chance of winning, just as a football coach is primarily a helper and only secondarily an instructor. Thus old negative patterns of pupil-teacher interaction may be avoided.

5. Approval is largely or wholly from teammates, who are peers.

6. Cooperation is necessary in team play and is a natural consequence of the desire to win. Discipline does not need to be enforced from outside in such a situation. Discipline is self-imposed by having to play by the rules.

7. If appropriate, real rewards such as money may be given for success in playing. Some authorities have advocated paying such students for learning. In a computer game, determination of how much to pay each student would seem quite fair and objective to the student.

8. The games may take up almost any problem area from those with strictly intellectual or mechanical content to those involving interpersonal relations. A game called the Family Game has a great deal in common with family counseling and could have a therapeutic effect on students whose family relationships are disturbed to some degree, as indeed many may be expected to be.

9. A great deal of factual knowledge can be gained from playing the game as well as from the requirement to marshal one's facts before entering the fray.

In the Career Game, developed in the Department of Social Relations at Johns Hopkins University (44), teams of girls are given information about a fictitious but realistic girl of 17. The players must decide what her life goals shall be, indicating the relative importance to her of marriage, children, occupation, personal development, and family standard of living. They then must decide about specific opportunities to fulfill these goals: when and whom to marry, how soon to have a child, how many children, whether to get a job, what kind of job to try for, whether to get additional education, and so on. In making these decisions the players use various resources ranging from a table showing how much time certain activities take to extensive information about training requirements, competition, and remuneration for various occupations.

After each set of decisions the players receive results indicating how well the woman is doing at achieving her goals and introducing certain events (whose occurrence is based on statistical tables) such as the birth of a child or success or failure at obtaining a certain job. A game may include ten decision periods, which take the woman to age 50.

Games developed at Johns Hopkins University, Washington University, and within the IBM Corporation, run the gamut from a family game, a school board game, democracy games, to games that impart specifics of scientific subject matter (44).

SIMULATION IN TRAINING SCHOOL ADMINISTRATORS

At a very much higher level of ability and educational achievement, computer gaming may be used to train school administrators or, indeed, to train any high-level decision maker. A famous example of such high-level training is the Carnegie Institute Management Game. Simulation studies for training and evaluating educational administrators have been carried out under the sponsorship of the University Council for Educational Administration (37). By using such in-basket techniques as memoranda, telegrams, and urgent reports, increasing amounts of stress are applied to administrators operating in the simulated environment. Those who have experienced the simulated situations feel that the simulated materials hold promise for evaluating and selecting new school administrators.

School simulation, which may range from the simulation of individual students to whole school districts or the total educational facilities of a state, offers special advantages to experienced professional people in updating their theoretical and practical backgrounds. (There is some reluctance on the part of busy administrators whose jobs provide well-deserved prestige to assume the role of the student and submit to "retreading.") Management or administration games, particularly when mediated by computers, represent a productive application of advanced technology well worth the administrator's time.

SIMULATION IN THE OPERATION OF SCHOOL SYSTEMS

It is a short step from the training of administrators to the use of simulation for the actual operation of school systems. There is no inherent limit on the amount of factual, valid information about the real world which may be fed into a simulation. The simulation that begins as a training exercise may grow into an analysis of an actual school system and, through repetitive cycling and correction, may come to serve as an accurate predictor of events in the real system.

This highly valid simulation may be used in two ways: to aid in operating the system as it is, and to try out modifications of the system in simulated form before having to make real policy and fiscal changes. Operation, modification, and scientific study of school systems (or government or management or military systems, for that matter) may be seen potentially to coexist, the lines between them becoming harder to draw.

Besides doing clerical chores in a rapid and errorless manner, computers may provide pictures of new roles for school personnel, modified interactions between teacher and pupil or between pupils, new ways to use school data, better ways to use existing or new space, or characteristics of graduating students (age, homogeneity, degree of achievement, quality of achievement) following modifications of the system (208).

In the area of administrative decision making, the application of heuristic or Bayesian procedures in support of the decision-making functions of the superintendent or school principal should find ready acceptance among educational administrators. Models could be used in the determination of short- and long-term objectives. Choices could be made in the selection of various alternative criteria for approaching the issuance of bonds or the planning of a building program. By storing the subjective biases of school board members or other decision makers in the community in a data bank, the superintendent could call on these decision functions to set a strategy for floating a bond issue or making other relevant decisions.

Predicting manpower availability by utilizing a skills bank of human capital would enable the administrator to plan for expanding programs. Alternative choices could be based on a data bank of standardized information or, if hard data were not available, on simulation procedures. Thus the development of models for simulation could result in maximum benefit to the administrator and the school system.

THE INFORMATION UTILITY OR CENTRAL DATA BANK

Two major applied programs and several research centers are exploring the feasibility of establishing a central data bank or "information utility" for servicing all the various needs of subsystems within educational institutions. In an educational system, one data bank might serve the needs of the administrator, teacher, counselor, curriculum developer, and student. For instance, in automated classrooms like those at Stanford University, students carrying on independent study with programmed materials leave a detailed record of their learning experience (164). These records are stored in the central computer facility. In the operation of tomorrow's schools, information thus stored would be potentially of interest to the counselor, for it reveals each student's up-to-the-minute learning problems. The curriculum programmer would have summary data covering the learning experiences of students for specific curriculum evaluation and modification. Teachers will have up-to-the-minute accounts of each student's information-need profile and thus can be guided in selecting special materials intended to meet some of the student's learning needs. In the ongoing school program, the rate of progress of the individual learner is potentially of vital interest to the administrator who will have a need to monitor and schedule individual study programs in the individualized, nongraded school system environment.†

APPLIED RESEARCH PROGRAMS UTILIZING THE DATA BANK

Project TALENT, as administered by the offices of the American Institute of Research and supported under grants from the U.S. Office of Education, is the first major effort to establish a data bank in the field of education. Although this file of data originally was conceived for research uses, it provides a longitudinal study or inventory of student abilities and achievements that could help determine in a very practical manner the effectiveness of many educational programs. As now projected in the long-range objectives of the program, the data bank will be used to aid educators and researchers in setting standards for educational and psychological measurement, helping to determine the initial state and/or aptitude of the student as the learner enters the instructional program, and establishing measures for better prediction of success through learning. For these purposes an updating record of more than 440,000 students will be maintained on magnetic tape for a twenty-year period.

The Bureau of Data Processing within the Chicago Public Schools maintains a "Total Information Service" which feeds data into six areas: (1) budget and finance, (2) personnel and payroll, (3) materials, (4) student accounting and scheduling, (5) research, and (6) computer education (30). It is this latter development that will eventually support the teacher in the classroom through on-line data displays. Tapping the central information file, instructors have at their fingertips most of the relevant information from the cumulative record file. Because data are so convenient, it is expected that teachers in the Chicago city schools

† The affective data that we have in storage may be a lot more interesting and more relevant to learning problems than cognitive data for planning the students' future courses, troubleshooting, developing courses of instruction that meet particular emotional needs, or developing feedback mechanisms that fit particular patterns of learning.

will make productive use of them to acquire a better understanding of their students' day-to-day learning needs and cyclical patterns.‡

INFORMATION-RETRIEVAL RESEARCH

The potential range of applications of a central information utility extends well beyond those already mentioned. Through the use of remote consoles, it includes decentralized instructional systems for the home (as in Columbia City, described on page 74). Joint utilization of identical data files for research and planning and student as well as faculty instruction becomes possible. Library and language-lab services can become centralized; decentralized networks of listening posts for musical or stenographic training are also a possibility.

It is not mere speculation to anticipate the day when information acquired during the operation of the central information-processing service feeds directly into decision mechanisms that regulate the scheduling and instructional programs of the educational institution.

Extrapolating from present trends in information retrieval, it is possible to envision some of the characteristics of advanced educational systems of the 1970's. Describing futuristic school systems in this manner will serve to point up current research and developments in the information-retrieval field.

The specialized information center for local school systems will be linked by data transmission lines to regional information centers. These centers translate and select items of information for automatic indexing, abstracting, and coding into magnetic tape files for subsequent feeding to a number of school systems. These central archives will gather from high-utility sources such information as reports of experimental and test results, technical publications, patents, doctoral dissertations, government reports, and so on. Archives will employ subject-matter specialists for locating and weighing the importance of incoming documental materials in specific subject areas. These specialists monitor the input to the computer-based information-retrieval systems which are optically

‡ Eventually, by utilizing the facilities of the computer witih centrally accumulated records, we may learn not only how to predict performance, but also how to prevent some of the predictions from being fulfilled. We will learn how to characterize the student so that he can be better understood by the teacher and counselor. His record will be reduced not to a set of numbers that are difficult for the teacher to understand, but to a set of categorical statements such as: This student exhibits the same patterns in third, fourth, or fifth grade that have characterized dropouts in the ninth grade.

scanning the contents of the selected documents and converting them to tape. Once converted, the material is translated, abstracted, indexed, and coded for efficient retrieval. Files are constantly updated and purged, with the most significant information in a particular field kept immediately accessible.

Information centers will supply to the school superintendent and local administration such data as economic and population trends, predictions of the outcome of projected bond issues based on past voting behavior of property owners in local school districts, and other information.

The school or university of the 1970's will have a dynamic system of information retrieval serving the entire school system. Instead of a passive cumulative record file and libraries waiting for customer requests, the information-retrieval system of the future school will direct information to a person "who has not yet asked a question, but who does have a need for the answer." As an example, the dynamic information-retrieval system would index the content of a new document and mathematically select customers whose interest or information-need profiles indicate that the content would be of some relevance to them. Automatic dissemination would then result. Feedback from the customer—that is, the student or the educator—would continually update the store of profiles of potential users. Student learning performance would also cause changes in these profiles, for as students progress through new subject material, both information needs and interests evolve.

The information stored in the utility just described might be used in the following ways by student and educator:

The Student.   Computer-based independent study cubicles will be much in evidence in the advanced school system of the early 1970's. These study areas will combine information retrieval and automated teaching equipment to give the individual student aid in compiling bibliographies and recovering facts for the preparation of essays, and assistance in reading text material of difficulty.

Since students enter the curriculum in different states of ignorance, the information-retrieval teaching machine would help each individual redefine his area of concern. The student might write a short essay describing what he thinks is the information he wants. The essay would then be handled in the fashion of an automated abstract, with words selected from the essay being compared with words similarly selected from the documents or facts stored. The teaching machine would encourage the student to explore new but related areas of knowledge, browse through updated information, and search for alternate solutions to problems.

The Teacher, Researcher, and Counselor. The same equipment used by the student for self-instruction can be utilized by the teacher for research purposes or for updating himself in his subject area. Rapid changes in academic subjects can cause a considerable information lag in the resource books used by the teacher. The computer-based information-retrieval system will help the teacher in assembling programmed instructional material and will serve as a source of current information and necessary data for upgrading an outdated curriculum.

For classroom management purposes, the teacher will have displayed, in the classroom, certain diagnostic information in an interpreted form helping him to individualize his instruction. To deal with classroom grouping problems early in the semester, the teacher can retrieve student information with suggested groupings of students along many different dimensions—for example, reading rate, interest profile, learning difficulties.§

The counselor in this advanced school system will use information storage and retrieval capabilities for doing a more efficient job of counseling. Using information-retrieval files for counseling purposes involves the storage of all student personnel records on magnetic tape. If these records include aptitude test scores, family background information, or the student's past grade record, as well as his current record of progress, the counselor will have at his disposal all the appropriate information he needs. As the stored information is continually updated by the daily progress of each student through the course material, the counselor will have the capability of monitoring the progress of any one student and of applying preventive measures *before* a student has developed a serious educational problem.

Researchers at System Development Corporation and Carnegie Institute of Technology are exploring the advantages of simulating a counselor's or teacher's diagnostic behavior for purposes of guiding the student through his educational program. By automated interview programs, students review their progress and are helped to plan a schedule of high-school courses (210).

§ People concerned with computer-assisted instruction want to diagnose the learning needs of the student through preassessment tests as he begins the program. But some authorities have suggested that preassessment is not really relevant today, now that we have the opportunity of making individual diagnoses on the spot as the student is learning. Then we develop some predictive tools so that we alter the daily instructional program on the basis of this real-time or real-learning experience.

PRODUCTION AND EVALUATION OF
CURRICULUM MATERIALS

A behavioral engineering approach to improving instructional materials has been the object of extensive research conducted over the past few years at the System Development Corporation and more recently by the Brooks Foundation within the School District of Philadelphia. With the support of the U.S. Office of Education, researchers have developed a technique of individual tutoring to modify and revise such instructional materials as standard textbooks, programmed instructional sequences, film and filmstrips, flannel board cutouts, and the like. Significantly improved learning has been evident among students with substandard verbal backgrounds.

The method of approach depends primarily on a systematic analysis of student learning behavior for the testing and revision of the commercially available text or instructional package.

As now projected this program of research eventually will lead to the establishment of a data bank of information on the different learning problems students encounter at different points in the instructional program. If the computer is used in the collection and analysis of student responses to diagnostic test items during the process of tutorial instruction, typical problems can be identified and related to the effectiveness of different strategies developed to resolve them. The result will be the storing of multiple media routines of individual instructional programs following the pattern of the most successful instructional strategies. This library of material will be stored within the school district's central data bank and brought to the classroom, the independent study carrel, or the faculty office at the time it is needed—by the teacher, student, or the curriculum developer.

Natural-language data processing, it is expected, will be used in Philadelphia as the means for building the data bank. Questions students have raised (and which have been tape-scripted) will be converted word for word onto machine-readable magnetic tape. It is planned that the computer program will automatically index the questions by building a concordance of the content words, and cross referencing them with the text being studied. That is, words used in questions revealing student difficulties could be maintained with a numerical listing of each chapter, page, paragraph, and sentence which was being read at the time the problem occurred. Successful strategies for modifying these passages that have been developed with other students of similar IQ, background, and difficulties, in identical tutorial sessions, will then be identified from hierarchical listings.

The research accomplished to date seems to point to the existence of half a dozen or so basic learning problems which are common to most students involved in a particular unit of study. Through the process of engineering their instructional sequences, or extracting from the data bank of prestored information, textbook authors will some day be able to identify these problems and prepare instructional sequences that resolve them.

A "textbook" or individualized instructional package resulting from this process could be defined as an amalgamation of film clips, manipulated objects, branching or scrambled programmed texts, workbooks, cathode-ray tube displays, and different textual materials. Packages could take a deductive, pictorial, or verbal approach to the explication of subject material.|| It will be the task of the educational engineer (and the instructor) to identify the patterns and typical problems of learning and it should be the responsibility of the publishers of instructional packages to reflect these patterns and problems in their instructional materials.

COMPUTERIZED INSTRUCTIONAL-SYSTEMS RESEARCH

Another approach to the generation of text material, and one that is more directly computer aided, can be seen in the work of researchers using the computer as a tool for instructional research. The materials being generated by researchers at the universities of Illinois, Michigan, and Pennsylvania State are entered into the computer through the use of simplified codes operated for the most part with natural-language inputs. (See description by Zinn in Chapter 8.) In this materials-production process the computer is used in five ways:

1. To aid the author in inserting instructional materials into the computer library file by permitting the use of natural-language inputs, obviating the need for knowledge of machine language.

2. To provide editing facilities that permit automatic hyphenation, pagination, and alteration of text material.

|| We might give attention to two alternative designs: a very flexible system that handles all kinds of student populations with varying needs, or a specialized system geared, say, to the child who does not have linguistic skills and needs a different kind of display and response mechanism than the child whose linguistic abilities are well developed. This is a question of general purpose versus special environments.

3. To allow for automatic diagnosis of the author's errors or weak passages in the sequence of instruction, identifying internal inconsistencies and omissions in light of diagnostic test performance of the learners.

4. To make syntactical and structural analysis of the author's material, i.e., identifying terms used before they are defined, frequency of examples, introduction of key concepts with familiar terms, etc.

5. To give the author access to a library of instructional strategies tested by experienced teachers in the classroom environment (as extrapolated from the data bank) and a file of unusual responses or questions students have raised while involved with self-instruction via the computer-assisted instructional system.

Apart from the work of researchers concerned with CAI systems, several other developments presage the era of fully automated production of sequences of instructional material. These developments have run the gamut from subroutines that produce example items such as might be appropriate for drill in addition and subtraction or spelling to the generation of natural-text answers to questions input in English. This latter development has been more closely identified with work in the field of information storage and retrieval but it is here represented as a possible resource for the automatic production of study materials for instruction. The information-retrieval system called Baseball, devised by Green and others at Carnegie Institute, allows an inquirer to present natural-text questions about the history of baseball to the system. In the computer program, the history of baseball is stored as lists and these are manipulated by means of an information-processing language, the IPL-V system, and answers are generated in English (361).

Techniques are being developed both for processing pictures into natural-language descriptions and generating graphic displays from verbal input. Computer generation of such nonverbal materials as sounds, graphs, pictures, or structured tables from verbal or numerical inputs may better serve the individual who is not verbally oriented or who is working in visually oriented subject areas. For example, as conducted in two special classrooms at M.I.T., the student can apply mathematical formulations to highway design problems and then visually assess the adequacy of his work by computer-generated graphical representations of various stress factors and their effects (18).

Licklider (101) describes the Bolt, Beranek, and Newman PDP-1 system in which the student types in the coefficients of an equation, and the computer immediately displays on the television screen a corresponding parabola. By causing the student to vary the coefficients in different ways, the computer-generated instructional sequence can help the student understand the relations between the coefficients. A further example of this kind of multidimensional display is seen in some work of Richard Wing of the BOCES Center in Yorktown Heights, New York. Here the IBM 7090 is programmed to sequence a series of color slides on the basis of student instruction during a simulated experiment in chemical analysis. This means that a chemistry student can sit at his desk and type directions to a machine that will "perform" chemical experiments step by step. The student has a viewer on his desk that shows him what would happen, for instance, if he orders potassium chromate to be added to a solution of hydrochloric acid. If the solution turns yellow, or the mixing causes an explosion, the student sees this on his viewer. The computer simulates what would happen if this were done in the laboratory.

THE THIRD-GENERATION COMPUTER

Since 1955 three major stages in the application of computer technology to education have been evident. The installation of the university computing center for the solution of mathematical and scientific problems came first. The second stage was the use of electronic data-processing systems in accounting, record keeping, and logistical control activities; this amounts to the automation of information and data-processing systems. The third stage, now barely under way, involves the use of time-shared computers with on-line teletypes and cathode-ray tube (CRT) display equipment for supporting educators and learners in a wide range of intellectual processes. It is this third-generation application that spells a revolution in American education, primarily because the development of time-shared systems promises to have a major impact on instructional processes. Through time sharing, the immense capacity and speed of the computer allow many students, working independently in different locations, to use a single computer at the same time with little delay in computer response to individual commands, questions, or answers. At the present stage of development, between thirty and forty students or a like number of classrooms, each working at a different task, can use the computer simultaneously. This time-sharing capability puts the entire potential of the computer at the service of the individual learner, and assures the maximum, and therefore the most economical, use of each machine.

It would be difficult to overestimate the full potential of large-scale, time-shared networks of inquiry stations for the improvement of learning. Computer-assisted instruction and the use of inquiry stations to teach computer mathematics and programming as they apply to certain academic and vocational subjects are only two of the potentially fruitful applications in this new generation of computer systems. These two rapidly growing areas of development have received much publicity of late, and justifiably so, but the impact of computer technology on the improvement of environments for learning is by no means limited to these areas of development.

COLUMBIA CITY—A TIME-SHARED NETWORK
OF COMPUTER STATIONS IN HOME AND COMMUNITY

A new dimension will be added to home television viewing if projected plans for a computer-based communications center come to fruition in Columbia City, Maryland. Research is under way to develop in the new urban community near Washington, D.C., a coaxial cable network, similar to community antenna systems now serving many localities, that will tie more than 10,000 homes into a single community computer center. The homes in Columbia City will have a two-way communications capability to be used for adult education, commercial, and recreational purposes.

Linking a home to a community computer center puts the services of a large digital computer "on call" for each member of the family. Current applications of the computer then become possible in the home from the playing of games with other television viewers to the retrieval of stored facts and documents from a central library source. All of this is within the present state of the electronic art of computing systems, but the various elements of the system that now exist need to be pulled together into a working prototype.

The Maryland State Department of Education is designing the system for its educational applications and plans are now projected for installation of the first neighborhood center in 1968.

A small keyboard device linking the viewer by coaxial cable and telephone line to the computer center makes the system possible by adding a feedback loop to television viewing and making the observer an active participant in the communication network. What does active participation mean to the average television viewer? Some of the early uses projected for the network system are:

1. The television set and keyboard response unit serve as a nucleus of a versatile teaching machine. Typically, and at his convenience, the student is presented with material related to his school courses or of interest only to himself. This material frequently is interspersed with questions designed to test the student's understanding, and the student responds to multiple-choice questions by means of the keyboard unit. Unless the student continues to respond correctly, he is not permitted to go on to new material. Alternative sequences of simpler material and variable approaches to the same instructional goals help the computer system to tailor the subject matter to the student's unique constellation of abilities and background. Immediate feedback on test results, cumulative scores matched against certain norms, and multimedia approaches to the explication of subject matter all serve to motivate the student.

2. The playing of two-person or multiple-person games becomes possible. In a typical bridge game the viewer logs into the system by identifying himself through activating his keyboard unit. He views his hand on the television screen and electronically responds with a bid or a pass. His partner's bid is revealed on the screen and card lay-downs are transmitted as the game unfolds. A closely coupled intellectual "conversation" is sustained either by the computer simulating players at appropriate levels of sophistication or by linking four players through the network switchboards. Chess, poker, and even bingo are amenable to the initial system.

3. Marketing applications for servicing the at-home purchaser become feasible. A parading of purchasable items across the television screen enables the home viewer to buy any item he can afford. Emergency provisions of drugs, food, or household items could be ordered. Instant look-up of a savings or checking account becomes not only possible but necessary if central billing is to be maintained by the computer center.

The near-simultaneous use of a large computer by more than 5000 persons cuts the cost of computer time to less than a fraction of a cent per minute per user and gives each subscriber access to the central facility as though the entire computer service was at his disposal. Time-sharing techniques combined with a multiplexing system enable the computer to service each customer with a single pulse of broadcasted information. Each customer or television viewer is ready for additional information or the next item under study. A Xerography process known as the "proxi system" makes it possible for the viewer to read the displayed information in high resolution form and also to make copies of what he sees on the screen. By interrogating the computer at will, the user can program his television viewing at his own convenience.

Much has been written about the problems that will face future generations living in an age of automation and increasing leisure. Convenient, individually tailored, and self-directed instruction and recreation via television in the home not only should provide an antidote to some of the problems of an automated society, but should help create the environment for a richer life.

chapter 8

Computer Assistance for Instruction: A Review of Systems and Projects
Karl L. Zinn

JUSTIFICATION FOR ON-LINE SYSTEMS

There has been and will be much debate about the value of computers used on-line in regular instructional tasks. Arguments have considered cost, distribution, reliability, ease of use, relevance to educational purpose, richness of instructional experience, effectiveness relative to alternative procedures, and facilitation of research or materials development. Several questions and alternative proposals are considered here. Partial answers can be given for some of the questions, but the problems must be explored with large investments in research programs and careful field testing of computer-aided instruction.

Most of the questions concern cost and efficiency. Is the expenditure too great per student hour at a teaching station? Is the smallest effective system too large for most institutions to support? Is the cost of materials preparation too great in relation to the educational achievement? It has been argued that computer assistance will limit the distribution of instruction in comparison, for example, with much more

77

portable programmed text booklets; on the other hand, the computer has been proposed as the amplifier or distributor of the best teaching talent available. Can systems be made sufficiently reliable to be trusted with significant components of education?

Questions about effectiveness or quality of instruction elicit another set of justifications and reservations. Can a machine adapt well enough to the individual student? Is there any way other than automation to achieve individualization of instruction for an increasing number of students? Might learning and retention be as good or perhaps better by other available methods? Is transfer to other problems and situations hindered by the impersonal technology of the teaching station? Will some areas and concerns of instruction suffer because they are not readily implemented on computer systems?

The immediate justification for computer systems in education today lies not in instruction value but in research and development payoffs. An electronic processor (usually a general-purpose computer) can present and monitor extremely complex and adaptive presentations to student-subjects in a natural environment. Facilities located in public-school classrooms, business offices, and engineering shops or laboratories can simultaneously instruct, record data, and test hypotheses regarding instruction and learning with great detail and over long periods of time. Such a capability may help bridge the gap between contrived laboratory situations and actual application of learning principles in the classroom. Laboratory results obtained under highly controlled conditions have been contradicted later in the natural setting when previously controlled factors are allowed to influence the student-subject. A computer system allows a better representation of the real world to be simulated in the laboratory, and permits laboratory control and measurement to be taken out into the real world.*

A computer-based research system allows interim and sometimes automatic decisions in the course of an experimental session. This is important in real-world experiments on humans where incidental factors such as fatigue and interpolated activity may confound the results. In addition to reducing the total elapsed time required for execution of an experiment and analysis of data, the computer-based system sometimes

---

* There are many valid reasons for simulation. For example, some processes are inherently so dangerous that the individual must be as well trained as possible before he undertakes them. But it depends on what we are trying to teach—whether we want to train a man in an approach to getting information from the world or to train him efficiently to copy certain set laboratory experiments. To take hold of something one knows little about and go to work and manipulate it would not be of much benefit.

eliminates the cost of bringing subjects back for additional sessions or running additional treatment groups. Another important advantage is the ease of experimental treatments allowed by computer control. Once the experimenter has clearly specified the alternative instructional strategies he wishes to test—that is, specified them so they can be programmed on a computer—the relevant parameters can be varied automatically according to the design selected.

Development of instruction strategies and curriculum materials demands a computer for collection of detailed performance records which, in turn, would result in mountains of paper if the machine did not also summarize the data. The selection of appropriate techniques of data reduction is important for each development purpose. For example, revision of instructional materials is a very expensive and time-consuming procedure when properly based on large amounts of data reflecting individual student performance. An "intelligent" computer routine could monitor many aspects of student performance and summarize them for the author on request. When a computer is programmed to accumulate all unanticipated student responses and questions, it should also be programmed to attempt some classification and display a listing or diagram for the author's perusal. The author could request greater detail whenever the summary was not clear. Other examples are discussed in the sections on author aids and performance data.

The use of computers for research and development also must meet cost-effectiveness criteria, and the answers can be expected to vary among users and problems. It has already been demonstrated, however, that much instructional research done with computers probably could not have been done without them. Such research promises better understanding of the technology of instruction even when it is determined that much of the instruction can be done just as well without mediation by the computer system.†

FUNCTIONS OF INSTRUCTION SYSTEMS

The field of instructional technology presents a rather complex picture. Any attempt at reviewing this new and rapidly changing field

---

† Curriculum-development specialists must attempt to establish criteria for determining the domains to which CAI is not applicable. Establishing what should be included and what excluded from a computerized system would lead not only to generalizations about the applicability of CAI, but also, by identifying areas for which CAI is inappropriate, it would allow the development of programs in those areas by other means.

must be incomplete and approximate at best.[1] In this review a system description is proposed to help clarify particular strategies and their alternatives. Comparison of a self-instructional system with a traditional text reveals significant differences in the communication or information flow among the elements during development and use of the text. The author of a programmed text obtains firsthand information about the performance of students on his materials while he is writing them. This important channel of communication is lacking in the traditional setting. With regard to a new text, feedback channels to the author involve him in the learning process and facilitate intelligent revision of the text. The author and student interact via the text or whatever medium is used for presentation, and are monitored by some data-processing system that records and summarizes this interaction for later consideration by the author. Similarly the teacher and author communicate via the manual which must be developed to do the job. A record of interactions between student and teacher provides the author with additional data that are related to the integration of the text into an instructional system.

In general, an instructional system includes the following elements: learner, materials, monitor, author-teacher, and administrator. The picture becomes more complex with the addition of other students, teachers, technicians, teaching assistants, special projects, and outside reading. The dynamic interaction of materials, strategies, and communication channels over time must be considered in any complete analysis. There are, however, a number of basic and distinct, though interdependent, aspects or functions of computer-aided systems for instruction and research on instruction. These will be discussed under six major headings: author language, author aids, performance data, display, response processing, and unanticipated student needs.

---

[1] Information from reports, proposals, correspondence, and conversations was interpreted and condensed for a preliminary draft. It was improved considerably through reader comment and criticism, and further revisions are intended to maintain the usefulness of this document. The preliminary draft was used as a background paper at the AEDS-Stanford Conference on Computers in American Education, November 1–3, 1965; the Commission on College Physics Conference on the Uses of Computers in Undergraduate Physics Instruction at Irvine, November 1–7; and the Irvine Workshop Conference on Computers in American Universities, November 8–12, 1965. For the original draft ideas were drawn from many persons, in particular: E. N. Adams, R. C. Anderson, R. C. Atkinson, D. L. Bitzer, D. D. Bushnell, J. A. Easley, G. L. Geis, R. Glaser, J. C. R. Licklider, W. Reitman, L. M. Stolurow, L. Uhr, and W. R. Uttal.

REVIEW OF EXISTING AND PROPOSED SYSTEMS

AN AUTHOR LANGUAGE FOR INSTRUCTING THE MACHINE WITH REGARD TO TEACHING STRATEGIES AND MATERIALS

A teacher-author is unlikely to have computer-programming skills or a programming assistant to code instructions for a computer. Certainly the user in such a system should be able to write in his own language with a minimum of restrictions the self-instruction materials he plans to use. This computer language should include general and special vocabularies natural to the author for describing his instructional materials and strategies. Presumably the user will employ the computer logic to treat students or subjects differentially, and it should be easy for him to so specify via a set of logics or strategies with which he is comfortable. A graphic input and edit capability would be convenient for describing patterns of instruction.

An essential characteristic of this author language is that it be user oriented without denying the author-instructor access to any of the system capabilities. For example, the novice should be able to prepare materials for computer instruction after only minutes of exploration of the system language, and the experienced author should be able to use the capabilities of the computer to the fullest, for as complex a procedure as he can construct. In the evolution of such a system a computer programmer works with the authors to implement each new request for system capability, but it is his purpose to program himself out of the system by generalizing each function that might be repeated in slightly different ways and by different authors.

Descriptions of five examples of author-input language (also called course compiler, lesson assembler, or source language) are available. IBM's Coursewriter has been documented in an IBM research report (106) and a systems description (93). In brief it is an interpreter language of about twelve executable instructions or operation codes and ten manipulative commands by which an author at an IBM 1050 terminal enters and edits text material and branching logic in the disc storage of an IBM 1401, 1440, or 1460 system. The edit commands include insert, delete, and type; they can reference text by line only. In operation with a student at the 1050 terminal the stored instructions are interpreted to present reading assignments, questions, and replies to student answers. Responses constructed by the student are typed on the keyboard, entered into the computer for comparison with alternatives previously stored by the author, and the next computer reply is determined by the answer with which a match is established. The author can specify that trivial characters such as space and tabulation are to be ignored in order to achieve a better match. Much experimental work is being done on partial answer processing (117).

The 1050 teaching stations have been adapted experimentally for control of accessory delivery hardware such as random access visual and audio files. The system has the capacity to accumulate and summarize data on student performance and frame characteristics for the author-experimenter. A limited records facility has already been announced. The instruction list can be extended by the addition of functions written in Autocoder. Further software development is in progress at IBM's Watson Research Center in Yorktown Heights (IBM 7010) and the Advanced Systems Development Division Laboratory in Los Gatos, California. The Los Gatos system (IBM 1500) is being used by the Stanford University project in computer-assisted instruction.

A second example of author language is the work of Leonard Uhr (173, 174) at the University of Michigan. His approach is similar to that of Coursewriter but imposes fewer restraints on the user in writing his text, questions, and alternative answers. In addition, Uhr includes a processing function that accepts partial, synonymous, and loosely stated answers. The programs are coded in SNOBOL and are being tested on an IBM 7090 with simulated on-line interaction. Some interesting provisions for semiautomatic editing have been included.

The PLATO group at the Coordinated Science Laboratory, University of Illinois (22), has developed a compiler language for writing teaching logics or patterns for their system. It incorporates a modified Fortran and can accept CDC 1604 assembly language statements at any point. The programmer has great flexibility and scope for preparation of basic patterns (such as tutorial, inquiry, and simulation) into which any author can later insert his particular teaching material. For example, using a tutorial logic an author need write only the text, correct answers, and diagnostics to obtain a computer-controlled sequence of instruction; the computer has been programmed in advance to fit arbitrary text and answers into a particular type of dialogue. In another preprogrammed strategy the author may insert any text that he wishes to evaluate; the computer has been programmed to ask questions and collect data during presentation to students according to a particular pattern. A third type of strategy being explored is simulation of laboratory or real-world situations.

Researchers at Bolt, Beranek, and Newman (66) are giving particular attention to a system in which an author-instructor can write training materials for such complex analytic tasks as diagnosing medical ailments, arriving at decisions in business and management, developing military strategy, and investigating scientific problems. They are currently implementing a context-dependent compiler called MENTOR with which an author can specify a strategy for complex teaching applications. The instructional program is in the form of logical expressions that determine computer replies and subsequent material on the basis of whatever aspects of the student performance history the author cares to designate.

Feurzeig and Bobrow describe the goals of the BB&N group in a list of ideal characteristics of a system for constructing programmed instructional conversations between student and computer: relevance of computer response; user freedom; appropriateness of computer response to any user remark; option to delay information requested by the student; capability for complex computations such as simulations; verbal interactions in natural language; questions or declarative statements may be put by student as well as author; and nonverbal exchange may include tables, graphs, pictures, and sounds.

A fifth example by Starkweather (154) is characterized by the ease with which a person untrained in computer programming may write sequences of material. In fact, an example written by third-grade students has been reported. The preparation and input of instructions to the computer is by cards, and no special provisions have to be made for editing.

Two other languages are in preparation at System Development Corporation (63). Authors and experimenters at Illinois Training Research Laboratory (155) use special programs for lesson assembly which do not operate on-line, although work is in progress to provide such capability. No other reports have been received of author-input languages in experimental systems, and it is assumed that all others code each instructional program in the assembly language of the machine, calling on subroutines to execute frequently used sets of operations.

Computer-instruction systems should provide author-input facility at three levels. In the first, as described earlier, the author enters only his text and rules for evaluating answers in some standard pattern of instruction (e.g., a PLATO tutorial teaching logic). No knowledge of computers is required. The second level allows the author to specify his particular pattern of instruction in a relatively simple language that can be learned in a short time (e.g., the IBM author language). At a third level an author having some training in computer programming writes out his own routines and strategies, and has access to the full capability of the computer system (e.g., machine-language programming of special experiments or complex simulated environments). The important point, however, is that computers are being programmed to carry out instructions written by an author in his own language. The exactness and organization required of the author should be no greater than that demanded for preparation of effective self-instruction materials that do not use a computer.

AIDS FOR COMPOSITION, EDITING, CHECK AND REVISION OF TEXT AND LOGIC

In four important ways computer routines and displays can assist the author in the preparation and revision of his instructional materials and strategies. This aspect of computer assistance can remove a major bottleneck in materials development and should receive attention.

The system can instruct authors in the use of the input language and other system characteristics through examples and exercises. Part of this instruction would be accomplished through a retrieval-system component covering the reference manual for the author-input language. In this mode the system would respond to requests for a list of functions which had been added to the language since the author last asked for new functions, or the expected execution time of a designated sequence of instructions. An on-line user manual is especially important if the language is continually being extended or otherwise modified. On-line instruction in the intended performance situation—that is, on-line composition of text—can facilitate the optimal transfer from the learning setting to actual use. Estavan and Donahue at System Development Corporation are preparing routines whereby one can be instructed in the use of a general-purpose display system while seated at the console carrying out one's work. Mayer (109) has completed studies of within-system training of system use.

The author should be able to compose and edit text and diagrams on a cathode-ray tube using typewriter and light pen or other such input and pointing devices. The commands to delete, insert, change, and move can be applied to any size segment from a single character to a lengthy concept drill represented by a symbolic name in a block diagram on the screen. Such systems are already in use to aid in the solution of engineering design problems. The skeleton of an author-oriented system has been programmed by Zinn for a PDP-4 computer at Michigan, and this section of the paper was originally drafted on a text preparation system developed at Stanford Research Institute.

The system should provide diagnostics on probable errors in a particular course, such as internal inconsistencies and omissions in the sequence of instructions, and suggestions or reminders of how to take full advantage of the computer system. Such diagnostic action might be cued automatically by the presence of a particular pattern of instruction which is incomplete, unusual, or equivalent in function to a simpler pattern or set of instructions. Or this information may be obtained by asking the computer, for example, which branches in the teaching logic have been specified but not provided for. Of course the user will have the option of overriding the automated diagnostics if he prefers to specify unusual patterns without interruption, much as the user of a fully automatic camera system can shift to manual control of exposure.

Syntactic, semantic, and structural analyses of instructional text are relatively unexplored and are potentially advantageous author aids. The results of searches might be well used to uncover premature use of a term before it has been defined, frequency of examples of a key concept, spacing of the introduction of new concepts, and so forth.

ANALYSIS OF STUDENT PERFORMANCE, AUTHOR MATERIAL, AND INSTRUCTIONAL STRATEGY

The immediate summary of student performance is very important to an author-instructor both for course development and individualized instruction. These data are best obtained with one observer for every student, but this arrangement is costly in both time and money. Instruction programmers usually have settled for tedious tabulation of students' written responses, obtained under poorly controlled conditions. The computer system makes possible proper data collection and summary in real-time interaction with the student-subject. First, the responses are obtained under well-controlled conditions; the author knows exactly what material the student has seen and when. Second, additional data such as response latencies and trace of choices are available for interpretation. Third, and in some ways most important, the on-line processing of student responses allows real-time program modifications.

That is, a "monitor" may be provided to execute prearranged changes on the basis of student performance summaries.

The Stanford system has been programmed to list student performance summaries each day for certain lessons (166). Easley at Illinois has proposed that an author-instructor be provided a general facility for retrieval and review of records on student performance. The user should be able to request a complete data listing, a graphic "trace" of student progress through a sequence, or summary statistics at any desired level of detail. The data display may be for individual or group performance, averaged over many observations or restricted to a single item. The data themselves may be performance records or questionnaire responses and spontaneous reactions, and they may be interpreted for diagnosis of individual student difficulties or overall effectiveness of the instructional program.

The instructor needs summary data on individual student performance for day-to-day scheduling of learning materials. The author needs frame-by-frame and strategy or pattern analysis for continual revision of a program in the development stage. Student error rate and frame difficulty have been used, but in the adaptive, real-time, computer-based system statistical treatment can and should become more sophisticated. New developments in data reduction for indefinite sequences, trends, and patterns may be employed, and Bayesian statistics are appropriate for processing partial data subject to later revision. The contributions of Smallwood (152) and Karush and Dear (94) have been important steps in achievement of useful on-line processing, but simpler algorithms or perhaps heuristic techniques that reduce only the most relevant information need to be derived (3, 76). In the interim the selection of decision logic and technique of data summary can be left to the author-experimenter. After an author obtains a summary of overall performance he may wish to inspect certain records in more detail. Graphic display of data may facilitate efficient retrieval at an appropriate level of detail.

DISPLAY OF INSTRUCTIONAL OR EXPERIMENTAL MATERIALS

Much of computer instruction to date has been restricted to typewriter input and output. Notable exceptions to text mode have employed taped messages, computer-generated sounds (169), transparencies or computer-generated diagrams projected on a television screen or CRT (22, 101). The important point is that the author not be limited in his controlled presentation of material to students. Inexpensive displays on paper, film, and tape will serve for much computer instruction, but a more elaborate display facility under control of the central system is necessary for some subject areas and purposes—for example, student construction of an electrical circuit, results in an attached physical experiment, and generation of additional exercises for each individual student.

The Stanford system represents an attempt to solve display and response problems in the instruction of young children. Glaser at the University of Pittsburgh is assembling a system with similar requirements. SDC's general purpose display system is a sixth example of a facility far more advanced than typewriter input and output.

STUDENT RESPONSE AND PROCESSING OF RESPONSES

The mode of response should be natural for the student and appropriate for the instructional purpose. If the task calls for discrimination and pointing the student should be able to point. If arrangements of elements or a free-hand diagram are required, a cumbersome translation into English should be avoided. If a constructed response is desired the student should be able to compose it without artificial restrictions.

Response processing is an important aspect of most systems and often creates a problem. A "comparator" function provided by the computer may be quite important when the learner cannot make adequate discriminations at the beginning of his study. Often it is too difficult or distracting for the student to compare his own response with the standard or alternatives provided by the author. The computer not only can make this comparison in certain instances but also can be programmed to give detailed feedback in regard to the discrepancy between response and standard. The student may have typed an English sentence, sketched an electrical circuit, or sung an ascending major scale.

In character input, trivial differences in spacing, punctuation, spelling, format, word choice, and sometimes word order should be allowed in answer matching when so specified by the author. One of the functions of the input language should be to allow an author-experimenter control over response processing without increasing the complexity of the language for another user whose needs are met by one type of answer matching. Eventually routines will have some of the characteristics of natural-language processing; that is, in some limited sense the machine will "understand" a student answer or request. Processing of mathematical and other symbolic expressions entered by the student requires another set of routines that will let pass trivial differences. In general, a symbolic interpreter is required to allow any equivalent algebraic expression where the author so designates.

An interesting example of response processing is the encoding of speech or music for comparison with a standard or model available on tape. Buiten and Lane (29) at the University of Michigan have developed an analog and digital system for research on the prosodic characteristics of speech. The delivery device plays the model recording of the word, phrase, or musical phrase, and asks the student to match it. As he makes his response, the wave shape of his audible response is compared on one or more selected dimensions with a replay of the standard, and the mismatch is displayed immediately as feedback to the student. Thus, when he is trying to play the first three notes of a major scale to agree in pitch with the standard, he sees immediately the direction and extent of his error. In attempting a Spanish phrase the student might set the comparison dimension for tempo and note at which points he is producing the syllables too rapidly or too slowly.

The capability of speech recognition with a very limited vocabulary may be available in experimental instruction systems in the near future, and vocal input of a general nature is likely eventually to become a regular component of computer systems.

Symbolic expressions or strategies can be processed for verification in reference to author standards. For example, computer programs designed by Easley et al (59) and Suppes check each step in a proof on the basis of a programmed logic rather than comparison with stored solutions. In this manner a student can follow his own path. Furthermore an instructor may not wish to require his students to write out in detail every step necessary in the proof of a theorem in algebra or geometry. When the learner makes a small intuitive step, as mathematicians frequently do, the computer checks for validity by carrying out the necessary steps in detail (15). This has interesting possibilities for instruction since a computer doing the processing task can also be programmed to accumulate the kinds of errors that the student makes, and generate additional exercises to assure acquisition of the skill.

Partial feedback on a student answer is an interesting and important concomitant of answer matching.‡ That is, the computer is programmed

‡ When we use computers, we obtain better data and more quickly, and feed it back to the teacher, the administrator, the curriculum maker—to the managers of the enterprise. What about the problem of getting data fed back to the learner

to print out those parts of the answer that agree with the model provided by the instructor. The feedback is typed out immediately below the student's response so he can compare and consider differences before making his next attempt. Uhr's (173) language and IBM's Coursewriter include this feature with the provision for specifying order in the elements of an answer. For example, an author can ask a student (via the computer program) for a list of examples; the processing routine searches for the keyword of each example in order (accepting the examples in any order) and prints out in the author's words those examples that the student apparently entered. The author could choose an alternative logic and print out those answer elements that were not included in a student reply. Morrison (117) has discussed response processing in detail and programmed a number of routines for IBM's Watson Research Center System. Response processing and partial feedback reduce the task of the author and increase the interaction between student and instructional program.

Adaptive Sequencing. In a programmed textbook off the shelf the student's pace and branching are based on only the current response. To achieve more than minor adjustment to individual differences, the instructor must maintain a library of parallel programs following different tracks and direct each student to the proper one on the basis of continual review of performance. A computer-based system makes possible a number of much more sophisticated adaptations which incorporate frame difficulty, frame relevance, student error rate, response latency, IQ, interests, and so on (155). When the author can provide a number of alternative frames or a rule for generating a frame at any point in the program, selection from a set of frames is determined by any one or a combination of frame and student parameters (186). In mathematics instruction a set of frames might include alternatives at varying levels of difficulty or perhaps based on applications drawn from different subject areas. The important dimensions in such adaptive selection or generation are not well known, but a system having such capability is necessary for research on these parameters.

Real-Time Generation. There are two practical reasons for preparing computer programs that generate instructional programs from the content elements and relationships provided by a subject expert. First there are instances, in subjects such as arithmetic, logic, or spelling, in which

about himself and all his operations? How can we use this new technique to give information back to the learner in such a way that he will understand it and have a better grasp of his own learning and development?

it is more efficient for the computer to generate exercises than to store all the possibilities intact. In programming a sequence for addition or multiplication drill, programmers typically do not store all combinations but only the digits and the operators, and generate the exercises from them. In author languages also one should be able to describe a class of problems rather than write out each problem of the class in detail.

Second, if our best theories or intuitions are any better than random guesses, the generation of material can be adaptive in a way that facilitates learning. For example, Uhr (172) has programmed routines in which the generation rule incorporates current student performance parameters in order to stress those combinations that are difficult for the student then receiving instruction. Both Stolurow and Zinn have written computer programs that generate syllogistic reasoning problems. In the development of reasoning skills or logical analysis, the student might be started on symbols, then advance to nonsense terms, and finally to meaningful material. For paradigms in which the student's performance suggests lack of mastery, additional exercises would be provided at the same or a simpler level until the student demonstrated he could proceed.§

Spelling is another subject in which storage of a dictionary of words coded by relevant spelling rules would provide a more efficient and powerful way of presenting exercises. A program to assemble reading and vocabulary exercises from sentence forms and lists of elements has been written by Stolurow and Lippert (159).

Another adaptive function that should not be overlooked is a diagnostic testing procedure by which not all test items need to be given to all students. For example, a difficult item in the application of a principle would be given only to students who could identify the principle. Others would be tested instead on knowledge and use of knowledge in other areas. In this way each student can be led to the depth as well as the breadth of his knowledge in a reasonable length of time. It has been suggested that this method of testing also leads to greater learning on the part of the student because he prepares more carefully and continues learning in the testing situation. This mixing of learning and evaluation will become increasingly common in regular instruction.

§ What about students to whom we are not able to communicate the subject matter at all; students whose own history prevents them from understanding the points we are making? We need to catch the computer up on this history to the point of impact. The students will be reviewed with what they should have learned, but they will not be prevented from visualizing the new piece of information because they have not learned the old one. This is the kind of organization we need to experiment with.

As a result the student generally will know how well he is doing and where he needs additional study, and the teacher will know in which areas the instructional materials are not meeting his objectives.

UNANTICIPATED STUDENT ERRORS AND REQUESTS

Unanticipated student response is an important consideration in a sophisticated and semiautomated author-program-student system. What today is unanticipated and unique should tomorrow become part of a more detailed and comprehensive program of instruction. An author must exploit the valuable data gleaned from these channels. There will always be new needs, however, requiring that direct communication be maintained. It is expected that there will always be a human monitor in the system with the learner; he can be called on when needed, and he can interrupt when he feels it to be appropriate. In the conference room, with tutorial and group discussions, unanticipated responses should be of central importance. Data from these sources should be introduced into the self-instruction components of the system.

It is a feature of the PLATO system to allow direct communication between an individual student and the proctor or teacher to be initiated from either direction; in the Stanford system an unsatisfactory level of student performance can initiate a "teacher-call" automatically. The machine maintains a record of the performance of individual students for guidance as well as research and curriculum-evaluation purposes. Certainly the student should be able to ask for help at any time, and the tutor responding should have the benefit of an immediate summary of current performance, and perhaps a list of possible difficulties if the author knows his subject and students well enough. Furthermore, the supervising tutor should be able to scan such a summary without the student having to ask for help or additional direction. Sometimes the tutor might, on his own initiative or at an alert call from the system, interrupt and help a student around an approaching difficulty, or introduce some additional guidance that would provide an interesting new direction for study. These aids not anticipated by the author should be noted and incorporated in revision of the instructional material and strategy. One tutorial logic on the PLATO system allows the author to make modifications in previously written material while monitoring a student's progress through instruction.

On-line Tutorial. Zinn and Reitman have proposed that the machine also monitor the individual interchange between student and author-instructor for the purpose of improving the program as well as studying the tutorial process. The record could be used in much the same way as tape recordings of tutorial sessions. Since the communication is stored via electronic media, further summary can be carried out by a computer. Ideally the editor function of the compiler should be able to store away and later use what an instructor adds to his course when interacting "on-line" with a student who is going through the preplanned sequence at a different terminal. Student-author interaction is routed through the program element so it can be monitored and processed for use in later student-program interaction, in revision of the materials, or in research on behavior of author and student in a tutorial situation.

Appendix
Current Projects

The preceding sections discussed functional characteristics of some systems and projects. This section summarizes hardware configuration, software, purposes, materials, and current operations of selected projects. Each project is identified by the person to whom inquiries should be addressed.

The information for this project file is maintained by the Center for Research on Learning and Teaching, 1315 Hill Street, Ann Arbor, Michigan, 48104.

Dr. E. N. Adams, Director
Computer Assisted Instruction
IBM Instructional Systems Development Department
Watson Research Center
Box 218
Yorktown Heights, New York   10598

also T. F. Hartman, W. J. Koppitz, H. W. Morrison, E. M. Quinn, J. Reddy, J. W. Schoonard, J. J. Schurdak, and G. O. Tarnawsky.

This laboratory is working on an experimental system using an IBM 7010-1440-1448 configuration with 1050 systems for remote terminals (106). Kodak Carousel slide projectors and Uher tape recorders have been adapted for rapid serial access to an 80-element video file on 35mm slides and a 30-minute audio file of separately addressable messages of 10 seconds or more on standard one-half-inch tape. Typically, printed text supplements are used for the core of a course presentation.

The Coursewriter language is undergoing further development. This laboratory is experimenting with additional features such as response editing and processing. Materials development is being conducted in the areas of second language learning, reading skills, and statistics.

Other development and experimentation is in progress by researchers not related to IBM using remote terminals at a number of university campuses, including Pennsylvania State University, State University of New York at Stony Brook, and University of Michigan.

Dr. Donald Bitzer, Director
PLATO Project
Coordinated Science Laboratory
University of Illinois
Urbana, Illinois   61801

The current operating system for the project called PLATO (Programmed Logic for Automatic Teaching Operations) is based on a CDC 1604 and includes twenty teaching stations with video capability. The author may project slides on a television screen via an "electronic book" and superimpose writing or diagrams by means of an "electronic blackboard" function. Student response is by teletype keyboard with user-defined characters or special symbols appearing on the television screen at a location predetermined by the author or programmer (22).

The software to specify the logical structure of an instructional sequence is written in an extended Fortran for the PLATO compiler, CATO (Compiler for Automatic Teaching Operation). Considerable flexibility is allowed the user familiar with the three levels of language: CATO, Fortran, and assembly. Special routines have been written for judging student answers by various complex criteria, plotting graphs on student request, plotting data from an on-line physics experiment, constructing and checking statements in a mathematical proof (59), monitoring physiological data entered over supplementary input channels, and controlling supplementary audio or visual displays.

Materials in many areas have been coded for PLATO (104). One regular credit course used the PLATO system in the spring of 1965 and three courses received regular instruction in 1965–66. University credit courses using the PLATO system are continuing in 1966–67.

Engineers associated with the project have developed a plasma-discharge display tube which will greatly reduce the cost of teaching stations.

Dr. C. Victor Bunderson
College of Education
5-A Sutton Hall
University of Texas
Austin, Texas   78712

also W. H. Holtzman, L. O. Morgan, B. Fruchter, and J. H. Ward, Jr.

The Laboratory for Computer-Assisted Instruction at the University of Texas began operation in January 1966 with an IBM 1401 Coursewriter System with five 1050 terminals. Two of the terminals were connected by remote telephone lines to Florida State University during the months of February and March 1966, and two terminals with audiovisual capability were added to the system at Austin later in 1966. The system was provided through a joint study agreement between IBM and the University of Texas.

The Laboratory is currently organized to perform both research and service functions. Two broad categories of studies are being pursued: feasibility studies in various content areas and basic research in human learning and instruction. The service function exists to further these goals as they express themselves in projects initiated from any department in the university (or, in certain cases, projects initiated in cooperation with outside agencies).

The four initial curriculum development projects are in simulated freshman chemistry lab, elementary statistics, scientific German, and heuristic problem solving, a research-oriented course drawing heavily on the books of George Polya. Research and development work at the college level will be expanded into the San Antonio area high schools.

Dr. Glenn Culler
Computing Center
University of California
Santa Barbara, California   93106

Culler (53) proposed an on-line computation facility for the solving of problems in mathematics and related subjects. UCSB has its own computer for the purpose with remote terminals at UCLA and Harvard computation centers. Numeric, graphic, and function operations have been programmed. Application is planned in experimental communications programs in psychology, biometrics, physical sciences, and mathematics.

An example of system operations is included in the report of a conference on The Computer in Physics Instruction sponsored by the Commission on College Physics, 1966.

Dr. Robert Davis
Educational Development Program
Michigan State University
East Lansing, Michigan

also J. F. Vinsonhaler, M. R. Denny, W. B. Lashbrook, F. Marzocco, and J. Kateley.

Using an IBM 1050 teaching station on the Watson Research Center experimental 7010 Coursewriter System, student attitudes toward computer-assisted instruction were explored. About 35 students in an introductory statistics course worked for 24 hours on self-instruction assisted by the computer.

Using the same facilities, comparison was made of traditional with automated administration and scoring of a multiple-choice test of scholastic aptitude. Further studies of automated testing are in progress.

A study of the interaction of individual differences with automated instruction is to be conducted by Marzocco and Davis. Vinsonhaler is conducting exploratory studies of retrieval systems used in support of instruction especially in the area of educational testing. He has produced a Fortran-based general-purpose indexing and retrieval system for educational materials. The work has been done on the CDC 3600, MSU's central computer.

Dr. John Fowler
Commission on College Physics
Physics and Astronomy Building
University of Michigan
Ann Arbor, Michigan   48104

Physicists associated with the Commission on College Physics have written short demonstration units in kinematics, momentum, and statics as part of a project at the University of Michigan. During a summer writing conference at the University of Washington in 1965, materials were prepared for instruction in optics, acceleration, and electrostatics using two IBM 1050 terminals with slide projectors on WATS lines to IBM's Watson Research Center. At an informal conference in September, summer users discussed the problems and potentials of computer assistance for diagnostic testing, remedial instruction, laboratory quiz, and other support for regular physics instruction. A conference on the uses of computers in undergraduate physics instruction was held at Irvine, California, in November 1966.

Dr. Robert Glaser
Learning Research and Development Center
University of Pittsburgh
Pittsburgh, Pennsylvania   15213

also R. Ragsdale, W. Ramage, J. Holland, and O. K. Moore.

This center has two years of experience administering programmed study for about 200 elementary school pupils, and plans have been made to use computer assistance in recording progress and scheduling new assignments for each student. However, the Center's PDP-7 is used primarily as the basis for a learning laboratory. About six typewriter terminals are being attached, two of which are augmented by a video display, an audio playback unit by Westinghouse, a pressure-sensitive display surface, an oscilloscope with light pen facility, a Rand Graphic Input Tablet, and eventually a position-sensing board.

A report on the interface between student and subject matter (72) discusses the conditions which subject matter properties and research goals place on the design of the student terminal equipment. Glaser and Ramage are now working on definition of learning strategies and on author language.

Dr. Duncan Hansen
Center for Computer Assisted Instruction
The Florida State University
Tallahassee, Florida   32306

Educational researchers at Florida State have been using an IBM 1440 system to serve as a nucleus for a research center in computer-assisted instruction. Earlier they operated on an IBM 1050 terminal with attached slide projector and tape recorder connected by WATS line to IBM's Watson Research Center system. Materials have been coded in Coursewriter for instruction in trigonometry, geometry, and educational measurement. Attention has been given to research on computer presentation of secondary-school mathematics instruction.

Mr. William C. Harless
Medical Center
University of Oklahoma
800 NE 13th Street
Oklahoma City, Oklahoma 73104

also Dr. Thomas Lynn.

The Medical Center uses five IBM 1050 terminals on a 1401 Coursewriter system. Interest is focused on graduate, postgraduate, and continuing education applications. These involve drill applications as well as information retrieval and dissemination techniques.

A course in medical backgrounds for graduate student enrollees in preventive medicine and public health is already in operation providing one hour of CAI material each week. The author, Dr. Thomas Lynn, dictates the content and instructions for answer processing and a typist trained in Coursewriter transcribes the material into code from the tape recording. After editing, the code is stored in the computer. Dr. Lynn reports about four hours of professorial time for each hour of CAI instruction for the students.

The Center expects a larger computer soon and eventually will have enough terminals to service all students for a major portion of the curriculum. Two more courses are now in preparation and three additional ones are planned.

Dr. Carl Helm
Educational Testing Service
Princeton, New Jersey 08540

also D. Payne and R. Ruderman.

Educational Testing Service has established a research team within the Developmental Research Division which will undertake a program of research in the new educational technology area. The program's objectives are to investigate the feasibility of utilizing machines and electronics in (1) developing verbal interpretations of test scores, (2) creating and assembling test materials, (3) test administration methods that will provide rapid feedback of test results and greater flexibility in presentation of test materials and results, (4) monitoring of learning in computer-assisted instruction, and (5) problems of sequence in instruction.

Dr. Richard S. Hirsch
IBM Advanced Systems Development Division
6450 Guadalupe Mines Road
Box 66
Los Gatos, California   95031

also B. Moncreiff and H. Jeans.

An IBM 1620 with attached typewriter and strip film projection system has been used to simulate a special-purpose, free-standing teaching machine. A conceptual version of one section of a qualitative analysis laboratory has been prepared using this system (89). The student is asked to identify properly each of the metals of a group by a sequence of tests on an "unknown" sample containing all of them. He instructs the computer by a code system representing drops, molarity, reagents, filtration, and so forth, and the computer responds with an appropriate color picture of the result of the operation and a typed verification when the student properly isolates the indication of a particular metal in the sample.

Staff members at the Laboratory are planning a sample exercise in a physics laboratory as further demonstration and test of the operation of their prototype machine.

In cooperation with Stanford, the Laboratory has developed the IBM 1500 Instructional System. In addition to typewriter or keyboard and scope capability there is a strip-film image projector and magnetic-tape audio recorder and playback.

Dr. Harlan Lane
Center for Research on Language and Language Behavior
University of Michigan
1315 Hill Street
Ann Arbor, Michigan,   48104

also J. Hemdel and D. VanderYacht.

Buiten and Lane (29) devised a Speech Auto-Instructional Device (SAID) for research on training in the prosodic characteristics of speech. It is a single terminal based on a PDP-4. The student console includes microphone pickup, indicator lights, and a meter display for feedback of the discrepancy between the student response and the model he is trying to imitate. The same computer is also used for research on speech analysis and synthesis, and a Galvanic Skin Response

(GSR) processing capability is in preparation for use in language behavior studies.

Mr. Harvey S. Long, Manager
Computer Assisted Instruction
IBM Field Engineering Division
Rt. 55, Building 956
Poughkeepsie, New York

also R. Valley and L. O'Neil.

IBM maintains two 1440-1448 systems at Poughkeepsie, each having twelve lines for servicing their own 1050 teaching terminals locally and at remote customer engineering offices. The 1440 Coursewriter system is used, except where modifications are necessary for special demonstrations and developments. Course materials have been developed which handle a substantial segment of instruction for the System 360 Training School and a short course on fundamentals of data processing. Field tests are in progress. Short demonstrations on number squaring and astronomy have been coded.

Dr. Sylvia R. Mayer
Decision Sciences Laboratory
Electronic Systems Division
L.G. Hanscom Field
Bedford, Massachusetts   01731

also Colonel Roy Morgan.

Mayer and Morgan (109) describe progress on the development of a computer-aided training program for users of an Air Force computer system. The training is provided as a supporting capability built into the computer system. Thus the training takes place within the same system for which the user is being trained. This approach presents important opportunities for additional on-the-job instruction when necessary, error detection with instructions for correction, and data for modifications in system or subsystem training procedures.

Dr. Harold E. Mitzel
College of Education
201 Chambers Building
Pennsylvania State University
University Park, Pennsylvania   16802

also K. H. Wodtke, K. A. Hall, D. W. Johnson, R. Seibel, D. Bjorkquist, D. Gilman, and J. Ritchey.

The Computer Assisted Instruction Laboratory at Penn State is operating four IBM 1050 terminals including slide projector and tape recorder connected by telephone lines to either the IBM Watson Research Center system or the Penn State 1410 used for the computing center tape-to-printer operations. Substantial progress has been made on four college courses written with IBM's Coursewriter: management accounting, engineering economics, modern mathematics, and audiology (115). The original project was designed to explore the writing of materials, reactions of students, advantages and problems of computer presentation, and the characteristics of a prototype teleprocessed system. Wodtke, Mitzel, and Brown (181) report preliminary results on student reactions and error rates.

The activities of the laboratory have expanded with a new project to assess experimental teaching strategies in computer-assisted instruction core courses for technical education programs. Computer operations have shifted to the local IBM 1410 system and now include two remote terminals at extension teaching centers in Altoona and Williamsport.

Dr. Omar K. Moore
Learning Research and Development Center
University of Pittsburgh
Pittsburgh, Pennsylvania   15213

The Edison Responsive Environment Instrument (ERE) is a computerized typewriter with capabilities intended to reproduce several of the response actions of a human teacher. When a pupil depresses a key on the typewriter keyboard, the key symbol is typed in large type on the typewriter paper and is pronounced at the same time. On a rear projection screen, letters, words, and sentences can be displayed automatically with accompanying audio explanations and pointer designations. The keyboard can be locked except for the key the child is expected to press. As well as playing the model soundtrack, the device can record and play back the child's voice for comparison purposes.

Typically the instrument is programmed to point out a particular letter, play the recording of the pronunciation, and free only the correct key to be pressed by the student. The program proceeds to the next letter or word or sentence after the correct key has been pressed.

Studies in the early teaching of reading and writing have been conducted for children of differing skills and abilities. Deaf and autistic children have been included, as well as those at the extremes of the ability distributions in typical schools.

A three-year trial program was begun in the fall of 1966 in the

New York City school system. The pilot study is supported by a grant from the Office of Economic Opportunity, and will emphasize instruction for preschool and primary grade children, dropouts, and illiterate adults.

Dr. Jesse O. Richardson
Board of Education
Commonwealth of Massachusetts
200 Newbury Street
Boston, Massachusetts   02119

This curriculum evaluation project is using teletype terminals on a PDP-1 employed in an information-processing project at Massachusetts General Hospital. The programming language is Telcomp, developed by Bolt, Beranek and Newman. The major purpose is to explore the efficiency of computer-augmented instruction in mathematics. Students in grades 6, 9, and 11 are using a computer to solve mathematical problems. Comparison groups receive a computer-oriented curriculum without access to the computer and a regular curriculum without reference to computers. The staffing and economic constraints of computer use will also be explored.

Dr. Harry Silberman
Education and Training Staff
Research and Technology Directorate
System Development Corporation
2500 Colorado Avenue
Santa Monica, California   90406

also J. Bratten, J. Cogswell, J. Coulson, C. P. Donahoe, D. Estavan, S. Feingold, C. Frye, R. Melaragno, J. Newmark, J. Rosenbaum, and Miss B. Rosenquist.

The CLASS facility (Computer-based Laboratory for Automation of School Systems) developed out of studies investigating branching effects in programmed instruction. An earlier experimental teaching machine at SDC used a Bendix G-15 computer, a random-access slide projector, and an electric typewriter (144). The current CLASS facility has twenty teaching stations and two teacher stations on a Philco 2000 computer. Each teaching station consists of a 2000-frame, manually operated, 35mm film-strip viewer and a multiple-choice response device including computer-controlled lights for indicating feedback. The teacher console includes facilities for monitoring the materials and responses of any student, and inspecting student records on a CRT. More recently this project has been using regular teletypes and experimental stations attached to SDC's time-shared Q-32V. The terminal configuration on this system can include CRT display, light pen and button input, and Rand Graphic Input Tablet in addition to keyboard facility.

Earlier hypothesis studies on the CLASS facility have given way to "tutorial" studies in which students are observed during independent work with a program and are assisted as difficulties arise. Each such interaction is used to improve the program, and the cycle begins again with another student (41). Hypotheses about programming strategy evolved from these empirical development efforts have been confirmed in further studies. A different type of instruction has been programmed to assist a student in solving statistics problems and to monitor his progress (63, 68). The student may follow any of a number of alternative routes to the solution of each problem. He may use the computer for computation and also as a source of further information. These routines are operating on teletype stations.

The author language developed for the statistics package (called Planit) is of general interest. The operating system will be changed over from the Q-32 to an IBM 360/65 and then to a 360/67 in 1967.

Another time-shared educational application is a computer-delivered "precounseling" interview (210). The computer has been programmed to ask diagnostic questions and suggest courses or provide further information on the basis of student answers.

Dr. John Starkweather
Computer Center
University of California
San Francisco, California   94122

also P. Moss and A. Milstein.

Starkweather originally designed a system with which a physician could readily specify automated procedures for gathering information for medical diagnosis. The first step was a simple language for communication with the computer. It was implemented on an IBM 1620 and proved useful as a tool for simulation and study of interview and counseling procedures as well as gathering of information.

The language, called Computest, is particularly notable for its simplicity, and in fact has been used by third-grade children writing question sequences for their classmates. The Office of Education is supporting a project in the Dixie School District north of San Francisco to explore the role of student-constructed materials in the learning and attitudes of fourth through eighth graders.

A revised Computest will be available on the Medical Center's IBM 360/40. Clinical applications, as in gathering information from patients, will continue to be explored.

Dr. L. M. Stolurow (on leave 1966–67)
Training Research Laboratory
8 Lincoln Hall
University of Illinois
Urbana, Illinois 61801

also R. C. Anderson and H. Lippert.

SOCRATES (System for Organizing Content to Review and Teach Educational Subjects) is based on an IBM 1620-1710 system with thirteen modified Autotutors called MASTER I/O stations for student terminals (102). The display is by microfilm and response is via a fifteen alternative button press. In the MASTER I/O modification, more flexibility is achieved through completely random access to 1500 35mm frames and additional key and display light options are included. The system is programmed in Fortran and SPS and a lesson assembler is available (157).

An effective program has been written to manage the system components, to accomplish the instructional logic of the educational programmer, and to accumulate the desired records. This program has been prepared in a modified SPS language introducing no new operations, but specifying system functions in a way that relates more directly to the educational programmer's needs. The logic of the educational programmer's set of strategies is communicated in a form that is more like the natural language. The system permits complete historical records of student performance and compilations of these records either individually for each student or cross-student, as desired.

The project has emphasized research on instruction using the computer-based system for controlled display of materials, execution of complex branching, and recording of both error and latency data on each response. A systems analysis has been proposed (155) in which student records, including aptitude and personality measures as well as current performance, may be used in selecting the best program for each student. Materials generation routines have been programmed for use off line (159).

The research and development activities may be combined with those of the PLATO project on the same campus. A university-wide laboratory is planned for research, development, and application.

Dr. Patrick Suppes
Institute for Mathematical Studies in the Social Sciences
Ventura Hall
Stanford University
Stanford, California   94305

also R. C. Atkinson, W. K. Estes, and H. Wilson.

This project shared with the Stanford Department of Computer Science the development and operation of a PDP-1 with twelve terminals, six for use by computer programmers editing and testing programs and six for on-line instruction and research on learning. The teaching stations include a number of modules which can be placed in any arrangement at each station. An IBM film display system can project any of 512 "pages" on a screen which accepts student response by light pen, i.e., the student touches the pen to part of the display screen. The author of materials may also prepare them for display on a Philco cathode-ray tube on which the student's keyboard input can be "written" within the display itself.

Audio messages of two to twenty seconds in length can be stored and replayed from a unit provided by Westinghouse. Usually students are brought to the laboratory, but remote teletypes have been placed in public school classrooms to test a limited set of arithmetic and spelling drills.

The project is committed to learning research with special emphasis on reliable data acquired over long periods of time. Its other goal is the development of "total" curriculum materials for elementary-school instruction in language and mathematical skills. By total curriculum is meant a reasonably self-sufficient sequence of instruction including oral communication with the pupils and strategy decisions about pacing, sequencing, review, and so forth. Materials now being tested include sets and numbers, logic, arithmetic drill, spelling drill, and practice in reading.

The project will continue working toward the goal of total curriculum with recommended testing in typical schools. An IBM 1500 Instructional System with sixteen terminals has been installed in the Brentwood School in East Palo Alto. The use of remote teletypes for drills associated with regular class instruction during the 1965–66 school year has been augmented by a cluster of cathode-ray tubes located in an elementary school. In addition to drill-and-practice material in mathematics, these CRT's will also be used for augmenting a course in mathematical logic given to fifth and sixth graders. The majority of the exercise work in the course will be given on the CRT's.

Dr. John A. Swets
Bolt, Beranek and Newman
50 Moulton Street
Cambridge, Massachusetts 02138

also W. Feurzeig and D. G. Bobrow.

Early work at this location was directed by J. C. R. Licklider (101). He experimented with routines for language vocabulary drill and graphic display of simple functions. More recently Swets and others conducted a series of experiments on identification of nonverbal sounds. Particular attention was given to mode of display and response. Swets has been operating a computer-based psychophysical laboratory since July 1965.

Currently, Feurzeig and others (64, 67) are working on the training and testing of complex analytic tasks such as diagnosing medical ailments, arriving at decisions in business and management, developing military strategy, and investigating scientific problems. For their "Socratic System" (65) they have developed a language called Mentor for teacher-authors to use in constructing conversational tutorial dialogues. The author of materials may, via computer storage and logic, take the role of advisor, monitor, interviewer, consultant, examiner, or tutor. Typically, a situation is established in which a problem may be solved by the gradual acquisition of information. The student types inquiries or declarations selected from a list of acceptable terms, and the machine identifies these even when misspelling occurs and types an appropriate reply according to complex conditional statements provided by the author.

In the current system teletypes are attached to a modified PDP-1 computer. The Mentor language is written in Lisp, and sections of instructional programs otherwise coded in Mentor may be written in Lisp. The same system is used with an on-line computational language called Telcomp for experimental instruction in the public schools.

Feurzeig, Bobrow, and Seymour Papert of MIT are working on the design of programming languages for student use toward constructive problem-solving study in mathematics, language, and logic. The current project on computer-aided school mathematics, being carried on under the direction of J. O. Richardson of the Massachusetts Department of Education for the U.S. Office of Education, employs one such language, Telcomp, noted above.

Dr. Fred M. Tonge
Computing Facility
University of California
Irvine, California 92650

also J. Kearns and W. J. Kopplitz.

An IBM 1410-1440-1448 computer system with disc storage and eighteen 1050 terminals began operation during the summer of 1965 (71). Faculty on this campus are trying out computer-assisted instruction using IBM's Coursewriter. A numeric manipulation capability has been added to the system. A symbol manipulation capability permitting algebraic manipulation, differentiation, and integration is planned.

Particular attention is being given to curriculum in mathematics and statistics in the general social-science curriculum. A second major line of development intended is the design and implementation of inquiry systems providing the capability for the computer to respond to questions asked by the student.

Dr. William R. Uttal
Mental Health Research Institute
University of Michigan
Ann Arbor, Michigan   48104

Uttal has designed a data collection and analysis system around a PDP-5 for research on physiological correlates of learning. Two teletypes, one with CRT, have been programmed for use in programmed-learning experiments. Plans include monitoring and processing data on tutorial interaction between teacher and student, and developing strategies for generating instructional material in mathematics.

Dr. Richard L. Wing
Coordinator of Curriculum Research
Northern Westchester Board of
Cooperative Educational Services
845 Fox Meadow Road
Yorktown Heights, New York   10598

Computer-controlled economics games have been tried with elementary-school children using several IBM 1050 terminals connected by telephone lines to an IBM 7090 with a time-sharing system (180). Experimental random-access slide projectors have been used to present graphic information supplementing typewriter output. The games are coded in Fortran Assembly Program (FAP).

Students respond at the typewriter, indicating decisions about social and economic affairs in the simulated society, and the computer displays the consequences of their decisions. The Sumerian Game (115) has placed sixth-grade pupils in the role of the ruler of a city-state in the year 3500 B.C. facing problems of grain allocation. The Sierra Leone Game simulates the economic problems of a newly emerging nation. A third project called the Free Enterprise Game has been written and partially programmed in Autocoder.

The Sumerian and Sierra Leone Games have been tested with sixth-grade students. Test results, interview reports, and other data are being analyzed. In addition to continuing experimentation with existing simulations, and development of new materials in elementary science and biology, this curriculum research office will operate as a demonstration center in the state of New York for computer-based instruction and other complex educational media.

Dr. Karl L. Zinn
Center for Research on Learning and Teaching
University of Michigan
1315 Hill Street
Ann Arbor, Michigan   48104

The Center is the focus of a program of research on computer technology in education. Pilot projects are being conducted in the areas of course development, author aids, retrieval and display information, student response processing, and "on-line" interaction between author and student. A number of authors are using Coursewriter on an IBM 1050 terminal including slide projector and tape recorder connected by telephone line to IBM's Watson Research Center. About twenty-five short demonstration or exploratory units are being developed in the areas of mathematics, natural science, social science, engineering, and medicine. The purpose is to obtain experience with a variety of authors and subject areas, and to explore the capabilities and restrictions of the author input language.

The group is planning now for on-line capability via the university's IBM System 360 model 67 to become operational in 1967.

The general assumption is that eventually there will be a large central data bank. Perhaps what we really want is to give everyone a credit card with a memory bank in it. Such an alternative may not be technologically feasible for at least a hundred years. But essentially it would have in it a map of where to go for every bit of learning; each time some information was received, a hole would be punched. The system need not store all the background. At the end of the day, a person would put his credit card in a slot, and some time during the night whatever information was required would be read into it. This type of system would avoid the horrendous problems raised by the question of centralization versus decentralization of data. One hundred million people in one data bank is a frightening idea. The real issue is whether it is intelligent or economical to do it that way.

chapter 9
Some Characteristics of
Educational Data Banks
Allan B. Ellis

Computer-based data centers exist throughout the country in a variety of forms and stages of development. To army generals, who call them command and control centers, they serve as storehouses of data relevant to the conduct of war. For the businessman, commercial data networks keep records, update inventories, post bills, produce summaries, and generally monitor daily business transactions. In the field of education, much of the interest in data centers has evolved from the establishment of data-processing facilities in which large amounts of data of various sorts accumulate as by-products of such services as the production of report cards, the scoring and norming of tests, the creation and updating of pupil cumulative records, and the maintenance of teacher personnel files. In a few instances, centers have developed as direct results of educational research projects designed to explore the relationships among a large number of variables drawn from a substantial population. In all these examples it is the power and speed of the computer that makes it possible to process and analyze what would otherwise be unmanage-

108

able amounts of data. It is a mistake, however, to consider any of these centers data banks merely because they contain data, whatever the quantity. It takes more than data to make a data bank, and, in fact, content is the least important of the determining factors.

Educational data centers which have been developed to date may be considered, for convenience, under three headings—archives, clearinghouses, and consortia—even though most of the larger, more sophisticated ones possess aspects of each type and are not so easily classified. The categories are useful nonetheless, not only because they isolate the various functions of such centers but because they emphasize the fact that the key to the identity of a data center—and therefore to whether or not it qualifies to be called a data bank—is in the way it functions and almost not at all in what it contains. Three data centers may conceivably be of different types, for example, even though they contain precisely the same data.

For the most part, archives are storehouses of data generally associated with a large research project and designed to facilitate research in a particular area by maintaining comprehensive files. Often called data bases, these archives—which function much like vaults, providing a place for safekeeping—can be thought of entirely in physical terms as places where one goes to obtain data on which to do analysis. One such data base has existed for some time at the Student Counseling Bureau of the University of Minnesota. These data archives consist, for the most part, of the information accumulated for the past thirty years from Minnesota's statewide school and university testing programs. The data, available on data-processing cards and magnetic tape, have been used for long-term follow-up studies, analysis of trends and changes, and the like.

Clearinghouses have as their concern the accumulation of all material relevant to a given research domain and the establishment of mechanisms for disseminating such material. They differ from archives in that they are more gregarious; their main function is dissemination, to which storage is merely a means. The Center for Interest Measurement Research is an excellent example of an educational research clearinghouse. This center was established at the University of Minnesota in 1963, with the following goals: "(1) to maintain an active research program in interest measurement; (2) to serve as a focal point for information on related research conducted in other places; and (3) to serve as a repository for basic data on interest measurement." [1] A second example is the National Center created by the Association for Educa-

---

[1] David P. Campbell, "Research Frontier, the Center for Interest Measurement Research," *J. Counseling Psych.*, 1964, 11, 395.

tional Data Systems (AEDS) to serve as a clearinghouse for all pertinent information in the area of educational data processing. The activities of this National Center will range from establishing a professional placement service to underwriting the costs of making data-processing consultants available to local school systems, but the central function will be dissemination. Clearinghouses obviously perform certain archival functions, but since they attempt as well to enhance the researcher's ability to deal meaningfully with educational data, they come closer to resembling data banks.

Of the three types of data centers, however, the consortium looks most like a data bank both in organization and in operation. Although the consortium is concerned with research and dissemination to a large extent, its major role is to foster communication among individuals and their institutions in order to encourage joint research or coordinated research on problems in a given area. One such educational consortium is the Inter-University Communications Council, Inc. (INTER-COM), a nonprofit corporation formed at the University of Michigan to provide universities with an effective means of collaboration on the study of communications made possible by computers and data-processing techniques. Individuals from the member institutions have formed task forces to examine such areas as information networks, educational systems and technology, and continuing education. It is by incorporating functions of the two other forms of data centers, with top priority placed on enhancing interaction among individuals, that the consortium becomes the most complex type of data center, and most nearly a data bank.

In fact, a data bank is a consortium, with the important qualification that it not only incorporates the major functions of archives and clearinghouses, but redefines them. Merely taking on the tasks of storing data and disseminating information is not enough because these operations are essentially one-sided: in the first case, individuals contact the storehouse for data they may need in their research; in the second, they periodically receive information which may be of interest to them. In neither instance is there ordinarily any substantial interchange among the parties involved. Within a data bank, however, effort is directed not toward storage but to access and not toward dissemination but to interaction. There is a shift away from the one-way roads of transmitting or receiving toward a two-way road of communication, and traffic should flow heavily in both directions. Where the data are stored—that is, whether or not they are stored in a single location—becomes operationally irrelevant, so long as one has access to them when the need arises and one's chances to be meaningfully informed are increased by greater communication with people working in related areas. The data bank becomes the organizational mechanism that creates and maintains the network of relationships necessary to ensure both access and communication. The data bank is an established environment of cooperation within whose confines are three ingredients: data, access, and communication—and whose major activity is to process the commitment of the individuals who fall within its bounds.

In the past few years there has been a growing interest in the establishment of data banks for educational research purposes. Experience suggests that there are two principal ways by which educational data banks (EDB) are likely to be developed. They may be part of large educational research projects, such as Project TALENT and the International Project on the Evaluation of Educational Achievement, where the goal is to examine thoroughly a large representative sample of students measured on a wide variety of educationally relevant variables. Or they may be part of regional educational data-processing facilities—such as the New England Education Data Systems—whose initial activity is providing efficient, automated accounting assistance to local schools, but whose eventual aim is toward providing impetus for the conduct of research in the school setting. The second method is preferable, because the EDB evolves naturally from existing relationships, and its development suggests that these relationships may be more interactive and perhaps more lasting. The assumption underlying this preference is that the function of a data bank within the field of education is to create and maintain a network of communication among those parties engaged in the education enterprise within a region—universities, state departments of education, local school systems—so that through such communication the full force of these agencies can be brought to bear on the major issues confronting schools.

The three large data centers mentioned cut across the categories of archives, clearinghouse, and consortium, possessing to some degree features of each of the three types. A description of their operations follows, to give a clearer picture of the functions and possibilities of different kinds of data centers.

PROJECT TALENT

Project TALENT emerged from an awareness of the need to conduct a comprehensive aptitude and ability inventory of the nation's secondary-school students. The developers of the Project felt that if the demands of a dynamic, affluent society were to be met, it was of the utmost importance to identify the talents of the nation's youth. Such a national inventory would allow schools to plan more accurately, and would assist them in developing the potentials of students with a greater degree of certainty. Included in the Project would be a study of the nation's secondary schools.

In 1957 preliminary plans were developed at the University of Pittsburgh by the Institute of Research in Education for a long-range, large-scale educational research project involving a 5 per cent sample of the nation's secondary-school population and 1300 schools. It was estimated that approximately 440,000 students attending grades nine through twelve would be involved.

During 1958 the Cooperative Research Branch of the U.S. Office of Education, the National Institute of Mental Health, the Office of Naval Research, and the National Science Foundation lent their support to the development of the Project's operational plans. The first year of Project TALENT was devoted exclusively to the development of a battery of tests and other instruments for collecting data.

The plans of Project TALENT called for:

1. A testing and information-seeking program to obtain data in areas of aptitude, ability, achievement, and interests, as well as demographic information.

2. Collecting information on a sample of approximately 1300 secondary schools that would yield the significant characteristics of secondary schools on both the 8-4 and 6-3-3 systems.

The selected sample of high-school students was given a two-day series of examinations during March and April of 1960. The cooperating schools also completed questionnaires which sought information on school and guidance programs. Administered to the sample population of students were the following:

1. Information test—information about knowledge acquired in and out of school.

2. Language aptitude and ability tests—including such areas as English usage and word functions in sentences.

3. Complex intellectual aptitude tests—testing specific aptitudes in creativity, in mechanical and abstract reasoning, and in visualization.

4. Mathematics test—including arithmetic reasoning as well as introductory and advanced high-school mathematics.

5. Clerical and perceptual aptitudes—object inspection and table reading.

In addition to the tests, three questionnaires were administered: a Student Information Blank, an Interest Inventory, and a Student Activities Inventory. Each student was also asked to write one paragraph on "my views about an ideal occupation," and another on "what high school means to me."

A School Questionnaire was designed to provide information regarding average age, years of teaching, degrees held, etc., of the faculty and the principal of the school. Also included were questions about the type of school, accreditation, grading system, pupil-teacher ratio, and the community background of the school. Questions were asked about extracurricular activities, advancement policies, and school curriculum.

Counselors filled out a Guidance Program Questionnaire concerning the nature of the guidance facilities and the services of the school. Guidance personnel were also asked to provide information about the types of tests administered, the nature of the problems brought to them, and the kinds of help offered. The questionnaire sought information about their level of education, experience, job duties, and the like. In addition, counselors provided solutions to hypothetical guidance situations.

Project TALENT includes provisions for follow-up studies. It will attempt to determine what the students involved in the initial sample are doing one, five, ten, and twenty years after graduation from high school, to provide a continuing record of the activities of each student for a period of twenty years. The long-range objectives of Project TALENT can be delineated as follows:

1. Develop an inventory of human resources that will identify the capabilities of the nation's youth. This goal will be accomplished through an extensive test and questionnaire program.

2. Develop a set of standards for educational and psychological measurements. The data collected will make available a set of reliable values for standardizing tests.

3. Develop a comprehensive counseling guide indicating patterns of aptitude and ability which are predictive of success in various careers. The data obtained from the initial study and follow-ups will allow attempts to develop measures for accurate prediction of success.

4. Develop a better understanding of how young people choose their life work. The follow-up studies should provide insights regarding

factors which are the most significant in influencing the students' decisions, as well as information concerning success or failure in their work.

5. Develop a better understanding of the educational experiences that prepare students for their life work. The information derived from the study will serve as a ground for developing basic policies regarding the use of manpower.

6. Develop a data bank that can serve as a source of information for future research studies in the problem areas of education. The data on file on tapes at the University of Pittsburgh are now available to any qualified researcher.

To date, Project TALENT has published two reports on the basic plans for the study and the instruments used, a summary of the information obtained about American high schools, a description of the achievement and characteristics of a large sample of 15-year-old youngsters, both students and nonstudents, and a detailed report on the achievement, aptitudes, interests, and personality characteristics of American high-school students.

INTERNATIONAL PROJECT ON THE EVALUATION OF EDUCATIONAL ACHIEVEMENT

The International Project on the Evaluation of Educational Achievement (IEA) is designed to conduct cross-national studies with the purpose of obtaining objective measurements of educational attainment. One of the primary objectives of the project is to foster cooperation at all levels through the pooling of talent and knowledge in the interest of a common enterprise. The task of developing a systematic study of educational outcomes in the school systems of the cooperating countries is merely a prerequisite to the attainment of continuous collaboration, pooling of information, and the establishment of a strong coordinating agency.

The fundamental goal, however, is better education throughout the world. IEA will allow educational systems to place themselves under scrutiny; the resulting diagnostic comparisons should lead to improvements and continuous progress. The attainment of this goal is contingent upon two variables in particular: the development of examinations reliable and objective enough to permit measurements of the degree to which aims are achieved, and the extent to which the founders of IEA will be able to bring nations to cooperate in the project.

In 1958 a proposal made to the UNESCO Institute for Education suggested that it explore the possibility of establishing an "International Study of Intellectual Ability, Achievement, and Functioning of Children of School Age." Representatives of thirteen research centers which had worked together in the past on projects similar to the one under consideration met in June 1959 and decided to develop a pilot project to explore the possibility of implementing the ideas of the proposal. Later it was decided that the IEA study should extend into a considerably larger project encompassing a long-range series of cross-national researches using instruments designed by IEA. In the meantime the pilot project would proceed to test and evaluate the machinery that had been developed in order to foster cooperation between widely scattered groups in Europe, the Middle East, and North America. Two other tasks of the pilot project were: (1) to search among the participating nations for technical and intellectual resources and decide on the best way to use them, and (2) to pinpoint the research problem areas that would be explored in carrying out the project.

As of February 1964, IEA listed Belgium, England, Finland, France, Israel, Japan, Netherlands, Scotland, Sweden, and the United States as full members, and Australia and West Germany as associate members. It was determined that the initial phase of the research effort would concentrate on studying the last few years of formal schooling and would be done in one subject only—mathematics.

IEA is financed by a grant made by the U.S. Office of Education, specifically for administration and coordination, international meetings, consultants, the printing of tests, and data processing. The UNESCO Institute will accept subcontracts to perform research of an international nature closely akin to the interests of the study.

In order to evaluate educational achievement, IEA felt it would be imperative to answer a number of basic questions, restated in the form of hypotheses. In formulating the hypotheses, the Standing Committee of IEA was concerned that the international nature of the project not be subordinated to interests of a national character, that the collection of data be kept to a minimum, and that the testing of formulated hypotheses be of primary interest.

The hypotheses were grouped into six classifications, designed to serve also as the set of concepts that would encompass the ideas in the study.

1. *Values and Philosophies.*   Each country has unique values and philosophical viewpoints which are intricately related to man and society.

2. *Policy.*   Each country attempts to express its values for the society it wishes to foster through the policies it develops and enforces.

3. *Educational Practices.*   Each society attempts to perpetuate its philosophy of the good society by shaping educational practices so that what is taught, and the manner in which it is taught, will reflect its policies.

4. *Cognitive Learning Outcomes.*   IEA attempts to determine the manner in which students have learned mathematics, as well as to measure how much they have learned.

5. *Affective Learning Outcome.*   A central concern of IEA is to determine the interests of students in learning mathematics and their attitudes toward it.

6. *General Attitudes and Values.*   IEA assumes that some of the results of exposure to education can be attributed to educational practices. Other attitudes, although they may be related to educational practices, are not so easily attributable to such practices. This is a most difficult area to measure, but IEA attempts to estimate it and has evolved a number of hypotheses about relationships between this area and the others.

Data to be used in testing the foregoing hypotheses will include a mathematics achievement test, a student questionnaire, school information, and information drawn from national case studies.

At the national level, the machinery established for the development of tests is the following:

1. Experts in each country will assemble relevant material that specifies subject-matter attainment for students in the age range of 13 to 17 and over.

2. The reports prepared by the experts are forwarded to one individual who is responsible for preparing a working paper.

3. The working paper is submitted to national experts for evaluation and comments.

4. The revised working papers are then submitted to subject-matter experts who produce the first draft of the test.

5. This first draft is submitted to national experts who field test it with selected subgroups.

6. After the field test a committee of experts prepares the final form of the examination.

These steps were followed in the preparation of the mathematics test that was field tested during February and March of 1963.

All data gathered by national centers will be processed in the United States by an IBM 1230 Optical Mark Scoring Reader, which transfers the information to punch cards. The initial step in the treatment of the data by the IBM 7094 computer is to organize and separate the data into four master files, each corresponding to one of the major levels to be tested. These files consist of magnetic tapes that will contain data on every student, teacher, school, and report collected by the project.

"Working tapes" will be made from the master files for everyday use of the data. These tapes will include scores rather than item responses, a number of derived indices, and a weighting factor for each student.

IEA will supply each cooperating center with a report that will include statistics on the scores of tests (frequency distributions, measures of central tendency, and dispersion). Although no national reports are to be published until the "international report" appears, outlines of research at the national level may be made available to governments or to qualified individuals from the national centers cooperating in the program.

The four master files are available to participating centers for the conduct of further research, particularly in areas not covered by the hypotheses. Qualified investigators will be permitted to use the data collected by IEA for research purposes, after IEA has completed its analyses and reports.

NEW ENGLAND EDUCATION DATA SYSTEMS

The New England Education Data Systems (NEEDS) is a political experiment created to provide research and services to the educational community by linking educational agencies at the state, university, and local levels. As viewed by the local school system, NEEDS exists to aid the administrator—by removing the inefficiencies attached to clerical tasks and by providing a mechanism to assist decision making—in conducting his school with a maximum concern for the needs and development of the individual student. At the base of every school system, of course, is the hope that the individual student will be adequately prepared for the society in which he will work and live. But such realities of school administration as production of schedules, report cards, class lists, and attendance records, because of their immediacy, require attention and time.

NEEDS seeks to provide ways to reduce the time and attention taken by these clerical tasks, thereby releasing the administrator and his staff for more important creative work. But this is only one function of NEEDS. Its other concerns are the improvement of communication among universities, schools, and state departments of education; educational research; and organization and dissemination of school data.

The overriding aim of the program is to accelerate the operating machinery of education so that the instruction of each student may be individualized. The pressure to develop ways of keeping each student "on target" is increasing as greater numbers come to the doors of the schools. To achieve this aim, NEEDS is seeking to meet a number of challenges:

1. To eliminate the information bottleneck in school systems that comes from traditional procedures of record keeping.

2. To provide quick, accurate information for the use of state and federal agencies in their planning and financing of education.

3. To establish effective machinery to relate the research of universities to the day-to-day life of the school systems.

4. To bring technological improvements within the economic range of the public schools.

5. To develop a body of personnel with technological skills in both education and data processing.

6. To close the gap between the sophisticated level of data processing in business and the low level of school data processing.

7. To aid in the revision of state legislation so that the machinery of government will not impede logical and effective change when and where it is indicated.

8. To develop in public education the quality-control techniques to promote greater sophistication in school administration.

Membership in NEEDS is open to schools that are members of the New England School Development Council (NESDEC), and to colleges, universities, and state departments of education in New England. The current membership costs per school system, subject to review and adjustment by the board of directors, consist of a basic charge of $300 plus a per capita charge of $2.50 for secondary-school pupils and $1.50 for elementary-school pupils included in the project.

The operating structure of NEEDS is divided into four sections: (1) data-processing services, (2) operations research and development, (3) in-service training, and (4) basic research and formal instruction. It is possible, through careful coordination of the efforts of these divisions, not only to provide data-processing services to the schools, but also to use such services as the context for reexamining educational procedures and practices.

The three coordinating committees which aid the board of directors in planning and coordinating NEEDS activities represent the three areas of education in New England that NEEDS is designed to serve. A project administrator and his staff give overall direction to the operational structure of NEEDS. A coordinator, the key contact between NEEDS and the member school system, is appointed by his individual school system to deal with all operational matters. His responsibilities to NEEDS and to his system are many. Within his system his job is one of data management, which includes acquainting the staff with necessary procedures for using data-processing methods, planning a processing schedule to meet his system's requirements, and seeing that the schedule is followed by all members of the school staff.

The data-processing service section of NEEDS supplies ongoing services to the school systems and coordinates all related dissemination functions. In this section are the technicians who operate the hardware and actually supply the member schools with the services that are currently operational.

All experimental work on operations is done in the operations research and development section. Its responsibility is to bring experimental projects up to the point of being operational, to supply the necessary documentation and publications, and then move to another task. Refinements and improvements are its constant job, requiring close cooperation with the other groups. This section is staffed by computer-programming specialists and systems analysts.

The in-service training section is responsible for training the member school systems' coordinators in using the facilities of NEEDS to increase the efficiency of their systems' operation. It conducts technical sessions and summer institutes to instruct the coordinators in the methods and techniques needed at all levels touched by this project. The coordinators in turn instruct the local school personnel. It is through this program that the full advantage of NEEDS is realized.

The section for basic research and formal instruction is staffed by Harvard University. Its goal is to develop a systematic program for educational research on problems confronting schools in the New England region. One of the first steps taken in this direction is the planning and development of a NEEDS regional data center. In addition, formal courses are offered to students at universities in the region to assure the requisite sophistication in computer skills and research techniques.

Services rendered by NEEDS to its members fall, for the most part, under five operating systems entitled: file creation and maintenance, scheduling support, mark reporting, automated attendance, and test scoring and analysis. The input and output of these systems form the universe of data from which the present contents of the NEEDS data base have been selected. Naturally the flow into the data base will intensify as the number of services increases, although only in the first stages of development will NEEDS limit the contents to data that are by-products of such service. As the data bank begins to function as a medium to foster communication among various agencies of the education enterprise, the NEEDS staff proposes to solicit other data directly from these agencies so as to establish a broad base of educational data.

THE DYNAMICS OF THE DATA BANK

Although these three data centers express concern for data, access, and communication, none of them is a data bank in the fullest sense. For one thing, to varying degrees communication is more the *means* by which they operate than the *product* of their operation. This is most true of Project TALENT, whose extensive network of schools was established in order to permit the collection of data on a national sample of students, but is not at all maintained as an educational community. The other centers are somewhat more involved in fostering communication among their members as a continuing force for the conduct of educational research. In fact, it is a major goal of NEEDS to create such a collaborative arrangement, and therefore, this organization represents one of the best examples of a functioning educational data bank. The operations of all three centers, however—whether or not they qualify at the moment to be called "data banks"—have helped to clarify many of the problems relating to the storage, retrieval, updating, checking, and maintenance of large amounts of educational data.

The first of these problems is simply, what should go into the data base? * Since it is impossible to include everything, one is faced with the task of deciding in advance what data are likely to be needed by some researcher at some future date. Attending this selection process is the likelihood that sins of omission will cause severe inadequacies, even if provision is made within the system for the inclusion of new variables when the need arises. Once answers are provided to these questions of what the data base ought to contain, there is another, perhaps more baffling, problem of deciding what data should be removed. Sooner or later, certain data will become outdated, inaccurate, irrelevant, or in some other way outlive their usefulness. Should these data be carried along and treated as vestigial organs to be cut out only when painful, or might the system be programmed to destroy part of itself periodically? These are a few of the issues which are critical not merely for practical reasons, but because the ways in which they are solved determine the essential character of the data center and the relationships among its members. The structure in which data are stored, for example, may have a severely limiting effect on the questions one may ask, or on the flexibility of the output form. It is dangerously easy for a data center to defeat its own purposes if care is not exercised. There is also the extreme of attempting such programming elegance to overcome these limitations that one loses sight of the original objectives. Perhaps the solution lies in viewing data not as the object of activity but rather as the result. In a sense this is what happens in a data bank; the foremost concern is with creating a meeting ground for continued discourse among people engaged in the educational enterprise. Conceivably the data base can be the by-product of such intercourse instead of the well from which it is expected to spring. That is not to say, of course, that the many problems relating to data and access need not be faced. Clearly, as the concepts of data, access, and communication are expanded within the context of the data bank, the problems expand as well, and the solutions become more pressing.

These concepts—data, access, and communications—while continuing to carry their usual connotations, take on special meanings within data banks. Data, for example, comes to include people—or, more broadly, resources—to which those involved have access. This is a major source of the dynamic quality of EDB's and is the reason why the con-

---

* Perhaps we should gather data only when we have a specific use in mind. When there is an existing set of data to analyze, the data often turn out to be wrong or inadequate. Why spend billions of dollars collecting information that will never be used?

cept of a data bank as a storehouse is so totally inadequate. In the case of access, the added ingredient is a sort of faith. It is a psychological state of assurance that a person's capability is generally enhanced by his involvement. Not only does the individual feel confident that the data bank will work effectively; he is confident about the relationships themselves, since he feels he can incorporate into his own functioning the capabilities and talents of other members. A partnership, insofar as it differs from a corporation, comes closest to resembling this dimension of access. When a partnership fails, its creditors can reach into the personal funds of the partners—and what one cannot bear, the other must —to gain satisfaction. This kind of commitment justifies the expectation that when one partner speaks, he speaks for the others, and not merely for himself. Each man incorporates into his own functioning the commitment of the others. This is the kind of commitment that is fostered and "processed" by the data bank.

Finally, the idea of communication is expanded so that the parties involved play active rather than passive roles in the enterprise. Schools, for example, do not, as is often proposed, become the recipients of good research, or innovation, or such; rather, they actively participate at all levels in the generation of such activity. There are no poor relations in an educational data bank, and to the extent that education is enhanced, it is enhanced in concert. The EDB is the key element in the process of confrontation, discourse, and participation in which the major educational institutions engage.

To view an educational data bank, therefore, as merely a container of data is to miss the point. The currency is data, to be sure, but they are ineffective as media of exchange without the commitment and the communication such exchange implies.

We are trying to deal with instructional values on an individual basis. We now have an educational enterprise in which 2.5 million teachers are trying to educate 50 million learners. To make improvements we must first take a look at what education is of most worth. In thinking about education we automatically assume institutions— buildings, a principal, and so on. But what if we did not have schools? No double-loaded corridors, no problems of scheduling and attendance. Let's say we had access to all knowledge in terms of a computer-assisted framework. Our problems would be to construct individualized curricular experiences; to deal with individualized activities; to account, in the counting sense, for the achievement of students in a program; to deal with the logistic problems of the right equipment in the right place at the right time. With the focus placed on these issues, school facilities would be designed to bring people together for human interaction, rather than for housekeeping blocks of rooms.

chapter 10
Higher-Order Needs in Contemporary School Design
Richard Myrick
Stanley L. Cohen, Barbara S. Marx

The last two decades have been a period of ferment for the American educational system. Technological advances and innovations in teaching methods have presented the educator with exciting possibilities, the future applications of which can be only partly envisioned at this time. New subjects and activities have been added to the curriculum. The new teaching methods being developed make use of teaching teams and emphasize flexibility and multipurpose spaces. Advances in computer technology and information retrieval, as well as in audiovisual methods and programmed learning, will bring about many changes and will require new approaches and creative decisions on the part of school administrators. Students can be placed in groups of varying size according to the kind of material being taught. School architecture, however, has lagged behind current developments in American education. The ways in which spaces in educational facilities are designed and used have remained for the most part traditional, and only recently has school architecture begun to move in a direction that will permit the new developments to be incorporated into the teaching process.

Clearly, if the American school system is to benefit from the advances now taking place in the technology of education, new designs in architecture are required. In addition, it is now recognized that architecture may influence behavior. Much research must be done before this influence can be demonstrated specifically, but it is an extremely important area for future architectural achievement. In studying what may be accomplished in this area of design, researchers will gain invaluable help from computers in analyzing how architecture can bring about desired behavior on the part of occupants.

The problems of architectural planning may be divided into two categories: those relating to the physical needs of the users of a building and those relating to psychological needs. In the former category may be requirements pertaining to the size, shape, and dimensions of classrooms and lecture halls, and the various relationships that must exist between these spaces. Often these requirements are expressed in numerical terms such as the size and number of spaces and items of equipment required. In the second category, the basic underlying consideration is that students using the educational facility must be able to integrate the various courses in their programs of study, must develop certain social skills, and must acquire favorable attitudes toward learning and its practical function in the adult world. To help meet these needs, certain relationships are necessary between student and teacher and between students. The architecture of the school can help influence these relationships. We shall place emphasis on these psychological needs, which have been given less consideration than, and may be as important as, physical needs in the design of schools.

ADVANTAGES OF INFORMAL LEARNING

If efficiency were the primary consideration in school operation the design of future school buildings would be a simple task. But the purpose of a school is not just to make maximum use of facilities or to convey information quickly. A high-school senior who has not developed attitudes appropriate for success in college or a job, or who fails to comprehend the broad meaning and application of principles he has been exposed to in his courses, or who fails to acquire the social skills that help him get along with others has not had a good education. His training has neglected areas that are vital to his progress. It is these areas of understanding that make up the "higher-order needs" of students, needs that can be met more fully when psychological requirements are taken into account in the design of schools.

Higher-order needs of students frequently are satisfied by informal learning activities. We shall consider as formal learning activities those that are planned in advance and controlled by the administrative system —for example, classroom lectures conducted at a specified time and meeting such specified conditions as having the results recorded by means of attendance records, daily classroom grades, and tests. By contrast, informal learning activities typically are unscheduled, occur spontaneously, and are not rigorously arranged to meet specified conditions. These activities may involve a student with one or more students, a student and a teacher, a student and some materials, or the student alone. Informal learning activities cover a considerable range that may include a brief conversation in the cafeteria about a forthcoming test, a discussion between a teacher and student explaining further some points made in a previous class session, or an individual student's perusal of an exhibit or bulletin board in the hallway before class begins.

Speaking in the terms of behavioral scientists, we may classify the situations that lead to informal learning as either "social" or "perceptual." Social situations refer to informal interactions occurring between people who make up the school population, whereas perceptual situations refer to the means by which the building allows an individual to see and understand the activities occurring within it. For example, the individual student may gain his understanding about relationships among ideas socially through interactions with other people, or perceptually by seeing a bulletin board display.

The educator may ask, as he sees students cluttering up the crowded school hallways with noisy conversations, "How does one define informal learning and what are its benefits?" When the focus of an informal social interaction or an informal perceptual situation is on any material relevant to school matters, informal learning is occurring. And although these activities do not fit into current educational pigeonholes and may often seem an inconvenience to the school administrator, informal learning is extremely important in that it complements and thus helps to complete what the student gains through formal learning. In fact, some of the steps needed to complete the educational process, such as reinforcing, clarifying, discussing, and generalizing what has been learned, can best occur through informal learning.

What are the characteristics of social and perceptual interactions that make these informal learning activities so important? Two of the most valuable products of informal social interactions in the educational situation are: (1) the development of mature intellectual and social attitudes that enable the student to understand better the meaning and usefulness of what he is learning; and (2) the mobilization of the student's energies and abilities in the direction of a worthwhile personal goal, so as to motivate him strongly. Informal social interaction between student and teacher is desirable in learning because it is generally benign in nature and encourages greater student participation in the learning process. In addition, social interaction of this kind contributes to realistic goal setting with an accompanying higher level of motivation because it can create a counseling atmosphere that is conducive to easy discussion of the student's future career plans, of his abilities and limitations, and of the standards and opportunities that exist for him.

With regard to perceptual learning activities, we have mentioned the desirability of a student's perceiving the relevance of what he learns in school to his later life, since the student's understanding of the relationship between present learning and its future application is a key factor in his motivation. Thus an important aspect of informal learning consists of the student's perceiving, as he moves about the building, the relationship between his present various activities and his general program of study so that he is able to integrate these into a meaningful whole, rather than viewing his courses in a fragmented, compartmentalized way. Designs of school buildings contribute toward the orientation of the student when they help him perceive the full range of learning activities and the relationships between them. The purpose of such orientation is not only to keep the student from being physically lost in the complex labyrinth of rooms and corridors that characterizes many modern schools, but also to keep him from being overwhelmed by the volume and variety of subject matter, the number of years he must spend in mastering it, and the seeming remoteness of his study program from his often vaguely realized goals.

The preceding comments suggest that informal learning in the social and perceptual areas makes an important contribution to meeting the student's higher-order needs in the school setting. The question now facing school planners is what kind of architectural design helps to promote informal learning and hence satisfaction of these higher-order needs?

REQUISITES FOR SCHOOL DESIGN

One design factor worth considering relates both to the places where important formal learning activities are conducted and to the routes taken from one location in the school to another. Routes can make certain formal learning situations more familiar and accessible by taking people past "contact points" where there are activities to be seen or people to talk with in a manner contributing to informal learning. The architectural design of corridors and the general layout of the school can encourage routes that maximize, rather than minimize, the number of such "contact points." The principal of a New England high school chose to have his office located on a main corridor in a way that made it easy for students to stop in briefly and talk with him. Clearly, favorable design will not suffice if the school's administrative setup creates an atmosphere that is unfavorable to informal learning; but the administration of the school, of course, lies beyond the province of the architect.

Besides functioning as a means of displaying a variety of activities to the student, routes can function as meeting places. The corridors of buildings are places where one student may see a hundred or more faces in the brief interval between class periods. If these corridors are used by a variety of individuals—students, teachers, and administrators—and provide spaces where people can stop and talk without obstructing the flow of traffic, then they provide opportunities for informal learning.

Therefore another kind of design factor that is important for school planners to consider is the "mix." The term "mix," as used here, refers to various ways in which groups of activities or people may be assembled in one location or along one corridor. Depending on the kind of mix, different goals can be attained. From the standpoint of the physical needs of people using the school building, it is probably most convenient and efficient to locate all similar activities in one place—all related departments, offices, or classes of one grade level, for instance. From the standpoint of psychological needs, a more heterogeneous mix is more desirable, one which provides a social environment making possible a variety of informal learning situations.

At present relatively little is known about how heterogeneous the mix of people should be in order to encourage informal learning. Successful interactions require a mutual satisfaction of needs, and if individuals have little in common it is difficult to obtain satisfaction. Depending on the type of educational program, it may well be that students one year apart will benefit more from a diverse mix leading to an increased number of interactions than will students who are three years apart. Furthermore, though interest in the benefits of informal learning is increasing, it must be remembered that great sociality is not always desirable. Certain activities are best accomplished without distraction, as with independent study or writing and painting. Other kinds of activities might require specific interaction with one type of individual but not another, as in the case of a person who seeks information or an answer to a specific query.

Recent ideas about office organization tried out by psychologists in a government agency suggest ways in which the development of the proper mix can promote both efficiency and constructive social interaction. In making office assignments, the question was how workers, some of them experienced and others new to the job, should be combined to meet the requirements of the task and to satisfy the workers' higher-order needs. It was found that placing two experienced workers at adjacent desks often resulted in run-of-the-mill performance. Much social interaction occurred, but little of it pertained to getting work done. When two inexperienced workers were placed at adjacent desks, their performance was barely adequate. Although the new workers showed much enthusiasm and offered many innovations, their social interactions were directed primarily toward trying to learn the proper steps and procedures for accomplishing their assignments. When the office was reorganized to place one new worker and one experienced worker together to work as a team, there were many favorable results. The inquisitive and open-minded new people, working with experienced personnel, awakened fresh enthusiasm for the task and caused a reexamination of traditional work methods while benefitting from the continuity of procedure and job know-how supplied by the experienced workers. By applying this type of experimentation to the school situation, it could be discovered how different mixes of students might best satisfy their higher-order needs through interactions leading to informal learning, without sacrificing the requirements of education.

Also important when considering mix is the extent to which architecture increases the chances of the student's becoming aware of the full range of subjects taught in the school. A restricted mix leads to the grouping together of teachers and courses belonging to one department of study, with science courses in one wing of the building, history in another. A number of educational disadvantages result from a restricted mix. One is that the student is prevented from gaining knowledge of the possibilities available to him. It may be that a substantial amount of current academic and vocational counseling of students is required simply to overcome restricted mix. A considerable portion of the counselor's time is often spent describing opportunities available in the school, when a more diverse mix of activities would give the student a greater chance of seeing and assessing those opportunities for himself.

A restricted mix also makes it harder for the student to see the relationships among the parts of his program. One newly completed school in the Southwest which offers a four-year dental training program is organized so the activities of each class occupy a separate floor of the building. This arrangement allows little interaction between classes and effectively prevents lower-level students from conversing with upper-level students. Increased interaction might help the lower-level student understand how his present studies relate to the whole program as well as to his occupational goals.

A restricted mix often occurs in colleges and universities built on the campus plan. This type of architecture tends to isolate the different academic departments in widely separated buildings, so the student has little chance of becoming personally familiar with the range of opportunities offered. He may spend his four years on the campus without ever setting foot in certain buildings, as a result learning nothing of the activities and interests of the students who frequent them. Campus-type architecture, then, tends to decrease the contact and interaction between individuals in different fields of study, limiting the sharing and diffusion of knowledge throughout the student body, and throughout the academic community as a whole.

Just as with mixes of people, there is a limit to the amount of mixing of departments which is favorable for the student and administratively practical for the school. In deciding what kinds of architecture will promote the optimal mix of people and activities, certain economic and construction factors must also be taken into account.

Another determinant of social interaction is an aspect of the school building which, adapting the terminology that Kevin Lynch applies to cities, may be referred to as "nodes" and "zones." Nodes are "contact points" or small areas where people gather. These may be obvious places like a student lounge, or less obvious ones identifiable as nodes only because people gather there. Zones are larger areas or "territories" to which "ownership" by a group or several groups can be ascribed. Traditionally, classrooms are "teacher zones," for the persons occupying the space at a particular time and the topics of conversation are determined by the teacher. Typically the interactions there are formal and planned. Some hallways are "student zones" in that these become areas where informal spontaneous student meetings may take place without interference. Each zone may carry within it certain expected behavior. In a city, for example, the automobile driver is expected to show behavior appropriate to the zone in which he is driving: to be quiet in hospital zones, and in shopping zones to be alert for pedestrians and the sudden stopping and starting of other vehicles. Similarly in school architecture different zones or parts of the school can evoke different behaviors.

THE COMPUTER IN DESIGN RESEARCH

In designing research to predict opportunities for informal learning in a specific architectural environment, using the notions of routes, zones, contact points, and mix, the computer can be highly useful. The computer already assists college officials who use information about room assignments to predict the traffic flow of students. But instead of trying to decrease the traffic in hallways, our purpose is to increase it along certain specified lines. Two groups of input variables must be taken into account: (1) student variables—sex, class level, and academic study program, plus such attitudinal and personality factors as interest in learning and gregariousness; (2) architectural and administrative factors—layout of the corridor system, size and location of classrooms, and the distribution throughout the school building of the different student class levels in terms of courses and activities.

It is hypothesized that these two groups of variables interact to produce those kinds of social contact that can lead to informal learning. Social contact can be described in terms of a set of output variables which are both architectural and behavioral in nature. These include routes, contact points, and mix. After the computer has predicted the magnitude of these output variables, one would be able to make statements about the number of opportunities for interaction between individual students according to their schedules, the routes they follow, and the amount of time available between classes. One could also make some predictions about the probabilities of these opportunities being used for informal learning. In other words, architectural and administrative variables determine whether there will be an opportunity for interactions to occur, while student variables determine whether the interactions actually do occur and whether they are relevant to academic matters. Because of the large number of students and the number of different behavioral and architectural variables, investigation of social interaction and informal learning becomes more feasible with the aid of the computer. By means of the computer it is possible to simulate interactional behavior in different architectural environments, and thus to study the effects of different kinds of school building design.

Computers can also aid in research related to the design of schools by making a cluster analysis of the needs of the student, teacher, and administrative populations using the school building. The object, as suggested by Christopher Alexander, an architect and mathematician, is to break down the design problem into logical and manageable subsections. To make a simple outline of this process, one first lists the needs, both physical and psychological, of the users of the building. The list might contain some fifty to one hundred needs. Although it could easily be made considerably longer, the inclusion of many more items would expand the complexity of the problem and make it cumbersome to solve.

Next, one asks a number of judges to compare each need with every other need in the list, asking whether a design action taken to meet one need would have an influence on steps that might be taken to meet any of the others. This is perhaps the most difficult part of the procedure. Large numbers of comparisons must be made—one hundred needs on the list would make roughly 5000 comparisons necessary. Furthermore, substantial quantities of data about existing school buildings must be incorporated if the comparisons are to be valid; for to carry out these comparisons, one must have sufficient data to understand the impact of satisfying one need upon satisfying other needs.

The interrelationships between all the needs can then be resolved on the computer, using an application of linear-graph theory, which is akin to factor analysis. The final product consists of clusters of needs in each one of which, ideally, all the needs are related but independent of needs in other clusters. The school building planners have then reduced their design problem into manageable subsections with comparatively few needs to consider in each one. Because each cluster of related needs is independent of the others, the planners may solve each separately and then assemble these solutions without fear that solving one part of the design problem will interfere with solving its other parts.

Aside from these examples, other research dealing with how architecture affects the learning process might be directed toward determining the architectural characteristics of school buildings, and the behavior and types of social interaction which can be attributed to them. Data could be collected and analyzed by computers to describe both the type of interaction and the location in the school building where it occurs. Explanations could then be sought as to why within one school certain types of interactions take place in certain locations and not in others, or why one type of interaction that occurs in a certain area of one school does not occur in a similar area of another school. Eventually it would be possible to determine which architectural features are desirable to include in a school building. Since it is believed that routes, zones, contact points, and mix are physically and architectually identifiable, further research might accumulate the knowledge necessary for creating zones for the desired interaction.

Flexibility is a much-used word denoting a much-desired attribute of modern schools. Through increasing flexibility, school architecture is beginning to meet the physical needs of students better. One way in which flexibility is being achieved is through the design of large generalized spaces that permit a variety of uses. This arrangement permits "plug-in" adaptable use of the space. At a high school in Long Island, New York, an overhead service network of ducts provides the utilities needed for a science laboratory, while movable laboratory modules on the floor can be arranged to meet a variety of requirements.

Comparable advances in school building design will be needed to satisfy students' psychological needs. Research on the effect on learning of different kinds of routes, mixes, and zones might provide concepts from which architects can benefit in designing buildings that allow greater amounts of informal learning to coexist with and enrich the formal educational program.

Higher-order or psychological needs have been neglected so far in school planning. This neglect is not so much due to the failure of educators to recognize the importance of such needs as to the fact that architects have not yet provided ways of meeting them. More information must be gathered about ways in which school architecture can contribute further to the satisfaction of psychological needs. At present, however, the relationship between higher-order needs and school architecture is obscure. It is becoming apparent that, to study the relationship, a redefinition of architecture in social-science terms will be needed. The next stages of development in the architecture of schools will not come about simply through study of traditional architectural variables such as color, light, size, and proportion, but rather through the application of certain social-science concepts. Research that draws upon the thinking of people in education, computer technology, social science, and architecture can lead to the development of school buildings that will increase the effectiveness of the American educational system.

selected readings

Appleyard, D., K. Lynch, and J. Myer. *The View from the Road*. Cambridge, Mass.: M.I.T. Press, 1964.

Barker, R. On the nature of the environment. *Journal of Social Issues*, 4, 1963, 17–38.

Barker, R., and P. Gump. *Big School, Small School*. Stanford, Calif.: Stanford University Press, 1964.

Chermayeff, S., and C. Alexander. *Community and Privacy*. Garden City, N.Y.: Doubleday, 1963.

Educational Facilities Laboratories. *Profiles of Significant Schools*. (A series of reports providing information on some of the latest developments in school planning.) New York, 1962.

Hall, E. *The Study of Man's Spatial Relations and Boundaries*. Prepared for Conference on Medicine and Anthropology. Harriman, N.Y.: Arden House, 1961.

Hereford, K., and S. Hecker. *Relationships among School Design, Utilization, Personnel Interaction, and Attitudes*. East Lansing, Mich.: Bureau of Educational Research, College of Education, Michigan State University, 1963.

Horowitz, H. The architect's program and the behavioral sciences. Lecture presented at Syracuse University. Syracuse, N.Y.: May 13, 1965, mimeo.

Lynch, K. *The Image of the City*. Cambridge, Mass.: M.I.T. Press, 1954.

Myrick, R. How to win friends and influence students. From *The Teaching of Architecture*, 1963, AIA-ACSA Teacher Seminar. Washington, D.C.: American Institute of Architects, 1964.

Myrick, R. A new concept in the architectural planning of dental schools. *Journal of Dental Education*, **29**, December 1965, 382–386.

133

Myrick, R., B. Marx, and S. Cohen. Is what is good for General Motors *good* for architecture? *AIA Journal,* **XLV,** March 1966, 62–66.

Sommer, R., and H. Ross. Social interaction on a geriatrics ward. *International Journal of Social Psychiatry,* **4,** 1958, 128–133.

Spring, B. Technology: "The plug-in" school. *Architectural Forum,* **119,** 2, 1963, 68–74.

Stea, D. Toward a psychology of environmental design: The impact of man-made ecology. Stanford, Calif.: Stanford University, undated mimeo.

part 3
Teaching the Computer Sciences

Leaving aside computer-assisted instruction, what is the place of the computer in the classroom? To what uses will it be put, not only for teaching about computers but also for the teaching of science and for problem solving? Does the computer really belong in the classroom? Or is it a device that might best be left out for a while, with students doing their basic calculations with pencil and paper? What is the best point educationally at which to introduce computers?

chapter 11

Computer Programming Courses in Secondary Schools
Sylvia Charp

That much of our present scientific, commercial, political, and social activity depends on the state of computer technology today is little understood and less appreciated. Our progress as human beings has been and continues to be accelerated as a result of computer applications. Yet education in computers is not reaching all levels of the population. Our young people particularly need to be educated to the widening variety of applications and the intellectual challenges that exist in the areas of computer sciences.

The place for computer education in the secondary schools, however, is still not clear. Though instruction about computers and their applications is considered part of the curriculum in many colleges and universities, the opportunity to use computers in secondary-school classrooms has been extended to relatively few students.

Until now, in the instructional program of the secondary school digital computers have been utilized by students in conjunction with certain academic courses and in some vocational programs. The mathe-

137

matics and science curricula have already been enriched by the use of the computer, and innovations in various subject fields are constantly being sought. Vocational training in data processing, which constitutes a wide variety of useful skills ranging from keypunching and use of unit-record equipment to operating and programming digital computers, is now being offered in some secondary schools.

The rapid growth of electronic data processing has created many misconceptions. Educators in particular must study the capabilities of modern computing systems more fully: the individual who lacks a grasp of the potentials and limitations of these devices can be severely handicapped. And students should be enlightened instead of frightened by the changes occurring in our society. No matter what career a student pursues, he should be alerted to the efficiencies of the computer so he can benefit from them. An engineer or a secretary may have to use the computer as a tool to solve problems or as a device for retrieving information. The clerk, the mechanic, the scientist, will each require some knowledge of the function of computers. The acquisition of basic concepts of what a computer does and how it operates will be of prime importance in general education.

While the large-scale computer is a twentieth-century marvel, in principle it is not far different from man's earlier attempts to understand and control his environment. An understanding of the historical development of the computer is as much a part of the student's general education as an understanding of the development of other machines since the advent of the Industrial Revolution.

A counting system can be designed with any number system as a base. Daily the student encounters different number systems, such as the decimal system of counting and the duodecimal system used for clock time. The familiar on-off position of simple switches can be related to the principle of the binary system of numbers in the design of digital computers. Working with different number systems enlarges the student's appreciation of number systems as a concept. Students are familiar with the existence of simple coding techniques like the Morse code. Coding converts everyday language into a form that is acceptable and adaptable and makes possible communication with a computer.

Careful planning and analysis are necessary to carry out tasks efficiently, whether one is programming a computer, building a house, or preparing for a trip. Flow charting is a graphic representation of a road map of activities. All students need this step-by-step approach to problem solving; the techniques gained can be applied to many life situations.

The objectives of a general education course on computers may be fourfold:

1. To familiarize the student with the field of data processing: manual, mechanical, electromechanical, and electronic devices.
2. To develop an understanding of the basic concepts involved in data processing.
3. To stimulate interest in careers in data processing.
4. To explore rigorous thought processes.

Information on computers introduced into the sociology course for secondary students would alert all students to the world of work as it is affected by data processing. This orientation could include the following topics:

1. Brief introduction to computers.
2. History of the development of the computer.
3. Description of how a computer solves problems.
4. Applications of computers as tools for control.
5. Design and simulation capabilities of computers.

A course in computers can be part of the general mathematics or science curricula. An introductory course requiring no knowledge of advanced mathematics could be offered to all students, and could be the basis for advanced work centered around the student's interest and aptitudes. Having a computer available to execute student problems is of definite advantage to any computer course; but a knowledge of fundamentals and the understanding of the principles around which a computer operates can be gained even without a computer. The value of hands-on or actual experience with the computer, however, should not be minimized.

The following topics can be introduced in either the science or mathematics curriculum:

1. Information flow in a computer.
2. Functions of sections of a computer.
3. Numbering systems.
4. Flow charting—concept of looping.
5. Communicating with the computer.
6. Machine language—coding—hypothetical computer.
7. Use of compilers.

8. Steps in computer analysis of a problem.

9. How computers work for us.

COMPUTERS IN CONJUNCTION WITH COURSES

The secondary-school curriculum provides for two types of students, the college-bound and the preemployment groups. Most of the work in computer education has been with the college-bound in the area of the sciences. Since the language currently in effective use with computers is mathematical in nature, and since learning in thought processes required in the flow charting of a problem must be performed in a finite number of steps, it has been recommended that computer programming be taught by mathematics teachers. Fortunately the present mathematics and science curricula afford many opportunities for the use of a digital computer.

USE OF THE COMPUTER IN THE STUDY OF MATHEMATICS AND SCIENCE

Many high-school programs of this nature are at present in operation in various parts of the country and the task of introducing the computer in the mathematics program is constantly being facilitated. The National Council of Teachers of Mathematics (NCTM) has considered the growing need of mathematics teachers for information concerning digital computers and for ways of fitting this information into the present mathematics program. In 1963 a book entitled *Computer-Oriented Mathematics, An Introduction for Teachers* was published and distributed to members of the Council. Also a Committee on Computer-Oriented Mathematics was formed in 1963 to consider the place of computers in the study of mathematics. A report, "Computers and School Mathematics," was prepared under the auspices of the Committee and appeared in *The Mathematics Teacher* for May 1965. As part of its continuing activity, the Committee proposes to sponsor the preparation of a series of booklets about the operation of computers, stressing the importance of algorithmic programming and the use of a monitor system, as well as a series of instruction booklets for teachers. Each booklet will apply computers to a mathematical topic in the present secondary-school curriculum.

Also completed is a twelfth-grade book on computing by the School

Mathematics Study Group (SMSG). This is concerned with algorithms and problem solving. The book consists of three separate texts, each with its teacher's manual. The main text can be studied independently of the machine and uses a "flow-chart" language. A Fortran text and an Algol text accompany the main text.

The objectives of the SMSG course are:

1. To introduce and provide opportunities for the students to use the step-by-step (algorithmic) process in the mathematics curriculum.

2. To use computer-oriented concepts in problem solving.

3. To advance the level of mathematical experience and maturity by the introduction of new methods.

4. To provide knowledge and experience in an area of study that is beneficial to the student's future education.

The National Science Teacher's Association has published two booklets, *Digital Computers, Theory and Uses* and *A Teacher's Guide*. These have been used effectively with science classes on the ninth-grade level.

Secondary schools preparing the academic student aim to provide experience and knowledge for college work. Since many colleges own computer installations and are using the computer as a tool in a variety of disciplines, college-bound secondary-school students are being exposed to concepts of digital computers. Many of the programs currently being offered, however, are outside the regular school program or held during the summer months, and are open only to superior students with top scholastic records.

In a recent survey, sixty-five schools involved in computer programming were investigated.[1] All of these had easy access to a computer. The feeling was expressed that computer programming should be taught in the high school; in about 30 per cent of the high schools surveyed computer courses had existed in the curriculum for over five years. Of schools with an enrollment of over 1500, about 65 per cent offered computer courses. It was felt by 90 per cent of the schools in the study that the course should be taught in the junior or senior year. For courses in computer programming that required a good aptitude in mathematics, only those students were admitted whose IQ was at least 110, and who

---

[1] "An Investigation of the Feasibility of, and the Content for, an Introduction Course in Computer Programming in the Mathematics Program at Morris Hills High School, Rockaway, New Jersey" (school year, 1964–65).

had successfully completed courses in beginning and intermediate algebra and plane geometry. A year was a minimum requirement for courses that offered advanced topics in mathematics.

The following topics were studied in the computer-programming courses: programming in Fortran, applications of iterative processes, flow charting, calculations with approximate numbers, determinants and matrices, symbolic logic, elementary number theory, Boolean algebra, infinite sequences and series, linear programming, analysis of errors of approximations, probability theory.

The foregoing are for the student in the junior or senior year. There are mathematical applications, however, for the use of the computer at earlier grade levels. Seventh-grade students could study number bases and the conversions from one to another, and could write a program to convert number bases. In the eighth grade a simple program might be written to test whether a number is a prime. A program to solve a quadratic equation could be given students in the ninth grade. Geometry students could compute pi or, given four points, determine whether they form the vertices of a square, a rectangle, a rhombus, a quadrilateral, or none of these. In the high-school curriculum many problems are adapted to computer solution.

Most of the programs that have been developed for computer instruction give students access to a computer. An interesting approach to hands-on computer instruction currently in use by the school district of Philadelphia is a portable computer with an added oscilloscope and an extra off-line flexowriter purchased to circulate among five schools. The instructor for the participating teachers, all of whom are from the mathematics and science areas, is provided by the manufacturer. Additional in-service classes are held as the need arises. The computer is scheduled for an initial three-week visit to each school, to be followed at a later date by a four-week visit in the same sequence. In each case the computer visit is preceded by the arrival of the off-line flexowriter to prepare programs. The curriculum as well as the number of students involved varies in the different schools. Two schools use the computer for extracurricular activity and classes are held before and after regular school hours. One course is taught by a science teacher who puts a strong emphasis on electronics and physics. One school uses the computer for general orientation for most eleventh- and twelfth-grade academic mathematics students. The course taught is not "computer programming" but "computer appreciation." The aims are to expose the student to computer concepts, acquaint him with computer vocabulary, and establish a basic understanding of how computers can be programmed. These aims are pursued with the machine present in the classroom, providing some students with hands-on experience, while putting all students in contact with a computer. The course, consisting of ten lessons, is taken out of the regular mathematics curriculum.

Dobbins Technical High School in Philadelphia has been teaching computer concepts as part of the student's class work in trigonometry and advanced algebra. Through this instruction the students solve a few of their homework exercises by use of the computer installed in the school's data-processing laboratory. The students thereby become aware of the usefulness of computers in solving their immediate work problems. In addition, students are encouraged to continue with further computer education. To accomplish these objectives, approximately 100 students spend ten of the 85 periods scheduled in trigonometry and advanced algebra in the computer laboratory. Instruction is scheduled about every two weeks, as follows:

Lecture 1:   General introductory lecture on the digital computer and its operation.

Lecture 2:   The basic Fortran programming method. This language is used since it requires little knowledge of computer circuitry and a relatively short period for instruction. It is also designed primarily for mathematical and scientific calculations, and its language closely resembles mathematical notation. Fortran is widely acceptable to many machines and is used for mathematical applications in many large-scale computer systems.

Lecture 3:   A simple problem encountered in the mathematics classroom is written in Fortran with the student's assistance. The flow chart is developed first and the algorithmic approach to problem solving is explained. The problem is solved on the computer by the instructor.

Lecture 4:   Lecture on flow charts continued and additional Fortran language explained. More problems are demonstrated by the instructor on the computer.

Lectures 5–8:   Problems from the trigonometry and advanced algebra texts are solved on the computer. The mathematics of the problem previously has been explained in the mathematics classroom. Students and instructor flow chart, program, and run the problems in the computer.

Lectures 9–10:   Students demonstrate the programming of their individual problems to the class.

A project to teach mathematics through the use of a time-shared computer was recently conducted in Massachusetts. Its purpose was the development of a mathematical laboratory based on a time-shared digital computer. Here a computer is brought to the classroom and used as a tool in the teaching of general mathematics as well as an aid to the teacher in demonstrating the more difficult mathematical concepts. The project dealt with students at three levels of maturity, grades 6, 9, and 12, in five different schools. It proposed to investigate whether:

1. A terminal teletype connected to a large computer operated in the time-shared mode will give the mathematics student the feeling of working on his own computer.

2. Having the computer on an "always-ready" basis will encourage students to engage extensively in voluntary extracurricular use of the computer terminal.

3. The presence of a continuously available real-time computer in the classroom will lead the student to acquire a more thorough grasp of mathematics as measured by the standard achievement tests.

The time-shared computer located in Cambridge, Massachusetts, was used with five teletype terminals connected by private telephone lines for approximately $5000 per year per terminal. All the programs written were to be maintained on a central computer file, so all participating schools could share the program.

The project was conducted in three phases:

1. An in-school pilot phase conducted during the spring of 1965 to install and test equipment and familiarize instructional staff with it.

2. A summer study session in which thirty teachers involved in the project worked together for six weeks to learn the fundamentals of computer usage and the potentials of a real-time computer in the mathematics and science classes, and to develop computer programs for the school year 1965–66.

3. The main experimental phase of the project, conducted for a school year at the three grade levels.

The Bronx High School of Science in New York owns its own computer and uses it for solving the problems in numerical analysis encountered in science and mathematical research. The school's principal feels that with students oriented toward scientific careers, a computer at this stage is as basic to their needs as a slide rule. The students undertake research projects in physics, biology, mathematics, chemistry, economics, and psychology. Typical problems that have been studied are "Predictions of Optimum Buying and Selling in the Stock Market through the Use of Finite Markov Chains," "The Multiple Correlation between Some Variable Factors of the Weather and Radiation," and "The Changes in Physicals Caused by Radiation."

In both physical and biological sciences there are many opportunities for using the computer. Physics classes offer occasions for solving problems involving complex computations. Some statistical studies in biology make the computer a necessity. The use of mathematical models in biology is identifying and developing areas of study. The computer is being applied in the study of chemistry to save time in solving tedious, repetitive problems and to enable the student to attack new problems too complex for solution by mechanical means.

The computer is steadily gaining recognition as a teaching aid to stimulate interest in mathematics and science and to reveal mathematical concepts and ideas. And so far computer education has been particularly successful for the young person of exceptional ability who can take a challenge beyond that available in his regular course work and who desires a career in science, engineering, or mathematics.

COMPUTERS IN BUSINESS EDUCATION

Business education is still another area in which interest in computers and data processing is growing rapidly. Job training in this field will be considered in another section. Schools are beginning to introduce units on automation into various sections of the business curriculum. Evanston Township High School in Illinois, for example, offers a ten-day unit on automation as part of an office practice course. In its orientation courses St. Rita High School in Chicago presents techniques of electronic data processing as they are applied to modern business.

The school district of Philadelphia provides a course of instruction to all commercial students in the secondary schools, approximately 4800 students a year, for nine weeks as part of their twelfth-grade course in office practice. The objectives of this course are:

1. To develop an understanding of data-processing systems and a familiarity with the operation of unit-record equipment and the electronic computer.

2. To cultivate a knowledge of the terms commonly used in business data processing.

3. To acquaint students with existing employment opportunities in the field of business data processing.

4. To stimulate in capable students an interest in further study.

The units are divided as follows:

Unit I   Data-processing cycle
    A.   Manual data processing
    B.   Automated data processing

Unit II   Unit-record card
    A.   Reading information
    B.   Keypunch
    C.   Interpreter

Unit III   Input media
    A.   Punched and mark-sensed card
    B.   Paper tape
    C.   Magnetic tape
    D.   Magnetic-ink-characters recognition

Unit IV   Processing information by electric accounting machine
    A.   Sorting
    B.   Collating
    C.   Accounting machine tabulating
    D.   Reproducing

Unit V   Application of processing by electronic accounting machine
    A.   Automated accounting applied to sales
    B.   Keeping of sales records

Unit VI   Electronic data processing
    A.   History and development
    B.   Classification
    C.   Functional units
    D.   Binary numbering system

Unit VII   Programming concepts
    A.   Computer storage
    B.   Coding
    C.   Flow charting
    D.   Writing of a simple program

COMPUTER EDUCATION IN OTHER SUBJECT AREAS

The use of computers in other areas is still in the experimental stage on the secondary-school level. Statistical research in the social sciences has been making applications of the computer, but few have been introduced in the high school. The electronic digital computer's potential is only now beginning to be investigated in the classroom, yet remarkable progress has been made by students working with it. Computers can parse sentences and translate from one language to another. One junior-high-school student has developed a computer program to identify the styles of various authors. There are vast possibilities for computer application in an English curriculum. The advent of computers already has exerted a profound influence on curricula in colleges. Experimental projects in automatic translation of languages, the composition of music, and information retrieval are just beginning to filter down to the high schools.

VOCATIONAL TRAINING IN DATA PROCESSING

Recent requirements of business and industry have created a tremendous demand for people skilled in the technical field of data processing. Good careers in data processing are available to those who know how to program, operate, and control data-processing equipment. Data-processing instruction has been introduced into the curriculum of vocational schools, technical high schools, and post-high-school programs. Through support from Title VIII of the National Defense Education Act, many states have developed educational programs for training individuals to become skilled EDP technicians. Training in keypunch operations, wiring of unit-record equipment, and computer programming are typical offerings in the field. On the undergraduate level the Department of Business Education of the Des Moines Public Schools offers extensive training in the electronic data-processing area for programmers, tab equipment operators, and keypunch operators.

The keypunch course runs one semester length but is arranged as two nine-week courses, the first of which is strictly keypunch drill, and the second a survey of the whole array of unit-record equipment.

The course of machine operator is a three-semester course that can be elected by any tenth- or eleventh-grade student with average grades who passes the qualifying examination. The topics include tab equipment 1 and 2, covering all phases of unit-record equipment, instruction in board wiring and machine operation, systems development and evaluation, and introduction to computers, demonstrating the relationship between record equipment and the computer.

The course for the computer programmer is very rigorous, and students are selected with care. An outline of the three-year curriculum and a sample curriculum showing another approach to training computer personnel at the Technical and Trade Center of Nassau County, New York, appear in Appendix 1 at the end of this chapter.

Most of the courses being offered in data processing are still on the post-high-school level. It has been found that the need for junior programmers and operators is being met by two-year post-high-school training programs in business and scientific data processing.

A two-year post-high-school course in business data processing trains individuals to handle business data and to assist in the design specifications for departmental procedures of common business problems. At the conclusion of the course, the graduates are of value to a business organization and require additional training only in the particular procedures and equipment used by that organization. Scientific data processing stresses mathematics and science instead of accounting and business procedures. The curriculum is designed to prepare an individual to program a computer under the supervision of an engineer, scientist, or mathematician.

Two-year post-high-school programs in data processing are being offered in junior colleges and technical institutes throughout the country. Most of the schools teach business data processing using the *U.S. Office of Education Bulletin* as the curriculum guide.[2] Scientific data-processing programs remain in the experimental stage, for the employability of the graduates of this type of program is still being investigated. Further it must be demonstrated to engineering and scientific personnel that a college education alone is not the central requirement for some of the positions in industry for beginning programmers.

Dobbins Technical High School in Philadelphia offers a two-year program in both business and scientific data processing. The curriculum in business data processing is based on the guide just mentioned. The curriculum in scientific data processing was developed at Dobbins.[3] The

[2] "Business Data Processing, A Suggested Two-Year Post-High School Program," Washington: *U.S. Office of Education Bulletin*, No. FS5.280:80024, 1963.

[3] "Scientific Data Processing Courses in Vocational and Secondary Schools," New York: IBM-E20-0092.

objectives and course offerings are to be found in Appendices 2 and 3 at the end of this chapter.

TEACHER TRAINING *

Teachers still are, by and large, inadequately prepared to teach computers and electronic data processing. Their training, therefore, is the primary task that must be accomplished. During the past two years science and mathematics teachers have indicated increasing interest in the use of electronic computers for more effective classroom methods. Teachers have attended National Science Foundation Institutes. The University of Oklahoma has sponsored a summer institute in which each teacher participating is permitted to choose a student to accompany him. The combination of teacher and student in the same classroom has proven highly successful.

At the University of Pennsylvania an eight-week course affords teachers an opportunity to learn such topics as abstract algebra, linear algebra, logic, and number theory, all presented in the context of computer programming and information processing. Applicants are evaluated with reference to their knowledge of mathematics and their desire to introduce computer mathematics into the secondary-school general-mathematics program.

An increasing number of colleges and universities are offering courses suitable for secondary-school teachers. Orientation courses in computer programming, data processing, and numerical analysis are appearing regularly in their curriculum offerings. And state departments of education are supporting in-service training for high-school teachers. The New York State Education Department with the assistance of Columbia University and the universities of Buffalo, Rochester, and Syracuse has established a program of in-service education in computer mathematics. Interested teachers apply directly to the universities. No charge is made for this instruction and no college credit given.

The Department of Education in Massachusetts took an active part in the development of courses by sponsoring a sixteen-week course, "Computer Mathematics and Scientific Programming," for high-school science and mathematics teachers. The state director of vocational education held a series of institutes on data processing for business-education

---

* The teacher on the firing line wants to know: "What is my responsibility? How do I fit in? How and when do I actually use the computer in the classroom?" Right now computer-assisted instruction is in an experimental stage, but teachers want to know how long it will be before they are using it, and whether they will be actively involved in its implementation.

teachers. These institutes proposed to develop the skill essential for teaching specialized courses for a two-year preparatory curriculum in business electronic data processing (under Title VIII of the National Defense Education Act of 1958).

A growing number of teachers in metropolitan areas have had the opportunity to work closely with industrial and scientific organizations where computer facilities are in use. There they develop skills in the use of equipment, and in turn use this knowledge to complement their classroom teaching techniques. A serious problem, however, confronting a teacher who wishes to make use of the computer in classroom teaching is the availability of "the hardware." Although much classroom work can be carried on without equipment, its availability is extremely important. Colleges and computer manufacturers can be of assistance; in addition, local groups wishing to develop programs of computer education, either for in-service teacher education or to complement existing classroom instruction, should work closely with local chapters of the Association for Computing Machinery (ACM), the Data-Processing Management Association (DPMA) and Association for Educational Data Systems (AEDS).† These organizations can substantially assist in every phase of the effort.

---

† If we are to develop systems of real classroom utility, we must design them to be usable by a broad range of teachers. Our systems must allow the teachers convenient means to arrange, rearrange, extract, and modify the material presentation and organization. Our systems must have enough flexibility so that teachers will not despair of their use, and enough real value to make the investment of teachers' time worthwhile.

appendix 1

A. Computer programmer curriculum in the Department of Business Education, Des Moines Public Schools.

Tenth grade:
  English
  Social science
  Mathematics
  Electromechanical machines
  Accounting and accounting applications
  Typing

Eleventh grade:
  English
  Social science
  Introduction to programming systems
  Computer programming
  System development and design
  Statistics
  Human relations

Twelfth grade:
  Communication skills
  Social science
  Computer programming
  Accounting
  Advanced computing programming systems

B. Programs in training computer personnel at the Technical and Trade Center of Nassau County, New York.

1. *Computer technology*: three-year curriculum designed to prepare students for beginner positions as service, maintenance, and repairmen with data-processing installations and/or equipment manufacturers. Courses included:

Tenth year:
Basic electricity
Drafting
Related mathematics

Eleventh year:
Advanced electricity and electronics
Electrical drafting
Related mathematics

Twelfth year:
Computer circuitry
Computer mathematics
Computer operations

2. *Computer program:* two-year curriculum designed to prepare students for positions as console operators, junior programmers, etc., in business data operations. The prerequisites are elementary algebra and general science. Courses included:

Eleventh year:
Basic electromechanical computer systems
Accounting and machine operation
Data-processing operations
Introduction to programming

Twelfth year:
Programming
Computer mathematics
Cost accounting
Introduction to statistics

3. *Data-processing operation:* one-year curriculum designed to train students for positions as keypunch and accounting-machine operators. Typing is a prerequisite. Courses included:

Twelfth year:
Keypunch and tabulator operation
Bookkeeping and machine operation
Business mathematics
Office practice

appendix 2
Business-Oriented Data Processing

Objectives of course:

1. To orient the student to the means by which information becomes data, and is then handled, processed, and presented in report form.

2. To familiarize the student with terminology and basic concepts of automation, integration of data-processing systems, and the stored program concepts of electronic computers.

3. To produce a programmer: This person will be a candidate for "on-the-job" training in the business world and will be qualified to:

    (a) Apply currently available programming techniques to a defined problem with a minimum of supervision.

    (b) Understand and master techniques as the "point of need" arises.

Admission requirements: high-school graduate with one year of algebra required for admission, good marks and an aptitude in mathematics.

First year:

Introduction to management mathematics: Linear equations in one unknown, functions, graphs, system of linear equations, exponents and radicals, quadratic equations, etc.

Accounting principles: Basic accounting concepts, elementary number usage techniques, accrued concepts and the income statement, bookkeeping, accounts receivable, and fixed assets, capital stock, surplus bonds, etc.

Technical English and report writing.

Computer laboratory:
1. Data-processing mathematics:
    Concept of notation, number systems, representation of a num-

ber with an arbitrary base, fixed and floating point numbers, precision, Boolean algebra.

2. Introduction to EDP systems:
   History and development of data processing, data representation, storage devices, central processing unit, storage program concepts, etc.
3. Fundamentals of programming:
   Flow diagramming, indexing, subroutines, machine-language concepts, assembly programs and compilers.
4. Programming applications.

Mechanized accounting equipment: Desk calculating machines, punched-card equipment, accounting machines, unit-record equipment including panel wiring and programming.

Second year:

Industrial management: Administrative problems experienced in computer system, management and scientific approach, management planning and control, human relations, etc.

Modern statistics: Advanced algebra, binomial expansion, probability, random variables, normal distribution, etc.

Advanced accounting: Cost accounting, organization levels of business.

Technical English and report writing.

Computer laboratory:
1. System development and design: Varies from a modest payroll procedure to the total information system of a large and complex business.
2. Data-processing applications to business.

appendix 3
Science-Oriented Data Processing

Objectives of course: Identical to the objectives of the business-oriented data-processing curriculum, with the additional aim of teaching concepts of electronics and instrumentation as associated with the computer.

Admission requirements: high-school graduate with two years of algebra and one year of trigonometry, one year of physics preferred, good marks and an aptitude in mathematics.

First year:

Advanced algebra
Advanced physics
Technical English and report writing
Basic electronics
Computer laboratory:
1. Data-processing mathematics:
   Concept of notation, number systems, representation of a number with an arbitrary base, fixed and floating point numbers, Boolean algebra.
2. Introduction to EDP systems:
   History and development of data processing, data representation, storage devices, central processing unit, stored program concepts, etc.
3. Fundamentals of programming:
   Indexing, subrouting, machine-language notations, assembly program and compilers.
4. Programming applications.

Second year:

Technical English and report writing
Analytic geometry and calculus
Instrumentation
Logic and design of computers
Advanced scientific programming, e.g. linear programming

We are concerned with computers in the schools at three levels. First, curriculum development in the area of computer science itself. Second, curricula in which the computer can or should be introduced as a fairly standard instructional aid. Third, computer-aided instruction behind the scenes, where computers are being used in sophisticated ways, without involving the students in the mechanics. How does one go about teaching computer research? What is the role of the computer in the development of standard curriculum materials? What special features arise in curriculum development when the curriculum is computer based?

chapter 12

The Computer Sciences in Colleges and Universities
Ottis W. Rechard

When the IBM Corporation first offered their 650 computer to institutions of higher education at 40 per cent of the standard commercial price, marketing estimates suggested that perhaps as many as half a dozen large universities might eventually desire to install such a computer. This must surely rank along with IBM's original estimates of the potential national demand for large-scale computers (it is said that when the 701 was first built, IBM projected a total market for such machines at something under ten) as one of the most short-sighted estimates of the postwar era. Fortunately IBM and other computer manufacturers were able to rise to the demands of colleges and universities until today more than 1000 computers are installed on approximately 500 campuses. Most of these machines were supplied by their manufacturers at generous discounts, yet even so, typical annual costs of operating a facility at a major university have risen from between $50,000 and $100,000 ten years ago to current annual costs frequently in the $500,000 to $1,000,000 range. During my tenure with the National Science Foun-
156

dation, I had occasion to review the programs and budgets of several computing centers at institutions with major graduate programs and came to the conclusion that today such an institution is typically investing half as much money in the operation of its computing center and the acquisition of computing hardware as it is in the operation of its library and the acquisition of books and journals.

This is a rather frightening figure for a university administrator to contemplate and, indeed, it would be beyond the financial capacity of most universities to absorb such a major budgetary increase, were it not for large amounts of federal assistance in the form of direct grants and indirect payment of computing costs on supported research grants and contracts.

Computers were initially regarded by university administrators as specialized research tools necessary in the support of a few research projects in the physical sciences and engineering. Today computers are rapidly assuming central roles in the total research and instructional programs of colleges and universities.

On many campuses instructional uses of computers can be traced to IBM's early policy of making its 60 per cent educational contribution contingent on the university's offering at least one course in scientific computation or numerical analysis and one course in business data processing. From these modest beginnings have sprung most contemporary departments and degree programs in computer or information science. Some of these programs have flourished while others are languishing largely from lack of adequate staff. A recent survey by the Curriculum Committee on Computer Science of the Association for Computing Machinery lists twenty-three colleges and universities reporting some sort of curriculum that could be identified as computer science. Since I am personally aware of at least ten institutions with such curricula that were not on the list, it seems safe to place the number of such schools somewhere around fifty. This, of course, does not count the many two-year colleges that are offering vocational training in computer programming and operation.

The diversity among these curricula is very great indeed, reflecting at this point little uniformity of opinion as to what represents adequate academic training in computer or information science. Beyond some basic instruction in algorithmic processes and a procedure-oriented language (usually Fortran or Algol), some numerical analysis, and some systems programming, it is difficult to find a common element. For this and other reasons, the numerous attempts to establish undergraduate majors in computer science seem premature and misguided. At a time when the field is still struggling with problems of identity, it does not seem fair to the undergraduate student to encourage him in the belief that a degree in computer science will mean as much as a degree in one of the more established disciplines. After all, it is reasonable to expect that two students majoring in mathematics at different universities will each have been exposed to a rather large common body of knowledge. The same is true of physics, biology, electrical engineering; but it is definitely not true of computer science.

In an attempt to deal with this problem, the ACM Curriculum Committee has recently proposed a curriculum for undergraduate majors in the computer sciences. While there is much to applaud in this effort, many of the recommendations are nevertheless puzzling. Why, for example, should a course in "combinatorics and graph theory" be listed as a basic course in computer science, while courses in "linguistics" and "analog computers" are included in a list of "supporting courses"? The catalog descriptions of certain of the courses can cause some confusion. In addition, if one regards courses such as "numerical analysis," "mathematical optimization techniques," and "constructive logic" as belonging as well to mathematics as to computer science, the proposed curriculum seems really to represent a sound major in mathematics with option in computation, such as has been described by Perlis (381) in the *Communications of the ACM*.

Of course, it must be admitted that probably the strongest force acting to hasten the development of undergraduate computer and information science majors is the position taken by some mathematics departments that the principal goal of a mathematics major should be the pursuit of an advanced degree in pure mathematics. In many mathematics departments the courses just listed are regarded as peripheral, and few of the best students are encouraged to enroll in them. Under these circumstances some administrative device by which interested students are encouraged rather than discouraged from preparing themselves for careers with computers is inevitable.

This qualified view of undergraduate majors in computer and information science should not be interpreted as opposition to undergraduate *courses* in the subject. Perhaps the most satisfactory arrangement *at the present time* is a department of computer or information science which offers a master's and Ph.D. degree and teaches a number of undergraduate courses, so that students can acquire a background in the subject ranging from simple experience with a procedure-oriented programming language to familiarity with compiler and operating system construction.

Most computer or information-science courses can be placed under one of the following major headings:

1. Computer programming and programming and operating systems.
2. Numerical analysis.
3. Computer architecture, logical design, and switching theory.
4. Artificial intelligence and heuristic programming.
5. Logic, automata theory, and theory of algorithms.
6. Information and communication systems.

Only a very few universities in the country, however, have faculty members prepared to teach in each of these areas, and most are fortunate if they can cover two or three. Part of the difficulty lies in the fact that most faculty members in the computer or information sciences have come to this new discipline from some other background and as a result are prepared to teach elementary courses in at most two or three of the six categories.

The mainstays of nearly all programs in computer or information science are the courses in computer programming and numerical analysis. Such is the case probably because the use of computers in the solution of numerical problems in the physical sciences and engineering was well established at the time most colleges and universities were installing their first machines, so that the men called upon to direct these fledgling computing centers were, by and large, mathematicians or physical scientists working in numerical analysis. At most universities where departments of computer or information science have been established, the courses in numerical analysis have migrated from the mathematics department to this new home. The wisdom of this migration remains to be seen. Where numerical analysis is languishing in an uninterested or disapproving mathematics department it may be necessary to provide a more hospitable environment for it in a department of computer science. On the other hand, those who are concerned with the health of applied mathematics must view with some alarm the removal of one of its most vigorous subjects. Whether numerical analysis is taught as mathematics or computer science, there is now almost universal agreement that it should be oriented toward computations on an electronic digital computer. The arguments that only by doing a significant amount of hand computation could one appreciate and understand the use of the computer have pretty well disappeared. The tendency these days seems to be to offer an elementary general course involving solution of polynomial and transcendental equations, interpolation, and numerical differentiation and integration followed by specialized and more advanced courses in matrix computations and the numerical solution of ordinary and partial differential equations.

Courses in computer programming are given at virtually every school that has access to a digital computer. These vary all the way from short informal Fortran courses carrying no credit to courses involving the most advanced topics of systems programming. The recurrent problem in all of these courses is to determine those principles and techniques that will have more than transitory relevance. Eight or nine years ago the IBM 650, the Burroughs 205, and the Bendix G-15 were the standard machines on university campuses; Fortran was just coming into use on the IBM 704, Univac was recommending the Mathmatic system, and Perlis was working on the IT compiler at Carnegie Institute of Technology. Most programming for the small machines was being done in absolute machine language and it was in these terms that programming courses were being taught. This meant that most of the course time was spent simply familiarizing the students with the order structure of the machine, teaching some of the rudimentary techniques of program debugging, and working out some painfully simple examples on the computer. Today, of course, nobody writes programs for a computer in absolute machine language, but such instruction nine years ago was certainly not a waste of time. To be sure, some students faced with the difficulty of programming even trivial problems simply gave up; but many others caught the vision of better things, have participated in the developments of the past several years, and are now moving into positions of leadership in the field.

It seems unlikely that over the next ten years the principles and techniques of computer programming for applications will change as radically as they have during the last ten years. Programming languages will, of course, evolve and change and there may even be drastic changes in the order structure of machines to accommodate such hardware innovations as associative memories and parallel processors, but none of these changes should have the same impact on the use of computers as did the shift from absolute machine language to the procedure-oriented languages of the present day.

Nearly every department of computer or information science offers one or more courses in systems programming and it is in these courses that the search for general principles and the rapidly changing hardware technology seem likely to have the greatest impact. Compiler construction and the structure of computer operating systems are undergoing rapid changes at the present time, and unless considerable care is taken, what is taught this year may well be obsolete before the students even leave the campus. Fortunately, at most of the better schools many of the students in these courses participate in the updating and modification of the compilers and operating systems of the school's own computers, so that their education in the subject is a continuing one up to the time of their graduation. This, in fact, illustrates one of the most appealing aspects of computer science in the academic milieu, namely that more than perhaps any other subject it embodies the ideal of a university as a community of scholars with the students participating actively as junior members of the community rather than as passive receptacles for the wisdom of their elders.

Strangely enough, although courses in numerical analysis have moved from departments of mathematics to departments of computer science, courses in computer architecture, logical design, and switching theory remain largely embedded in departments of electrical engineering except at those universities where the computing center developed around a locally designed machine. Some notable exceptions exist, perhaps the outstanding one being at the University of Illinois, but by and large this situation again reflects the fact that most departments of computer and information science have developed around university computing centers, and these have been staffed largely with computer users rather than computer builders. There are, of course, several departments of electrical engineering around the country with strong programs in computer design, and in some institutions these programs may serve as the nucleus of future computer or information-science departments.

Turning from the discussion of computer and information science courses per se to examine those courses in other departments which do or could make use of the digital computer, attention should be directed to the rather disturbing fact that although computer and information-science departments and computing centers have been staffed mostly with mathematicians, apart from specific courses in numerical analysis (which, as we have seen, are tending to move out of departments of mathematics), the computer has had little or no impact on the mathematical curriculum. For the most part, pure mathematicians have been content to ignore the computer revolution, secure in their opinion that it has nothing to offer them. One might hazard the guess that, apart from computer professionals, not more than 10 per cent of the academic mathematicians in the country have even bothered seriously to expose themselves to the computer. Of course, one reason for this situation is that until now the computer has not been a particularly useful research tool for the pure mathematician. As we gain more experience in the manipulation of symbols and the use of displays with computers, the situation will most likely change, and more and more pure mathematicians will find the computer to be a useful if not indispensable adjunct to their work.

But in the meantime the bulk of our students are being deprived of the help of a magnificent tool for the enhancement of their mathematical understanding. The following are only a few ways in which a computer could be used effectively in the standard mathematics curriculum.

Many beginning students have difficulty distinguishing between the definition of a function and the value of the function at a point. For a student who has written a computer program to evaluate an algebraic expression and who understands that the program defines a sequence of operations on whatever number is stored at a specific machine location to produce a new number (the value of the function), such a distinction should be trivial. From there it is an easy step to the consideration of functions defined by other than explicit analytic expressions—for example, indefinite integrals and implicit functions.

Another area in which the computer could be used to advantage is in clarifying the concept of approach to a limit, particularly as it is used in the definition of such things as derivative and definite integral. Simply because of the computational difficulties involved, most students have never evaluated the definite integral of a function for which they could not find an antiderivative in closed form.

As displays become more common, the possibilities for effective instructional use of computers grow enormously. It now becomes possible effectively to illustrate the mapping of one complex plane into another, the convergence of successive iterations in Picard's theorem, the concept of the direction field defined by a first-order differential equation, and numerous other topics. Dr. Glen Culler of the University of California at Santa Barbara is experimenting with a classroom equipped with displays and keyboards typical of what has come to be called the "Culler-Fried" system, after its chief architects, Dr. Culler and Dr. Burton Fried of U.C.L.A. The results of his efforts should hold considerable interest for the entire mathematical community.

At most engineering schools around the country, students are now required to take at least one elementary course in computer programming. Following this the computer is available as a tool to the student and instructor for purposes limited only by the imagination and sophistication of the faculty. As a minimum they can now assign more realistic and difficult problems in such traditional courses as "servomechanisms," "heat and thermodynamics," and "structures." Virtually every course in engineering design is a candidate for extensive computer utilization. For example, complex electronic circuits can be simulated before they are constructed in the laboratory; the stresses in complicated structures can be calculated and the design thereby improved; or the characteristics of a particular reactor design can be computed.

An experimental project at the University of Michigan four years ago demonstrated the possibilities for the incorporation of computer methods into the engineering curriculum. This project was followed with interest by engineering faculties throughout the country and can probably be credited with the rapid movement of engineering schools over the past several years to require of all graduates some knowledge of computer programming. The upgrading of the students in this respect could be accomplished by fiat; unfortunately the upgrading of most faculties is a slower process, and it must be reported that success in this regard has been less than 100 per cent. The majority of engineering students today do take at least one course in computer programming, but many excellent opportunities to capitalize on this knowledge in other engineering courses are lost through lack of understanding on the part of the faculty.

The situation in chemistry and physics parallels that in engineering except that design is no longer a major consideration. Once again, the advent of on-line systems and particularly on-line displays would seem to have important implications for the use of computers in the physical sciences and engineering. An interesting example is afforded by the work of Becker, Cusachs, and Longenecker(338) at Tulane in representing molecular orbitals computed on an IBM 1410 computer and displayed on the face of a cathode-ray tube through an IBM 1401.

The biological sciences have been rather slow to utilize the computer for instructional purposes, and perhaps the most interesting work has been done in adapting computer-aided instructions to the teaching of clinical diagnosis in medical schools. Computers are now being used extensively, however, in biological research for both statistical calculations and simulation of complex systems. This work has already begun to penetrate the graduate curriculum; for example, Washington State University now offers a course entitled "Modeling and Simulation of Biological Systems" as part of the information-science curriculum; and it seems safe to predict that undergraduate courses that use computers will be fairly common in the biological sciences in the next five to ten years.

What has been said here in regard to the biological sciences can be repeated for the behavioral sciences. The use of computers for statistical computations and for the simulation of social systems has progressed to the point where many schools are including these topics in their graduate and undergraduate courses. In addition, many departments of computer or information science now offer courses in such areas as artificial intelligence, pattern recognition, and self-organizing systems.

In the areas of business administration and economics, the use of computers is well established. Most departments of business administration either teach a course in data processing or require their students to take such a course offered by a computer or information-science department. In many of the more quantitatively oriented departments, as at M.I.T., Carnegie Tech, and U.C.L.A., a major portion of the curriculum is oriented toward the use of computers in the application of mathematical methods to business management. Specific courses in operations research and econometrics typically make heavy use of computers, since by and large the methods employed in these areas require a computer for their fruitful application. The business game is a well-established adjunct to the curriculum of most business schools, and simulation techniques in general are used extensively.

This report began with a comparison of the costs of university-operated computing centers with the costs of libraries. The comparison was deliberate since I hoped to demonstrate in succeeding pages that computers have come to occupy a place in the university scheme second only to the library in centrality and universality. And the story is only beginning. Some day in the not too distant future, familiarity with computers will be expected of every educated man and woman.

part 4
Information Processing for Education Systems

A new technology is needed for two purposes: for developing and understanding new theories of educational administration, and for finding out what happens to a child in that experience called "he learned." How do we process data about the learning act? This is information we are awed about finding, much less collecting and assessing. We need a new theory of education and a new theory of data collection. We do not know how to achieve either of these even with today's dollars.

chapter 13

Meeting Information Needs in Health, Education, and Welfare

Shelton B. Granger

Any attempt to discuss the programs of the Department of Health, Education, and Welfare in terms of their implications for collecting, storing, processing, and reporting data must fall short of the mark. The programs are so vast and the administrative machinery so complex that an exhaustive presentation would consume many pages. Despite this, we can examine pertinent statistical data related to recent legislation and make a few projections about information and data needs.

Few people will doubt that history will make note of the legislative accomplishments of the 1960's. The 88th and 89th Congresses tackled extremely difficult and controversial subjects and produced new laws destined to affect the lives of millions and to make indelible impressions on our culture, influencing our way of life for generations to come. These actions have taken into account the fact of the accelerating rate of social change in the United States as well as the relationship of domestic to international change. Some of the changes can be expressed demographically.

The population of the United States has doubled in the last fifty

167

years, reaching 195 million in mid-1965—an increase of almost fifteen million over the 1960 census. One-half of this net growth in population occurred in the school-age group of 5–19-year-olds.

The birth rates have declined for women of all childbearing ages, 5 per cent for women aged 15 to 24 years and between 2 and 3 per cent for older women. The birth rate for the nonwhite population, 29.2 per 1000, continued to exceed that for the white population, 20 per 1000. The rate of nonwhite births decreased by 2 per cent between 1963 and 1964 and that of white births by 3 per cent.

The death rate dropped to 9.4 per 1000 population in 1964, a slightly lower rate than that of the two previous years. The infant death rate in 1964 reached a record low of 24.2 deaths per 1000 live births. Life expectancy at birth for the total population is now about 70 years. Since 1900 life expectancy has increased greatly—by about 20 years for males and 23 years for females. The increase in nonwhite life expectancy, for both males and females, has been about 30 years.

The population under age 20 totaled 76.9 million in mid-1965—two-fifths of the total population. The number of school-age children in 1965 was 1.6 million more than in 1964. The population aged 65 and over reached 18.2 million at the middle of 1964. Of special significance to trends in health and welfare is the fact that the proportion of persons aged 65 and over to the total population has more than doubled since 1900. Today one out of 11 persons is over 65.

There has been a steady rise in school and college enrollments over the last fifteen years and this trend will continue. Projections of elementary- and secondary-school enrollments indicate that the 48.5 million enrollment in the fall of 1963 may increase to 55.4 million by the fall of 1975. Recent figures show 41.7 million in public schools and 6.8 million in nonpublic schools. In the fall of 1965 the number of classroom teachers reached 1.7 million, continuing the trend over recent years of improvement in the pupil-teacher ratio.

These figures are another means of expressing what has been stressed frequently—that the American population is on the increase with heavy emphasis on the young and old. The simple mathematics involved suggests new dimensions to the problems and programs affecting these age groups.

Research findings have made it clear that we must produce an understandable strategy for comprehensive systems of social planning and action. Such systems must take into account the roles of the various levels of government as well as the roles of nongovernmental institutions in the United States. And it is hardly necessary to say that the structuring and operation of these systems must be based on reliable information systems that are adaptable and sensitive to social and political processes. The task is far more than the simple assembling of raw data of relevance and value; it is more than the very necessary quantification of social problems. Rather, the task seems to extend to a qualitative analysis of raw data and to the quantification of *resources* in relation to problems—the latter requiring *methods* of dealing with the numerous variables in any set of human equations.

To illustrate the problems we can consider some of the legislation passed by the 88th and 89th Congresses.[1]

Health insurance for the aged under Social Security marks a monumental advance in protecting American workers and their families against major economic risks. As a result of Medicare, people growing older are assured of protection against costs of hospitalization.

The expanded Kerr-Mills medical-assistance program will bring more adequate medical care and other health services to the aged poor who are blind or disabled. It will also ensure that they receive those services in a way that is consistent with fairness and dignity, and with the ultimate objectives of restoring them to health and self-sufficiency.

The Child Health Amendments will increase federal support to make more health services available to expectant mothers, to infants, and to crippled and retarded children. They will also enlarge our efforts to train people to work with the crippled and retarded. They authorize a five-year program of special project grants to provide comprehensive health care and services for preschool or school-age children from poor families.

The Elementary and Secondary Education Act of 1965 is designed to bring better education to the millions of disadvantaged young people who need it most. Of the 50 million school-age children in this country, more than five million are in families earning less than $2000 annually. The majority of these children go to schools providing inadequate education. The relationship between poverty and retarded educational development has been apparent for some time. Yet evidence shows that environmental conditions and inadequate educational programs, rather than lack of basic mental aptitude, are the major reasons for the failure of these children to perform adequately.

To attain excellence in education for all children we must put the

---

[1] For additional information, see *1965 Year of Legislative Achievements*, available from the Superintendent of Documents, U.S. Government Printing Office, Washington, D.C.

best educational equipment and ideas and innovations within the reach of all; yet today 69 per cent of public elementary schools do not have libraries. With the limited resources available, individual school districts are unable to provide the necessary services that quality education demands. We must advance the technology of teaching and be able to provide incentives for learning.

Title I of the Elementary and Secondary Education Act of 1965 creates a three-year program of federal grants to establish special programs, including construction of school facilities, to meet the needs of educationally deprived children of low-income families. Title II provides $100 million to buy library resources, textbooks, and other instructional materials required by modern schools and good teaching.

Title III allocates $100 million for a new program of supplementary educational centers and services. The centers will be available to both public- and private-school students as well as to out-of-school youths and adults.

The overall improvement of American education requires additional research, more advanced training, and expedited transfer of this added knowledge to our classrooms. Title IV provides $100 million over a five-year period for programs of educational research to reduce this gap. Although these provisions help to meet the immediate national needs in education, Title V assures that education will remain a matter of state and local responsibility by providing grants to strengthen state departments of education and to stimulate them in the development of programs for identifying and meeting educational needs.

The enactment of the Elementary and Secondary Education Act of 1965 was a great beginning. After years of controversy the federal government has entered into a creative partnership with states and communities across the land to provide good education for all our children. Special programs for educationally deprived children will help us to break the cycle whereby ignorance and poverty in one generation are directly translated into poverty and ignorance in the next. This legislation is putting books and other educational materials into a great many schools where they have been lacking. In other schools textbooks, maps, and other tools of learning are being brought up to date to reflect new knowledge and scientific achievements. Supplemental educational centers will enrich the lives of children and of entire communities by bringing all the resources of the community to bear on the educational process.

Title IV is enlarging our educational research effort by establishing regional research centers at major universities. These centers draw on the skills of persons from many disciplines to develop curriculum materials, to train teachers, and to find better ways of teaching the country's children. The new law strengthens state departments of education, consistent with its general purpose to foster and reinforce local control and direction of educational programs.

Among the provisions of the Civil Rights Act of 1964, which seeks to end the deprivation of personal dignity suffered by Negroes in every aspect of American life, is the clear directive that federal programs shall be administered in a manner that will assure no discrimination on the basis of race, color, or national origin. Title IV authorizes the Commissioner of Education to establish training institutes and to provide technical assistance and financial aid to deal with problems incident to desegregation. Applications for federal aid must include, as a condition for approval and the extension of any financial assistance, an adequate assurance of compliance with all of the nondiscriminatory requirements imposed by Title VI of this Act.

These specific programs must be viewed in the total context of our democratic social and political system. Each step leads to the realization of additional means of achieving progress. But there is no end to the need for enhancing our understanding of human aspirations as these are related to our social circumstances. What makes the secure elderly seek more security? What makes the highly skilled and educated seek better skills and more education? What makes the free seek more freedom? The closer we come to answers to such questions, the closer we will be to the full realization of our society's values. The steps we take in the future must depend on innovative methods of assessing our potential for human and social development. Such answers will not come from "snapshot" views of social data. The tools for more advanced and sophisticated examination are at hand, and we must depend on persons with the technical and professional competence to fashion appropriate systems for analysis and projection.

There are at least four areas in which people competent in automatic data processing can make a unique contribution. First, because of the rapidly changing conditions under which we live, there is a continuing need to refine the raw data that are gathered as a means of analyzing social problems. Too many of our social institutions make major judgments and decisions on the basis of simplistic reasoning that might have been suitable at some time in history, but is now no longer so. In the field of education we can find many examples. Our data gathering on race, during the initial efforts to desegregate schools, was more in the nature of head counting than research. We now know that to combine the process of desegregation with the process of upgrading our educational systems, we must do a qualitative analysis that will fit the necessary simple quantifications. We do not want to know simply how many white or Negro students attend a school in a specific district, but rather what are the social, economic, cultural, and ethnic similarities within racially divergent groups that will have a bearing on success or failure of desegregation efforts. We do not want to know how many schools have submitted what kinds of desegregation plans, but rather which schools in which cultural areas have found that certain kinds of desegregation plans are adaptable to their educational needs and meet the demands of current civil-rights pressures. These are cited simply to show that the job of identifying the appropriate raw data is not yet complete.

Demands for improving educational planning are clearly with us and our inabilities to meet new demands are a matter of record. We have yet to identify the basic informational sources that will contribute to a solution of the double-barreled problem of extending democratic concepts of equal rights while meeting demands for the creation of more efficient systems of education.

A second area of professional challenge can be called the inter-disciplinary association of demographic and other social data. The public interest in the fields of health, education, and welfare has expanded at an uneven rate. The result, in part, has been proliferation and fragmentation of programming. The challenge before us is to integrate these many activities into an understandable comprehensive package of federal participation in local programs. This means, for example, that the educational component of welfare and health programs must be isolated so that a balanced relationship between the disciplines can be achieved. In many communities educational programs are running ahead of health and welfare. In other communities welfare may outstrip education and health. What seems to be called for is an information system that will contribute to the task of coordination for planning in these fields.

A third challenge lies in the area of human-resource development. If we think for a moment about the vastness of our medical needs, as they are anticipated under the Medicare provisions of the Social Security Amendments, we can begin to focus on the national and local resources required to implement these programs successfully. Although no serious question has been raised about our present competence to initiate Medicare, few persons would be bold enough to speculate about the spread of services in the medical field that may be stimulated by the Medicare approach.

The same anticipation should apply to educational programs. We have every reason to feel confident about the speculations we have made thus far concerning the impact of federal programs on elementary, secondary, and higher education. We have no reason to doubt our initial projections in the developing preschool programs such as Head Start. The resources available in thousands of communities around the country for the effective implementation of programs requiring trained personnel in human-services fields, however, will need careful and continuous analysis. As the programs go into effect there will be serious alterations in the professional services necessary to carry them out. The elementary-school teacher of fifty years ago had clear-cut duties; today's teacher is far less certain about the demands of future programs.

How, then, should the human resources for teaching be divided? What are the responsibilities for professional social-welfare services and what are the anticipated needs for subprofessional supporting services? What percentage of high-school graduates with college potential will need to go into which of the human-services fields? Systems for gathering, sorting, and clarifying vital information must be adaptable across disciplinary lines and must be able to make a major contribution to effective social planning if we are to identify the resources within our population for the attainment of national goals.

Finally, we should focus on what has taken place internationally to add to our store of knowledge about our domestic development programs. If we accept the concept that societies are constantly evolving and that within this country there are many levels of development identifiable in different geographic areas and different population segments, it seems that we would have much to learn about the development process from the experience of less-developed countries. It may be as important to us, in the long run, to learn about manpower-development programs in Latin America, for example, as it has been to some Latin American countries to receive loans, grants, and technical assistance from us. What has happened in textbook programs in many countries may enlighten our efforts to revamp textbooks in our educational system.

The task seems to be the continuous development of systems for programming information as a means of improving planning and administration of vital human services. The growth and development of the American population demands experimental and innovative efforts in this direction. Proper conceptualization of the sociocultural context and a firm knowledge of the substantive content of programs are essential to the creation and maintenance of large-scale data systems that will facilitate the provision of vital human services.

chapter 14
Measuring American Education
James K. Rocks

The National Center for Educational Statistics must cope with four basic problems concerning data processing. It must determine what data about education should be gathered; it must devise means and policies for collecting them; it must analyze them; and it must transmit them to interested parties.

In some respects these points hardly differ from the objectives which the Office of Education has had since its formation in 1867. Continuing expansion and vast new responsibilities involving the efficient disbursement of federal funds, however, make it impossible to continue in the limited framework of the past. In addition to simply counting the components of the educational system, it now becomes vital to evaluate federal expenditures. We must determine if the transfusion of approximately four billion dollars from the general tax revenues into the educational activities of the nation is being allocated properly, and to what extent it can be said to be doing measurable good. The Center, in

174

short, must perform the same kind of cost-benefit analyses on federal educational expenditures that are now standard in defense planning.

No matter how complex the ultimate analysis of educational expenditures may eventually become, we begin with a set of basic items of data which must be collected about pupils, teachers, other staff, facilities, programs and funds; about policies, customs, and laws; and finally about the socioeconomic environment in which the educational system exists. First then come these simple counts of obviously denumerable elements. Unfortunately, even this process remains immensely difficult.

Picture then the steps to follow where, in order to make allocations and evaluations at any level, some sort of value judgments must be made of achievements in various areas, most of which defy purely monetary measurement. Some efforts have been made to measure the value of an education in terms of lifetime income as related to the grade level completed, but even here one is immediately caught up in the paradox that a large number of well-educated people in the society, school teachers and civil servants, are not well paid.

Conceptual problems like these emerge immediately as we begin to choose items of information to collect. Even when a satisfactory list of items is compiled, theoretical problems of data synthesis remain. These relate to what can be termed the "hinge" problem, that is, to select the echelon of the real world where characteristics shall be defined and counted. Consider that there are some fifty million pupils. We may identify them variously by age, sex, race, grade, religion, family status, curriculum, health, IQ, aptitude, attitude, aspirations, classmates, teacher, school, social adjustment, and accomplishment to date, to name just a few possibilities. If each characteristic can take on any one of ten values, and there are ten characteristics, then there are ten billion conceivable ways of describing a child. This is a number more than two hundred times as large as the number of children in the nation. Of course, we can operate on all these empty "vectors" to reduce the number of possible values such a characteristic may take on by combining the empty vectors with those adjacent to them. We find also that a good many of the vectors will be occupied by more than one student, so that the number is further reduced. Suppose we now have a set of ten million vectors about individual pupils, and we wish to synthesize these into some general picture of the student body of the nation. We may of course simply sum up the number of students who have any one characteristic, such as boys or 10-year-olds or pupils taking American history, and thus finish with one hundred numbers: the quantity of children who have one of ten values in one of ten characteristics.

Although such information is interesting, it tells us little of significance. For purposes of allocation and evaluation, we must make a finer analysis, namely, of the relationships among countable objects sharing a set of vectors. To present all possible intersections is a task whose magnitude ranks with listing every possible game of chess. Thus the decision involves determining how many of all the possible configurations to present; next devising a method of choosing them; and finally discovering a scheme to vary the configurations upon demand.

Although the actual data being gathered do not change very rapidly, the requirement that any configuration may be requested (from the set of all possible ones) indicates a large-scale, on-line computing problem in a vast system of data acquisition.

We find, for example, that for a given pupil, unless the set of descriptors includes the interplay of students and teachers and the impact of certain sequences or groupings of curricula and their contents, a meaningful measure of a child in terms of the effect of education on him cannot be made. We must consider the whole social community of which he is a part.

In some respects it is feasible to hinge the system on the student, since each one is a clearly delimitable subject—a person who occupies space and time and has characteristics that can be described in generally acceptable terms. If we hinge the system on the classroom or the class, we have another set of definable elements (the facilities, contents, children, and teacher therein, etc.). Or we may prefer to hinge the system on the teacher, since we have again a single human being who can be described in terms of his class, the pupils, his personal attributes, background, experience, and so on. Other possibilities are the school as a whole, the district, or even, as is quite commonly done these days, the state as a whole. With each aggregation we reduce the number of elements that require description, but we increase the number of descriptors required to make the information meaningful. This is true because the descriptors must include functions of items as well as items themselves, thereby permitting the evaluation of interrelationships of the characteristics measured.

The theoretical problem, of course, is to devise an algorithm through which we may decide at what level to begin aggregation (simple summations of characteristics and functions), which to aggregate specifically, and which to retain as a lower-hierarchy data base to be tapped as the need arises.

Record keeping in varying degrees of detail exists, of course, at the school-teacher-student-curriculum-facilities level, as there are some aggregations at district and state levels. The national *Digest of Educational Statistics* is the synthesis of many federal surveys and other publications. The way the information is presently gathered, aggregated, and organized, however, makes it somewhat difficult to know what is really going on in the sense of constructing meaningful indicators and being able to make good allocations. Obviously what is needed is a concerted effort to construct a uniform, efficient, and accessible hierarchy of information banks to provide national totals as required. Again the system must penetrate to the level of detail required to develop data in response to functions that were not aggregated originally. It would become relatively simple to test interesting conjectures if such a structure existed.

COMPILING STATE DATA

The state and local educational agencies have been the chief policy-making groups for public education in the nation. While local school districts have their boards of supervisors, the state generally has controlled teacher accreditation, curriculum standards, textbook authorization, and frequently funding as well, at least to the extent that there is a substantial veto power existing at that level over local school board activity. Historically, the role of the federal government has been observational rather than operational and, except for the Land-Grant College Act, only recently has there been any substantial participation in school matters by Washington. The Elementary and Secondary Act, for example, is the first piece of federal legislation to disburse public funds to aid school districts in proportion to the number of their children from underprivileged families.*

The interest in free and voluminous interchange of information about education grows generally, and the federal government is seen as the feasible agent for drawing together common facts from all the states. This feeling is intensified of course by the existence of large sums of federal money which are being made available to states.

Thus, as the educational effort burgeons, the states have become

---

* Who has the authority to run the educational system? Primarily the state legislatures. Unless we recognize that it *is* the states and give them an effective professional arm, we are in trouble. Perhaps even private consultant services could be available to assist school districts that want to improve data-gathering or instructional programs. They might constitute a computer corps with mobile units of some kind.

even more important, since good management assigns to each level of a hierarchy the decision-making functions at which allocations can be optimized. As funds available for education have increased, so has the size of the job of the states, who need more information, not only about their own operations but about activities in every other state. Thus there is in operation an amplification of existing institutions with the stipulation that for the role of the national government to be optimized, each of the federated elements must somehow come up to some reasonable level of competence in gathering information and implementing standards throughout its own bailiwick. Fortunately funds have been made available for this. The application and volume of these funds, however, is neither fast enough nor large enough to do the job successfully. Therefore the amount of money available must be increased or some ingenious system to improve efficiency must be devised. Certainly the use of administrative data processing at the state level is a sensible idea, but we are talking about an investment equal to that required to build and staff a new junior high school in each state. The question is not whether a data-processing facility at the state level is necessary; it is instead whether it is more vital at present than some other allocation for the same amount of money.

An alternative is to assign to the federal government the entire data-collection job, so that information flows from the schools to the federal centers and then returns to the states and districts in the form required. Still another alternative is the establishment of regional data-collection bureaus, an idea which has been proposed in a number of regions. Then, of course, it is imaginable that the existing Title X of the NDEA could be expanded from its present $50,000 per state to approximately half a million to cover the costs of an adequate ADP system, properly staffed, with sufficient support at the lower levels to make it work, and sufficient effort at higher levels to assure everyone involved that the information acquired is the exact information desired.†

† Suppose a state were divided into county or multicounty units, each of which would have computer capacity for serving a number of schools. A central computer facility in the state department of education could probably schedule all the schools in the state over a two-week period, from input supplied by the auxiliary computers. These countywide computers might be provided data on "Information Day" in the schools each September. The teachers would fill in once-a-year data, describing their classrooms, students, and so on. Basic data would then be fed in by school, by school system, by county or multicounty units. Some things the schools and districts need every year the state department might need every three years, and the U.S. Office of Education every five. The greater the number of schools that were completely automated around this kind of purely informational system, the more effective each individual system would be.

The hardest activity to justify is acquisition of information when the need for information appears at best to be academic. Yet we are spending billions to find out what Mars looks like, and there is no evidence that the information will do more than satisfy our curiosity. We can only deduce that if people are not willing to satisfy their curiosity about education (or perhaps are not curious), some negative phenomenon is discouraging such an expenditure. One possibility might be our own unawareness of what really good information, ingeniously evaluated and studied, might tell us. Among the purposes of the reorganization of the Office of Education has been the attempt to spark this kind of sophisticated curiosity within our own house. Hopefully it will emerge to spur demands for better information elsewhere.

THE NEED FOR A MODEL

The third major activity of the Center in which ADP can be a substantial contributor is in determining what the information gathered from the institutions of education all over the nation actually implies. *Meaning*, of course, is a slippery term that has attracted the attention of epistemologists for some millennia. We prefer to avoid the theoretical and concentrate on operational definitions as far as possible, relating them to the explicit functions of federal allocations of resources. These resources are not limited of course to money; they include the research effort which must be directed, the management function with its objectives, and recommendations and standards for general use. Thus it would seem that the correct approach in the development of allocation programs (as opposed to philosophies) is to pose alternative courses of action with regard to the nation's educational goals and then try to decide which of these alternatives to apply.

Suppose, for example, that one national goal were that everyone be granted the opportunity and be urged vigorously to complete as much education as he could, independent of his own financial resources. (This is an alternative to the current situation which permits anyone as much education as he wants and can afford, given that some resources are available in the form of private grants, scholarships, and the like.) The question then arises, what would be the outcome of such a policy on other federal policies, or in fact on life in these United States generally?

Naturally such a policy has implications for the quality and kind of education offered. People may discontinue their education because what is taught is irrelevant to what they want to know, or the means of teaching are personally unsatisfactory to the student, or the rewards for further education do not appear to be worth the effort required. We might have to admit the rather dismal fact that sections of our system alienate potential students of a certain psychological cast, particularly those who would rather figure things out for themselves than be told the answer. (A large number of dropouts maintain that for them school was an environment in which they could not win. To call these young-sters *born losers* is to sidestep the issue. We have not learned how to teach a loser to be a winner, and after all this is clearly one of our primary functions.)

Certainly, we must envision some kind of a mechanism—perhaps a simulation of the society which permits us to assess the general impact of various alternative strategies, at least in a rough numerical sense, provided we have some rough model and a way to delineate the alter-natives. In particular, we are probably able to define some aspects of the society in terms of years of education, jobs, job requirements, rates of change of job requirements, people at various age levels, and the like. A certain change in one category can cause a change in another category and so on, and given a time-based simulator it is quite possible to see the outcome of various policies appearing as shifts in the quantities of people in various roles in society and, of course, shifts in the flow of wealth through the economy. One would hardly care to argue for the accuracy of such a model. More likely it would serve to establish limits on functions and parameters on the basis that alternatives give rise to ridiculous results. Nevertheless it is probable that such a model, which would obviously have to be computerized, could give us a much better grip on the implications of policy decisions than any other method of analysis. (We are assuming, of course, that those who used the model had formerly been making policy decisions without it.)

The problem is compounded by the absence of any really solid con-cepts of what belongs in a model. There are many conjectures concerning the flow of people into, out of, and from point to point in the system, in terms of salaries and working conditions. Other notions are that the educational process is some kind of a gestalt involving teachers, pupils, history, laws, money, administration, the community, parents, libraries, what is known, and on and on. Until one can erect some kind of a model of this organism, the detailed measurement of any one part of it may develop information that is biased. Computers can help by providing a tool to explore these complex systems, but not until we know exactly what help is needed. We must then specify what we consider a school to be before we can begin to model education in any sense pertinent to the allocation of federal funds.‡

MEASURING THE UNMEASURABLE

If I were asked to pin down what should be measured in the system, I would try to develop some sort of a quantitative model of a school in terms of the socioeconomic status of the community, teacher preparation and experience, student mix, facilities available, and curriculum—sorting all the schools in the nation into approximately one hundred categories on these relatively objective measures. I would then try to get some internal and external measure for the success of the school. My assumption would be that the school represents the formalization of universal human activities devoted to improving abilities to cope with the problems of life. Schools, it is well to remember, exist because they can accomplish certain tasks better than the family or community. They are an invention of society to perform a set of operations, which in more primitive cultures is done within the family.

One can measure the effectiveness of the schools by measuring their performance in building the skills that society requires: ability to read, write, attack problems logically, handle logical abstractions (like arithmetic), learn something about man, history, the world, the institutions of men, the works of men; ability to perform some set of tasks for which society is willing to provide rewards; ability to mix comfortably with other people, to participate in social, governmental, and economic activities, and to employ the resources of society in amelioration of individual ills. In short, one can manufacture some sort of test (and success in life itself is such a test) to measure the ability of students to succeed at the sorts of tasks they are ostensibly taught to succeed at in school.§ The

‡ The technical development of a simulation program would be simple compared to describing the performance variables exhibited as learning at the end of the education process. One fundamental problem is that, in trying to build any model, we do not have the real equation: what conditions affect behavior. We do not know how twenty children versus thirty per class will do; or a teacher with a Ph.D. versus a teacher with a master's degree; or a female teacher versus a male teacher; or what variable really affects learning behavior. So we are playing with the trivial parts of education, and not dealing with its essence—the learning process.

§ Is it possible to establish some criteria sufficiently behavioral in statement that they can be checked against what we are trying to do in designing an educational system? To talk of changing values is nice philosophy but we need to get down to a statement of how we expect this to happen behaviorally. Behavioral definitions could be checked against a set of criteria to give us some kind of objective guidance. This line will lead us down to basic subject matter sooner or later.

critical issue is whether what is taught in school is pertinent to the world in which the student is to operate as an adult. It sometimes seems that the influence of the schools is so pervasive that society is being made over into a system in which well-educated people can operate successfully on the basis of what they have been taught, rather than being taught for the society in which they live.

Such conjecture, however, complicates the problem, for the system now ceases to be steady state and becomes dynamic in that the role structure of society changes in response to the training people receive to fit them for what teachers believe their roles to be. If one now has a list of school gestalts and a list of role-playing abilities of graduates of the schools, presumably one can with sufficient statistical sophistication tie the two together to come up with some evaluation of the aspects of the system which gave rise to success or failure in each school.

In short, it is insufficient to state categorically what data should be collected on the basis of what has been collected in the past. It is fairly evident that if there had been this sort of conjecturing (and perhaps it has never been more than an academic discussion simply because no one ever before had to decide about an ADP system for 50 million children), we would see considerably more evidence of it in terms of the quality of the average high-school graduate. One can argue that poor quality is simply a reflection of inherent stupidity, but I believe it is more likely that some schools are simply a very poor simulation of the real world their students will enter, and that the bulk of the skills taught are irrelevant. There are very few people in our society who cannot make change from a ten-dollar bill for something that costs $6.39; but there are a great many people who are unable to add up a column of figures (as achievement tests show).

So we must ask ourselves what we are measuring before we can sensibly start measuring. We need to know what all these numbers are going to mean, and judge our data-acquisition procedures by their pertinence to our fundamental task (federal, state, and local alike) of allocating the resources of money and people for specific goals.

With regard to problems of standardization, it may be that the lack of a common language of descriptors arises from the lack of consensus about the function of education as a whole. In many instances the lack of standards is a result of differences of locale and tradition. In the worst cases so substantial are differences in outlook between communities that it is difficult to find a means of establishing common denominators. How, for example, can one compare a course in paleontology in a school that denies the theory of evolution to one in a school that accepts it? Or compare the dropout situation in a state where school attendance is mandatory with the situation where there is no compulsory education law.

We are attempting to collect terms which are carefully defined to produce a uniform vocabulary, and it is fair to say that the bulk of the states are assisting in this effort. Discouraging, however, is the fact that with the proliferation of education laws, even at the federal level, there is a concurrent proliferation of meanings for the same term. "Average daily attendance," for example, has several current legal definitions, and each of these results in a slightly different allocation of funds. Standardization could profitably begin at home. A long step is the dissemination, to those charged with the responsibility of using them, of precise meanings for terminology commonly employed in the profession, presently assembled in the U.S. Office of Education's handbooks of educational terminology.

The functions of the National Center are never independent of the functions of the rest of the Office of Education. Everything that goes on at the federal level is to some extent determined by what we believe education in the nation to be. In turn, our view will be determined by what information we gather and what questions we ask. In the end, there remains some idea in our minds regarding the nature of education: a dynamic fundamental component of human life in a complex social environment. And, perhaps, the immediate role of the Center is not strictly the acquisition of particles of data, but rather the formulation of a quantifiable model of the real and dynamic world of education.

This view is the basis of the model-building effort in the Operations Analysis Division of the Center, which is working to develop some picture of the flow of countable objects through the educational universe. The primary problem being faced now in America is the allocation of sufficient resources in the form of cash to permit people to do what they already know how to do and judge to be good. The second step, more difficult still, is to determine when a particular allocation is approaching saturation with respect to other possible allocations, and to which of an innumerable list of possible alternatives further resources should be assigned. Before this can be accomplished, some clear idea of what goes on must be established, and after that, the proper information to evaluate the magnitude of these phenomena must be gathered and analyzed, and finally recommendations made. It is a formidable task for even the most gifted thinkers in several fields, including politics.

Plans are now underway to organize the categories we feel are necessary. We will gather the information and then spend time examining it curiously. The information we want is not sophisticated. There will be routine numbers about schools, teachers, facilities, funds, programs, and products: enough at that to keep us busy for quite some time.

A point worth making about the Center's data-acquisition program is that the interrelationships among the various factors that make up a school are so complex and potentially unmeasurable that their effect masks to a very large extent the effects of the factors which *are* measurable. The only way to extract some significant signal from this "noise" is by the statistical analysis of an extremely large number of schools. Although we can conjecture about what is fruitful to implement a policy, we cannot really test our conjecture unless we can somehow clean out the random effects that plague sociological analysis. The famous Hawthorne experiment is a good example: no matter what the experimenters did to create poor working conditions for the selected group of girls, the girls' production improved. It was finally discovered that appreciation for the personal attention given to them as individuals was more significant a factor than everything else combined in determining their work output. It may be so in the field of education: the fact that people are becoming more and more concerned with the problems and that the money is being made available in larger quantities may do more to improve the productivity and efficiency of schools than the particular allocation of funds to each specific area. Nevertheless, attempts must continue to be made to provide an accurate basis for the measurement of educational performance, and to devise the mechanism for this monumental effort.

The time has passed when a small school system can perform adequately the job that needs to be done. We must spend $1000 or $1500 for each child per year to get a good strong educational program. In order to accomplish this, we shall have to strengthen structures. Local school districts cannot bargain directly with the federal government, although there is some effort by the federal government to deal with the larger school systems. Our only hope may lie in cooperative organizational structures, perhaps completely different from anything we now know.

chapter 15

Expediting Decision Making at the State Department Level

Lorne H. Woollatt

One hundred years ago, on March 11, 1867, Henry Barnard left the presidency of St. John's College at Annapolis for Washington. What prompted the successful educational philosopher, practitioner, and statesman, who had formerly held the positions of superintendent of schools for the states of Rhode Island and Connecticut, to resign such a post? It was his own frustration at the lack of information about schools across the nation. He had made speeches about the necessity for gathering information about the progress of education in the various states, and had been so persistent in his attitude and expressions that President Andrew Johnson had invited him to head the new Department of Education as its first Commissioner. Under Barnard it became the Office of Education in 1868 and the Bureau of Education in 1870. In 1929 once again it was known as the Office of Education. It was attached variously to the Department of the Interior and the Federal Security Agency, finally growing beyond the stage of merely gathering statistics to its present partnership rank in the Department of Health, Education, and

Welfare. There are even some indications that a separate national department of education with cabinet status is to come. Of major significance is the revision in the U.S. Office of Education structure to establish a National Center for Educational Statistics. This is open recognition of the need for a unified data program, bringing together the information from the states which in turn have gathered information from localities.

How significant even today is Barnard's statement in his Report as Commissioner of Education for 1867–68:

> None save those who have had personal experience in this field of labor can appreciate fully the difficulty of obtaining complete statistics, or even general information, of the organization and operation of systems and institutions, located in forty-six different States and Territories occupying half of the American Continent —these systems, where they do exist, differing from each other in organization, management, and returns; and these institutions, whether in or out of the general system of the State, differing from each other in all the great centres of population. This difficulty of obtaining precise and uniform statistics, not inconsiderable even where there is legal authority for requiring the information, and forfeiture of some kind, or pecuniary advantage is attached to withholding or giving the same, becomes almost insuperable, when, as with this Department, there is no organic connection with systems or institutions in the several States, no authority to require, no pecuniary advantage for furnishing, no forfeiture for declining or neglecting to furnish the information sought, and no means to supply the deficiency of written returns by personal inspection. If a comprehensive and exhaustive inquiry, on some general plan, was instituted every year in each State, into its educational condition and progress, including institutions of every kind and grade, a compilation and comparative view of the results would be very easy and satisfactory and it is hoped that one of the results of the labors and publications of this Department, and of the annual Conferences of State and City Superintendents already inaugurated, will be the adoption of some uniform plan of gathering annually the statistics of schools of every kind, both in States and in all large cities. At the present time, there are not two States or cities in which the statistical returns as published include the same particulars, or between which a rigid comparison as to schools can be instituted; in more than one half of the States the returns are so incomplete as to institutions, or omit so many vital points in the condition of the schools returned, as to be worthless as indications of the real work attempted, or done, in individual schools,

or by all the schools of the State; in nearly all of the States, no attempt is made to secure inspection or returns of private, denominational, or incorporated institutions; . . . .[1]

Or consider the perspicacity of an educational leader in the Baltimore Public Schools about fifty years ago. Superintendent Henry West found it so impossible to make comparisons using statistics reported by the schools of his system that he decided to establish a bureau of research of his own. Records show that within the following two years information reported by the schools of Baltimore became sufficiently standardized to permit an overall statistical assessment of schools. The Baltimore Schools' Bureau of Research at about the same time began to use the standardized test, administering to pupils the early Stone Test of Arithmetic Reasoning.

In his annual report submitted "To the Honorable Legislature of the State of New York," Gideon Hawley, the Superintendent of Common Schools, declared: [2]

> That in pursuance of the act for the better establishment of common schools, reports have been made to him from some of the counties in this state relative to the condition of their schools. But that these reports are so few in number, and, in general, so extremely defective in substance, and artificial in form, that no rational estimate can be drawn from them. The superintendent has not, therefore, thought it necessary (although aware of the duty enjoined on him by law) to transmit, at this time, to the Legislature, what, if in their possession would serve only to incumber their journals, or, if made the basis of calculation, would lead to erroneous conclusions. He has thought it more advisable, and at the same time a sufficient compliance with the spirit of the law, to defer the performance of this duty, until, from more perfect returns to be made(the forms of which he will prepare and distribute), he shall be enabled to discharge it to some beneficial, and a more satisfactory end.

By 1817 Gideon Hawley's report listed for the various counties of the state and for the state as a whole the following: the number of towns and said counties, the number of counties making returns, the whole number of school districts, the number of districts making returns,

---

[1] Henry Barnard, *Report of the Commissioner of Education for the Year 1867–68*, Washington, D.C.: Government Printing Office, 1868, pp. x–xi.

[2] Gideon Hawley, *Annual Report of the Superintendent of Common Schools 1814–1828*. Albany, N.Y.: New York State Education Department, p. 183.

the amount of monies received in said districts, the number of children taught therein, and the number of children between the ages of 5 and 15 years residing therein. Of the 3713 school districts only 2873 responded.

By 1905, when the New York State Board of Regents and State Education Department had been unified for a year, more comprehensive statistics were available. The New York State Education Department was probably the first to introduce Hollerith techniques to a Bureau of Statistical Services, which by the 1940's was using electrical accounting machine punched-card methods. Today the Department has an electronic computer in use, a practice in which it is joined by many other state education departments.

The major school districts and state education departments as well as the U.S. Office of Education have been making marked strides in the computerization of statistics to refine data and facilitate the application of data to administrative decision making.

For a long time information has been gathered about the various aspects of schools, colleges, libraries, museums, and related organizations. Most commonly, data have to do with the number and characteristics of the students of a given school, district, state, region, the nation. These include figures for attendance, enrollment, and number of classes in a given subject. Then there are questions related to program types: general, academic, technical, vocational, business. Also there are data about staff, centering largely on teachers by grade in the elementary schools, and by grade as well as subject matter in the high schools; and supplemented in recent years by information regarding assisting personnel such as counselors, psychologists, and librarians. Information is gathered about facilities: school buildings and equipment, type of construction, amount of floor space, date of construction, assumed value, costs of maintenance and operation of plant. Materials and supplies for instruction are also reported although less frequently in terms of quality and kind than in terms of cost. And always elements of finance are gathered, including current operating expenditure, debt service, construction funds, and within current operations a breakdown of instructional salaries, instructional materials, administrative costs, retirement allowance. Community and neighborhood economic and demographic data are also essential to a modern system. These areas of information are basic. They provide major areas in which to study the adequacy, accuracy, necessity, and timeliness of data.* We must ask whether the definitions are suffi-

---

* We are concerned about the problem of the meaning of various measures that are used, and how comparable they are. We collect masses of numbers and use them,

ciently sharp to get the same information everywhere. What data essential to the educational enterprise should be added, and what can be dropped with no harm to the process?

EXPANDING THE DATA BASE

New categories determining the nature of data to be collected now must be considered. Six of these are:

1. *Race.* Much soul searching has been associated with the matter of reporting race. Until 1954 this question was asked frequently. Then some schools and states dropped it. Consequently the very information necessary to improve school facilities for Negro children in crowded areas of cities under the neighborhood-school concept was unavailable. Educators have gone through a period of "color blindness" to ensure the equal treatment of all children without reference to race. Within the last two years there has been a reversal: race is looked upon as a significant feature in educational planning. We are consciously trying to overcome the disadvantages which Negro children have met in the past. The new civil-rights legislation is reflected in all aspects of life: housing, voting, and education. This problem, therefore, must be resolved without delay. For example, are the terms *disadvantaged* or *children of poverty families* sufficiently sharp to cope adequately with the problem?

2. *Occupational Information.* Educational offices are now in the process of linking information on eventual occupations to the vocational and academic goals professed by students. The U.S. Office of Education is currently developing an information system for vocational education which may well serve as a model for all types of education. Seven states are cooperating and working with the Office and a consultant team to develop a system which is to be installed and tried out on a pilot basis in California. The states involved are California, Illinois, Iowa, Maryland, Tennessee, New York, and Texas. In addition, occupational information about parents has proved useful; taken in conjunction with achievement and program data it can improve the programs substantially.

3. *Welfare Data.* The Elementary and Secondary Education Act of

but what do they mean? When we compare California with New York, for example, do the numbers mean the same thing for each state? Early in the game we need to identify those things that can be measured accurately and comparably. These are the things to collect for large-scale data banks.

1965 in part bases its formula for allocations to local school districts on the number of children in families receiving social insurance. First attempts to get at these figures in a state where school districts are not coterminous with municipal boundaries have shown the need for better methods for identifying the locations of individuals within particular school districts.

4. *Income and Economic Data.*   Although the New York State Quality Measurement Project has already made good use of data about occupation of parents, sharper data regarding income would help in administrative decision making. The machinery for securing such information is frequently absent, however, due to a general sensitivity in the matter.

5. *Scheduling.*   The scheduling of high-school and college classes using electronic data-processing techniques is still in a developmental stage. Scheduling by computer soon will be not only feasible but practically mandatory for keeping student cumulative records, reports to parents, and similar internal housekeeping procedures in the school districts.

6. *Data Systems.*   One of the immediate needs is valid data system beginning at the source; for example, data about pupils beginning inside the classroom, moving up to the school, then to the school district report, to the state report, and finally to the federal report. It is recognized generally that a system must have in it all the elements necessary for complete reporting; yet not all of the elements need to be transmitted every year up the line. In other words, some data about pupils are consistently used by teachers for the development and guidance of students, yet may be useful for federal planning or state assistance only every three to five years.

A LOOK AT THE FUTURE

Data from the past augmented by current information needs help us look forward to the future. Seven areas of future need are:

1. *Equipment Systems.*   Computer master stations and computer substations must be able to talk readily one with another. The closer the machines conform in their elements, the less problem there will be. Currently there seems no breakthrough in this matter of standardization of equipment to permit a school district, a region within a state, a state, and the U.S. Office of Education to transmit information in exactly the same way.

2. *Compatibility.* We are now at the stage where we talk of having machines that can speak to one another through a machine language. In order for the machine of one manufacturer to speak to that of another, it is necessary to have a sort of Esperanto or Computeranto, a language that will permit one machine to work with another. Fifty states at present are sending information to the U.S. Office of Education Center on Educational Statistics in every form, from typed distribution tables to the electronic tapes of various manufacturers. The Office has set up a complicated means of translating these into a common system which its own massive computer installation can handle.†

3. *Matrices.* Much of the analysis of educational data can be handled readily by matrices of either two or three dimensions. A start has been made in this technique and more will be required.

4. *Programs.* The great need for the immediate future is a store of programs for the application of standard mathematical and statistical treatments to educational data. Such a relatively simple application as that of chi square to classified data requires the development of a new program. Some programs have been adapted to given machines to provide simple two-way matrices or multiple matrices, but the first-level statistical treatments seem more difficult to come by. With the great number of pertinent data about special fields available, it is mandatory that we be able to run intercorrelations, partial correlations, multiples, predictive regression equations and factor analyses. In other words, educational accounting programs in terms of money and pupils seem available more readily than programs in the area of scientific investigation.

5. *Input.* Still greater is the future need to simplify and speed the entry of accurate data into a system. Mark-sense techniques appear to be a solution but the combination of manmade marks and machine-sense responses is not yet totally coordinated. This problem will no doubt be overcome within a very short time and we will proceed to more sophisticated methods such as voice input of data. Again we hope soon to be able to synthesize and mechanize data so that certain information practically enters itself into a system (for example, birth date related to age).‡

---

† High priority should be given to language—the development of machine-readable languages that are more readily usable and understandable.

‡ I would like not to have to collect data, but to have data flow from the processes themselves. Rather than collecting information on achievement tests, we should collect information from the teaching-learning process. This is looking ahead a few dec-

6. *Output.*   At the moment, more promises have been made than output
   delivered. In the New York State Education Department, a Committee on Forms and Reports meets monthly to cope with general
   problems and to approve specific forms. Such identification data as
   number of teachers and number of pupils tend to be sought repetitive-
   ly from one form to the next. In a sense this serves as identification
   information. If the Committee insists that these data be completely
   removed from all forms but one with the information to be supplied
   by machine listing, then the user of data within the Education Department must search two lists. Clearly, when a school system or an
   education department or the United States Office of Education lives
   with data that are partly automated and partly manual, it is more
   difficult to control forms procedures than when the system is completely automated. No doubt within a few years the Office will be
   totally automated. Then, assuming sufficient capacity and sophistication of electronic equipment and personnel to operate it, it will be
   possible from one set of input data to generate the variety of output
   tabulations and information which will serve supervisors and administrators in carrying out their duties. Going one further step, it
   should become possible not only to tabulate and classify data for the
   state and its regions, counties, and school districts, but also to give
   information about selected teachers in a given subject for the use of
   a department supervisor. When this is accomplished, supervisory
   staffs will see for themselves how very useful the system is.
7. *Research.*   The discussion of programs (see item 4) suggests the research field. Electronic data processing makes it possible now to do
   some research of the kind formerly done with pencil and paper or
   accounting machine. The future must carry us forward into more
   sophisticated arrangements. One thousand astronomers sitting shoulder to shoulder could not have accomplished what the one electronic
   system did in the machine discovery of the surface of the planet
   Mars. Similarly the use of electronic data processing should make it
   possible, within a reasonable period of time, to do a complete analysis of the less than one hundred key items of information which should
   describe a school system, whether it be local, state, or national.

ades, perhaps, but the best data are collected from the operations. For instance,
rather than asking a school district how many students its buses carry, we should have
an automated process of bus scheduling or bus building, and draw off the data in
miles traveled from the operational system itself. In one state we ask every secondary-
school student what courses he is taking, what teachers, and so on. For those schools
that are operationally scheduled, we do not have to ask. We have the data as a side
benefit, already on tape.

THE "ED" IN EDP

When we speak of educational data processing, we must remember what the real purpose of education is. It is not sufficient to gather data which our predecessors have gathered or to hypothesize new data. The purpose of education is twofold: the development of an individual to his highest potential and the cultivation of our society for the service of all mankind. It seems a far cry from EDP to these purposes of education. But it need not be so; individuals can be described and the elements of the good society can be delineated as well. Further, such description often has mathematical concomitants whose concepts can be expressed by number. What data then, we must ask, are of the greatest worth in achieving the purposes of education? §

We may follow this by seeking a criterion measure against which to assess the various pieces of information available. Such assessment depends on the scientific programming of research formulas; for instance, analysis of variance and covariance, chi square, the F test, various correlation and regression techniques and factor analyses. The most penetrating analysis of this nature was begun by the late Paul R. Mort in the 1930's and is being carried forward by the Institute of Administrative Research, Teachers College, Columbia University. Mort and his coworkers developed a so-called simplex of characteristics composed of a core element of "quality of schools" and four panels or families of data drawn together through correlational and factor analytical studies. The panels were termed "individual school," "school system policy," "educational climate," and "community." [3] From this and a recent discussion among members of the Committee of Educational Data Systems of the National Council of Chief State School Officers it seems reasonable to expect that something in the neighborhood of 72 data characteristics would be sufficient to describe the entire universe of education, at least through the secondary-school grades (six possible panels of information times 12 items of information in each panel). Putting 72 such items into such a complex of computer programs based on six 12 × 12 matri-

§ The function of the schools becomes one of finding ways to bring to bear on the child his own history and abilities, about which we collect information. The schools offer another ingredient: the skills for evaluating, for making decisions about what the child will do next. To help enable the student to make those decisions himself, in school and in the rest of his life, is the role of education.

[3] The most concise approach to the understanding of the sequential simplex appears in *Administration for Adaptability*, edited by Donald H. Ross, Metropolitan School Study Council, 1958, pp. 119–127.

MAXIMUM AVAILABILITY OF DATA-PROCESSING
EQUIPMENT AND SERVICES TO STATE *
EDUCATION AGENCIES
(as of January, 1966)

Type of Equipment	State Education Agency	Centralized State Unit	Other State Agency	Unit of College or University	Other Educational Organization	Total Number States
Electronic computer	14	7	15	1	2	39
Basic mechanical equipment	9	..	3	..	..	12
Less than basic	1	..	..	..	..	1
None	4	..	..	..	..	4
Totals	28	7	18	1	2	56

* Refers to fifty states plus the District of Columbia and the Territories of American Samoa, Canal Zone, Guam, Puerto Rico, and the Virgin Islands.

At the present time, 39 (70 per cent) of the education departments in the 56 states and territories have computer facilities available to them; of these, 14 have their own computer while an additional 22 make use of state facilities. Only 4 of the 56 state education agencies (all territories) have no data-processing equipment available.

ces, one huge 72 × 72 matrix with an assorted complex of statistical formulas from analysis of variance through factor analysis would give a remarkable starting point for decision making or at least for identifying the elements most closely related to decision making. Such an analysis could represent a pioneering venture into the measurement of attitudes, the quantification of processes, and the application of new mathematical treatments in the social sciences. These are most exciting times in which to be living when one conceives the potential for adapting such mathematical processes to the social scene.

chapter 16

Gaps in Educational Information Systems

Robert W. Marker
Peter P. McGraw

Gratifying as it might be to dwell on the successes of educators in harnessing the computer for professional purposes, it is not our purpose to laud the past. Nor do we propose to make predictions about the future; undoubtedly the number and quality of these achievements have been significant and even greater advances lie ahead. We shall avoid documenting the current state of the art on the assumption that readers are familiar with the basic uses of computers in state educational agencies, colleges and universities, and local school systems. Adequate references are available for this purpose.[1]

This paper proposes to report the unsolved problems and observable gaps in our efforts to apply computer technology in education. The hope is to illuminate these gaps rather than to solve the problems they rep-

[1] Among these are A. Grossman and R. A. Howe (243), R. A. Kaimann and J. P. Van Uxem (264), and J. W. Whitlock (328). See also, *Report of the NDEA, Fiscal Years 1961 and 1962*, Washington, D.C.: Department of Health, Education, and Welfare, 1962.

resent, though presumably judicious spotlighting might generate research activity to provide solutions eventually.

In general, gaps exist all along the spectrum of feasible computer applications. Three major areas can be delineated:

1. How we organize and administer education.

2. How we teach.

3. What we teach.

The discussion here will be limited to the first of these areas.

SOME DEFINITIONS

The problem of applying the computer effectively in organization and administration is largely one of developing an information-processing system. Such a system utilizes hardware, software, and personnel.

1. *Hardware:* the physical devices from pencils to filing cabinets and mechanical and electromechanical equipment, transmission networks, and electronic gear available for recording, processing, transmitting, and storing information.

2. *Software:* the procedures, forms, flow charts, instruction manuals, and computer programs needed to handle the information, and most important, the identification, terminology, and definition of items to be incorporated in the system.

3. *Personnel:* everyone who is involved in the recording, processing, transmitting, storage, and use of information. Students, parents, teachers, and administrators are included, as well as the technical staff directly involved in the design and operation of the system.

THE NEED FOR AN INTEGRATED SYSTEM

At the present time the processing of information is largely limited to antiquated paper and pencil records. As one wag expressed it, we have progressed from "quill pen and eyeshade to ball-point pen and eyeshade." In truth, we have moved beyond this point. As electric accounting machines have become readily available we have applied them to many problems. Our first computers taught us to perform even greater feats. The work, however, has been done piecemeal, without a proper concern for the entire problem.*

A good information system must serve all of the units in the educational structure. Local information is needed in more and more detail at the state level. And it is no longer practicable merely to summarize local statistics into a state report at the end of the fiscal year. The number of persons required to administer state responsibilities effectively is becoming staggering. The best solution to this problem is to store the individual unit records in one file from which they can be retrieved in any format desired. Thus all of the information in the file is stored in five groupings or tracks. These five major areas should include: pupils, staff, facilities, program, and finance. This integrated filing system can be used, for example, to relate selected students to their teachers, the courses they are taking, and the facilities being used. The concept of integrated information must depend on the authority of the state educational departments to develop and establish compatible systems. The states, in their turn, must respond to national system parameters to ensure integrated information on the broadest possible scale.†

It is probably fair to say that the concept of a completely integrated system is a product of our age. Society has been specializing over the years. Division of labor, for example, has contributed to productivity throughout business, industry, and education. The integrated-systems concept demands that a holistic analysis be applied to our information needs. For the first time we must combine the many specialized needs for information and the many divided tasks into a workable system network to collect, store, retrieve, use, and evaluate information.

As total knowledge and record-keeping requirements have increased, the capabilities for processing data electronically have increased apace. Demands for new and more complex educational programs must be met

---

* In the field of educational data processing there is a need for a central repository to collect the information from all of the various studies that are underway, so that somebody can take a look and translate the findings into the total system requirements. We need a clearing house of information, and someone should be looking at the problem from a systems point of view.

† There is a question here of when complete enumeration is necessary and when only sampling is required. Perhaps large-scale information systems as here described can provide a bootstrap operation for the theory of sampling. For the first time we have an opportunity to enumerate fully criteria by which we can judge sampling techniques. For example, would samplings from different classrooms yield, at significantly lower costs, reliable measures of daily attendance? What are the advantages in cost? The disadvantages in reliability of data? What about longitudinal studies of the "follow-back" type? We should ask what data and what equipment are of most worth. What about confidentiality and the protection of the individual?

with better information systems, systems that combine computers and communications in ways we have never used them before.

Most of the tools and techniques to solve the problem are available to us. The new generation of computers has the capacity to handle most of our needs. We have also witnessed increases in printing speeds but up to now have been plagued by the lack of good machine-input methods. Attempts currently are being made to close this gap. Possible solutions may be found in optical character scanning, magnetic character reading, optical position scanning, or by direct electronic interchange from terminal to central computer hardware.

Two recent developments at the University of Iowa indicate how rapidly hardware gaps are being closed. Our engineers have completed two new optical scan devices: one of these will read both ordinary pencil marks and punched holes on both sides of a card in one pass at the rate of 400 cards per minute; the other will read 8½ × 11 sheets on both sides at the rate of 500 sheets per minute. Our new computer will have a capacity for storing eight billion characters of information in random-access storage.

One remaining problem in low-cost transmission devices for use in small schools and individual offices will probably be solved through recent developments in telephone service and equipment. The touch-tone telephone is directly compatible with hardware input requirements. It can be used as a very low-cost data-collection device appropriate to the geographic dispersion of operational units found in education. Intensive testing of automatic card-dial telephones has already begun. If these tests are successful, we will be able to transmit data from any location merely by installing a telephone.

The six major steps in the organization and administration of an integrated system are:

1. To develop cooperative arrangements between local, state, and university systems for the establishment of centralized data files.

2. To make further efforts on the problems of uniform terminology and definition of data items.

3. To do extensive testing of low-cost transmission devices to be used for data input and output.

4. To make comparative studies of the relative merits of local, regional, and state centers for processing.

5. To develop equitable arrangements for financing these centralized systems.

6. To clarify our state laws with regard to the ownership, control, and privacy of information.

THE NEED FOR CAREFULLY DEFINED OBJECTIVES

The totally integrated system envisaged requires careful planning and clarity of objectives. Broadly we can conceive of these terms as the improvement of service, management, and daily efficiency of operation. In trying to define these objectives more specifically we discover several gaps.

1. It is not clear what information is needed by various individuals responsible for education because local administrative units vary in size and organizational structure. Administrative processes vary drastically from one unit to another. The unit with a twenty-thousand-dollar budget and a part-time superintendent obviously has different needs for data than a school system with a twenty-million-dollar budget.

2. It is difficult to judge how sophisticated to make the information system in order for it to be most useful to the majority. We have early indications from our current research that professionals vary widely in their ability to use information wisely. Certain data can be successfully applied only when tempered with experience and sound judgment. There are gaps in our ability to identify the dangerous situations and tailor the data to more useful formats to avoid any misinterpretation.

3. Very little is known about the timing needs of much of our information. The best information system will make outputs available at the time of need. Too early they cause redundant handling; too late and they are ancient history. We need to do a better job of analysis on the value of timing. For example, does a parent need a grade report the day after the end of a semester? Would a three-day delay make any difference?

4. Even less is known about cost versus value of certain information. Similarly, we have not developed sound unit-cost measures for these comparisons. It is estimated that we spend approximately three hundred million dollars each year in attendance accounting. Is the record worth this cost?

5. There is no measure of value of certain data now available for the first time. We have always kept some record of pupils and finances in education but facilities records are practically nonexistent. The smallest corner filling station has more elaborate equipment records than most of our largest school systems. Is this because they are not needed?

These and other lacks exist in our specifications for an educational information system. Some will be filled with adequate research, others will continue to exist until we do a better job of training educators to use information. Both tasks will require personnel who have a broad understanding of the fundamental bases of education and sound knowledge of information technology.

THE NEED FOR A CENTRALIZED FILE

The concept and operation of an integrated information system call for a central mechanized master file. Here would be stored all of the basic data about students, staff, facilities, program, and finances. The records would be so constituted that a student's history could be examined longitudinally over his entire school experience, and so integrated that student, teacher, classroom, course, and cost could be examined in one total horizontal picture as well.

The basic information for this file in an average-size state, such as Iowa, will amount to one billion characters in the first year. The hardware to handle this volume is now available. The software has several deficiencies.

1. There has been insufficient research in the design and maintenance of large integrated files. Although many algorithms have been proposed, they have not been tested operationally.

2. Experience of transmission systems is too limited to allow for a clear statement of the needs. Again, although many varieties of transmission services and hardware are available to us, they have not been examined carefully enough to enable us to select optimum configuration.

3. The software that will allow a computer to accept dozens of input items from thousands of locations, edit the input, store it, and retrieve it automatically has not been developed. This effort will require many man years of effort from highly skilled programmers. Some of the techniques are available from other applications in industry.

THE NEED TO EXCHANGE INFORMATION

Although a few leaders have been aware of the duplication of effort going on throughout the country and have foreseen the problem of exchanging information, we still find many people struggling to "rediscover the wheel." Much of the development in educational systems has been accomplished in isolated centers by individuals or small groups. These individuals proceed with their immediate problems without documenting their findings. As a result very little of the information is disseminated to those who need it. The gaps may be summarized as follows:

1. We do not have an efficient organization to collect, document, and disseminate present knowledge. A large centralized effort such as the Association for Educational Data Systems National Center in Washington, D.C. needs adequate support to get its work underway.

2. Research efforts in system development have not included adequate documentation of failures and successes. Research grants should include funds for this purpose and research proposals should include the necessary procedures.

3. Little emphasis has been placed on transferability of systems. Large-scale efforts in systems development should be oriented to procedures, hardware, and software (particularly programming languages) so that the results will be transferable to other organizations.

THE NEED FOR PEOPLE

It is axiomatic that what goes into an information system will be no better than the people who plan it, and the output will be useful only so long as there are people to put it to work. An integrated information system requires many people of various skills and abilities. Its development will demand a resourceful blend of our knowledge about educational administration and our knowledge of information science. As educators responsible for molding young minds, we must look to ourselves to fill these gaps.

1. We need to educate highly skilled specialists at the graduate level who can direct the development of information systems in state edu-

cational agencies, colleges and universities, large local systems, and in federal agencies.

2. We need to establish in-service training programs for those presently employed who are trying to do the job.

3. Before we can do an adequate job of training, we must identify the body of knowledge that is needed by various professionals responsible for education.

4. We need pilot demonstrations of school systems actually using an integrated information system. These pilot systems should test the revisions of organizational structure and operating procedures that can be effected by a complete system.

The design and phasing-in of large-scale information systems in education is a staggering job. It will require years of effort and millions of dollars. This revolution can be brought about only by calculated evolution. Though the first steps on the journey have been taken, continued progress depends on our ability to fill the gaps in the roadway.

The ideal administrator of the 1970's will have three basic attributes. First, he will be ultimately and primarily concerned with individual children and their thoughts, their needs, their education. He will plan for them as individuals, considering the worth and dignity of each child and each adult who is part of the learning complex. Second, he will have a new set of attitudes regarding national, state, and local relationships and the opening up of the information flow. Third, the administrator will use technology. No longer will he be discussing the feasibility or the importance of technology—he will be using it effectively.

chapter 17

Educational Data Processing in Local School Districts
G. Ernest Anderson, Jr.

APPROACHES TO DATA PROCESSING

The diversity of local school districts creates a major problem in any attempt to survey their use of data processing. The districts differ in size, administrative organization, educational objectives, and resources made available for data processing, to say nothing of the state laws under which they operate. There is little consistency in the ways data processing is perceived and used by educators. The job to be accomplished often is not well defined beyond the general concepts of saving clerical effort, providing accurate information more quickly, and, if possible, increasing "efficiency." The relative newness of data processing may be one reason for the present lack of consensus about it.

It is not surprising, for example, to find that schools are using data processing in very different ways. School districts similar in size attempting to do similar-sounding things may have quite different approaches and results. Description of a school district is not an indication of what it might be doing with data processing, nor is the specification of a machine installation an index to the kinds of uses to which it is put or

204

to its effectiveness. In this context we find wide variation in what is meant by any given application, such as attendance accounting. To one person, it may mean nothing more than a listing of daily absences by machine; to another, the computation of summary statistics by machine. The following inventory of data-processing applications must be taken in this context.

The great variations in the uses of data processing are exemplified by school districts whose data-processing operations range from very sophisticated machine installations as advanced as those found in business and industry to those operating very simple data-processing equipment or buying spot services not systematically related to other uses of the same information. A cross section of districts with essentially different approaches to data processing can be seen in the following examples.

Chicago, Illinois. The Bureau of Data Processing is well staffed, well equipped, and is using a total-information-system approach for both business and pupil personnel records. Several computers are installed, and a specially built optical scanner is being used experimentally to fill a vacuum not filled by commercially available machinery. Chicago has not been constrained either by what was commercially available or by traditional ways of doing things.

Memphis, Tennessee. The Division of Business Services has done an outstanding job of automating the information system in this area, and has also offered some services to the schools for pupil-data services.

Wilmington, Delaware. Business applications have been developed to the computer level of sophistication, but attempts to provide pupil-record services to date have not been so successful.

Nyack, New York. An early small punched-card installation did an effective job with high-school records, with occasional business services secondary. Data services have now been incorporated into a Board of Co-operative Educational Services.

Palo Alto, California. A sophisticated punched-card installation, handling both pupil-personnel and business services, now includes a small computer. Extensive use is also made of large computer facilities located elsewhere for jobs such as school scheduling, utilizing locally prepared data and returning data ready for entry into the local machine-records system.

Sharon, Massachusetts. A high level of pupil-personnel data services is being obtained through the New England Education Data Systems project, with no data-processing machinery installed at all on the school's premises.

In general, administrative uses of data processing in school districts may be considered in two categories: business records and student-personnel records. Some of the same data may be used in both categories: teacher information and space utilization, for example. The major reasons for considering these categories separately are:

1. Business data processing is relatively better developed and understood, at least by data-processing personnel, after many years of effective use outside the educational enterprise.

2. Business operations tend to be better defined, more specific, and much more rigidly controllable. For example, the rules for assigning pupils to classes are far more nebulous than those for payroll.

3. There are subtle but important operating differences between the two areas. For instance, neither school scheduling nor report-card preparation is done often enough to become routine to operators in the same sense that a weekly or monthly payroll can.

4. Business data processing can often be justified in economic terms alone. It is rarely possible to justify student-personnel operations on this basis since teachers are paid no less nor are they hired in reduced numbers when data processing takes over some of the clerical work.

BUSINESS APPLICATIONS IN THE SCHOOLS

Business applications are better understood and therefore will not be covered here in as great detail as the student-personnel-record applications. A concern with this, however, is by no means trivial. Many school districts should take better advantage of what data processing can offer in the business areas. With a better control of the money available, more of it can be directed to the educational program with less administrative time spent rectifying discrepancies.*

The spectrum of business applications in various school districts includes the following:

1. *Budgeting and accounting:*
   (a) Analysis of requests and estimates.

---

* There are school superintendents today who overspend their budget without knowing it, or underspend and turn back thousands of dollars they wish they had known how to use. Data processing is the logical approach to solving this problem. Even if not one bit of machinery moves in, the processes involved and the systematic thinking required may help to set up a better manual system.

(b) Allocation to specific categories.

(c) Establishment of amount available in each category and maintenance of amount remaining after each transaction affecting that category.

(d) Detail accounting of how monies in each category were spent.

(e) Cost analyses of goods and services and of programs.

(f) Projected costs in each budget category of proposed courses of action, such as salary increases.

2. *Payroll:*

(a) Preparation of salary checks.

(b) Maintenance of employee accounts of amount paid, taxes withheld, Blue Cross, insurance, retirement, etc.

(c) Preparation of accounting documents for tax, retirement, and insurance officials.

(d) Withholding tax statements.

3. *Purchasing:*

(a) Batching requisitions for quantity discounts.

(b) Fund encumbrance and release when payment made.

(c) Follow-up uncompleted purchase orders.

(d) Prompt payment to earn discounts.

(e) Analysis of product consumption.

(f) Analysis of vendor performance.

(g) Analysis of disposition of purchased goods and services.

4. *Supplies and Inventory:*

(a) Requisition procedures for stock items.

(b) Automatic reorder of stock items at a certain level.

(c) Allocation of costs to budget categories and projects.

(d) Delivery routing.

(e) Inventory of materials stocked or in use.

5. *Accounts payable and receivable:*

(a) Generation of bills.

(b) Crediting and debiting of proper accounts.

(c) Follow-up for bills not paid promptly.

6. *Maintenance:*

(a) Preventive maintenance schedule.

(b) Repair scheduling and costing.

(c) Replacement scheduling.

(d) Analysis of product durability.

Obviously there is considerable overlap among these categories. In general, the kinds of data-processing activities mentioned here contribute to a general accounting system to keep a complete, accurate, and timely record of the cash position of a school district. This accounting system would provide for control information on how products have met specifications or expectations, whether vendors have met intended commitments for delivery and quality, and similar information usually obtained from critical incidents if at all.

Immediate extensions present themselves in several directions. Cafeteria accounting, for example, can be included. Sophistication in using the cafeteria accounting system could even extend to the analysis of available commodities and their prices in relation to balancing the diet and providing for consumption habits of pupils in purchasing for the following week.

Textbook accounting might save the teacher time as well as indicating what is *really* used in the school district. Library books might be listed, or a semiautomatic catalogue might be maintained as part of the purchase-order procedure in buying books, with frequent notification to all concerned of new books available. As unusual instructional programs are launched and exceptional or rarely used equipment is obtained, notification of its existence in the school system may stimulate other teachers to make greater use of it. Technology is no barrier here; instead, limitations in the creative imagination of school officials and resources to implement ideas retard the uses of information.

The list of possible "business" applications can be continued beyond the financial and property-management areas. For example, a personnel office might use the following data-processing applications:

1. Analysis of applicant qualifications and interview reports.
2. Qualifications and experience of staff members.
3. Job evaluation.
4. Salary levels.
5. Credits earned towards next level.
6. Leave record, including illness.
7. Staff studies of geographic origin, eligibility for certification, mobility patterns.

School officials responsible for building construction may also want to use some form of PERT or CPM analysis to determine if anticipated progress is being made, and how to readjust construction schedules in view of realities.

STUDENT-PERSONNEL APPLICATIONS

We turn now to examine some of the possible applications of electronic data processing to student-personnel records. By extension, to include the total activities of the educational program, such as those in a particular high-school building, some of the so-called business applications (e.g., roster of library books and special instructional equipment) are in a "gray" area. An almost endless variety of similar lists comes to mind. To name a few at random:

1. List of seniors for cap and gown measurement accounting.
2. List of audiovisual equipment available and requisition procedures.
3. List of films, slides, records, models, wall charts, and other instructional materials not automatically placed in classrooms where they might be of use.
4. Analysis of use of audiovisual equipment.
5. List of available space, with indication of seats, lighting properties (for audiovisual presentations), and other special features.

Any systematic consideration of student-personnel records must begin with the master file, or, as it is sometimes called, the basic pupil-census file which is the heart of the machine-records system. This file maintains the pupil's identification despite moving, school changes, name changes, and other occurrences that can cause confusion in school records. Such a master file usually contains considerable demographic information about pupils: name as used, legal name, birthdate, sex, residence, guardian, parental employment, year of entrance into the school system, year of anticipated high-school graduation, school attended at present, and special considerations such as physical defects, etc. Some possible uses for this information are:

1. Pupil directories for all school offices.
2. Address directories for capitation purposes and to indicate the number of children from one household in the schools.
3. Federal employment of parents survey (PL 874).
4. Mailing of official school communications (or PTA information), one per household instead of distributing this material one per child through the schools.

5. Age in grade reports.

6. Availability of verified birthdate (and hence age) for tests using age as part of the norming process.

7. Checking to see that attendance and test files are complete.

8. School-bus transportation requirements.

A master file may be extended in two directions. One is to include *school information* as it becomes available: test scores, attendance records, courses taken and marks earned, special comments, physical fitness and health reports, and subsequent career information. Whether this information is formally included in a defined master file or kept as a set of separate but related files is a matter of operational convenience.

The other direction in which a master file might be extended is toward *community surveys*. In any city, a complete pupil-census file will cover the majority of households anyhow. With some additional effort, at least upon occasion if not on a continuing basis, information can be included on all households. Such factors as condition of housing, income and background of family, and family mobility can yield valuable information for school planning. Related community information such as anticipated land use, tax and assessment evaluation rolls, court records, and welfare records can sometimes be very useful in such planning to amalgamate information from all sources. It should be possible for such planning surveys to do an improved job in predicting the number and type of pupils to come, and in bringing this community information to bear on the understanding of the children.† A word of caution: Too free an interchange of information for purposes not comprehended or approved by the public can be a source of danger. At some ill-defined point, the possibility of invasion of individual privacy needs to be considered, along with the desirability of ensuring that children have a "clean slate" at certain points in their careers.‡

---

† If we had a central type index of all school districts, all schools, and all teachers, with some count of pupils by age, race, and economic status, and some measure of the money spent, by whom, and for what, we could go to Congress and say, "This is how much money it's going to take to do a certain class of activity in this country," or, "If we do this, here's what will happen."

‡ By the time you collect all your school's data, you have information that is valuable to a whole other group of state and local agencies. Health people need it, the poverty program needs it, insurance underwriters need it, and so on. We are going to have to deal in the next few years with the possibilities and dangers of tying in with other data systems. It is all very well to build a centralized data-processing system with terminals in all the school districts. But what about the confidentiality of information? Questions of ethics are raised, and we are remiss in our duties if we do not consider them carefully.

Another paper has considered in detail the problems of scheduling. It must be noted here, however, that scheduling does imply many different things to educators, ranging from complete computer manipulation of facilities and requirements to produce the master schedule and pupil assignments, to simple counts by sorter to provide information for a manual scheduling process. Scheduling has been the most important reason for school use of data processing to begin with, and in many schools remains the one area where it is functioning. The varied tasks closely related to scheduling accomplished by data-processing methods include:

Recording of anticipated instructional programs for pupils.

Tabulations of course requests as a basis for teacher hiring, curriculum planning, and section determination.

Lists of pupils requesting specified courses for screening (e.g., advanced placement, band, courses to be withdrawn).

Determination of the interaction or potential conflict between pairs of courses.

Projection of enrollment in higher-level courses in future years based on requests for beginning courses.

Counselor notification when pupil course requests deviate from anticipated or planned program.

Summer-school registration that may affect fall course changes.

Generation of "dummy" student requests for anticipated new pupils not yet in the school district.

Trial runs of proposed master schedules (simulation).

Class lists.

Homeroom lists.

Unhonored pupil request list for counselor action.

Pupil schedules.

Teacher schedules.

Room utilization studies.

Extracurricular-activity time assignment.

Checks to see that pupils have met course prerequisites.

Locker assignment and lock combination records.

Attendance accounting has been automated to varying degrees in many school systems. Some of the specific applications are designed to do little more than assist the main office to compute summary statistics; other applications actually record attendance information at the source. Some data-processing operations for attendance accounting have cost so much that attention has been directed to the high proportion of our resources going into this area. Typical attendance applications are:

Daily attendance bulletin showing pupils absent, tardy, or dismissed.

Period-by-period accounting of pupils not present and not on the daily attendance bulletin.

Preparation of register pages for manual recording.

Preparation of optical scanner sheets for recording.

Printing of register pages from recording documents.

Processing of pupil summary data, hand counted for school summary statistics.

Notification of school officials when consecutive or cumulative absence for any pupil reaches a predetermined number of days.

Analysis of absence and tardy patterns for individual pupils.

Production of pupil summary statistics for report cards and permanent records.

Production of state reports.

Automated mark reporting has been well received by most high-school faculties. There is some loss of face-to-face contact with pupils when marks are given, but much gain of teaching time in schools that formerly had pupils carry their report cards around with them for marking in class. There is a tendency for teachers to mark more honestly when they do not know what other teachers have given, and it is believed that teachers make more comments when these can be made easily. It is also thought that more report cards actually get home and are read by parents when the report cards are mailed with no return needed. Analysis of both mark and comment information has been facilitated by electronic data processing. Here are some of the applications related to mark reporting and analysis:

Printing of report cards.

Printing of gummed labels for permanent records.

Printing of transcripts.

Mark analysis by course and by teacher.

Comment analysis by course and by teacher.

Failure and incomplete lists.

Notification of counselors when pupil marks change from past performance, or type and number of comments change.

Computation of pupil summary and average statistics.

Honor roll computation.

Rank in class lists.

Underachiever identification.

Class lists showing marks.

Preparation of anticipated mark distributions for each class from distribution of tested ability and school's marking practices for the course.

Test data have been handled by electronic means for many years, and until recently may have represented the major application of data processing in the schools. Many schools that did not have a test-scoring machine of their own have used commercially available services, and the very process of test construction and validation required considerable research work involving processing of data. Because of the way the standardized testing movement developed, there is an ethical problem today if schools that are able to do their own test scoring do so without using forms provided by the test publishers or without some form of royalty payment based on pupils tested. Perhaps the biggest potential gain to education from a school's ability to do all its own test processing could be the analyses of teacher-made objective tests as part of the scoring procedure. Uses of data processing for handling test data include:

Count of the number of items right, wrong, and omitted on a test.

Raw scores as a function of items right, wrong, and omitted.

Scaled score conversion from raw scores.

Computation of local distributions and norms.

Table look-up or computation of national norms.

Class rosters of test results.

Group averages.

Item analysis of tests, including difficulty level, per cent correct answers as a function of total score, and inter-item correlation and cluster analysis.

Reliability and validity studies, including locally constructed tests.

Prediction and expectancy studies.

Gummed labels for posting to permanent records.

Profile reports to counselors, teachers, and parents.

Development of banks of items with known statistical properties.§

From test scoring we move into research uses of data in schools. For example, the evaluation of various instructional techniques may use test and achievement data as both background (preexposure) and post-exposure measurements. And, whether it is intended or not, the managers of the growing data-processing effort in schools are building banks of data as a by-product of various automated reporting procedures. It is becoming possible to consider using such data for extensive research studies which would be completely unrealistic by hand methods of data manipulation.

Nor does this exhaust the list of possible data-processing applications in local school districts. Among many others that might be listed are:

College admission studies: what kinds of pupils are accepted and make good where?

Library circulation control and analysis.

Misconduct reports and analyses.

Bus passes.

Athletic tickets and accounting.

Identification cards.

School insurance accounting.

§ One grading program that has been worked out can take objective-type tests and analyze the students' answers, tell the student which questions he missed, and provide him with up to 9000 lines of feedback telling him why his answer was incorrect, what the right answers should have been, and where he can go to find additional information. An item analysis is provided for the teacher so he will know what students missed what test questions with what degree of frequency.

In building a test, a teacher should be able to draw on a test bank which would contain, say, 5000 test items for a unit in American history. From these 5000 items on random-access storage discs, the teacher can select questions appropriate for the particular objectives of his unit and for his students.

Health and dental records.

Physical education skill and achievement records.

No one school district is actually using all the applications mentioned here. Yet all are possible and all are being used in one or another place, one way or another, and with varying degrees of success. Some are in operation because the machinery is there, or because a neighboring district is doing them, without regard for utility and appropriateness. In many cases, data-processing applications have developed in advance of the readiness of school officials to make full use of them.

Despite some soul searching and uncertainty, there is increasing evidence that electronic data processing is successfully automating routine information management in school administrative tasks. But today the real challenge to educators is not merely to perform these tasks more effectively; it is to use the information becoming available to us, the time formerly spent on routine activities, and resources formerly constrained by tradition and manual methods for reevaluation and reshaping of the educational enterprise. And only if we retrain ourselves to capitalize on the new tools of automation can we meet this challenge.

chapter 18
Computers in Higher Education
John Caffrey

The computer evolved in the academic world, both in concept and engineering, with major assistance from the electronics industry, and in many colleges and universities it remains essentially an academic possession. As the need for computer scientists has expanded in recent years, the computer has also become an object for instruction. There are demands on freshmen in many colleges today to know computing, and the expanding interest of secondary schools in teaching computer science has made the computer as popular a tool for problem solving as the slide rule and desk calculator were two decades ago.

The use of punched-card equipment for administrative purposes antedates the use of the computer for similar purposes by many years. Until fairly recently, few managers in higher education knew much about computers, and in many institutions the academic community posted a clear "Keep Out" sign on the computer room door. As computers became better understood, and as smaller ones became available, some institutions converted their punched-card procedures for card-

216

based computer systems, essentially doing more quickly and economically what had formerly been done with cards, and a small minority even introduced more advanced tape systems.

Not until recently and only in a very few cases, however, has attention switched from the how-to-do-it stage to the nature of the system itself. "It," in this context, has proved most often to be such pedestrian yet massive tasks as student registration, grade reporting, test scoring, analysis, accounting, personnel records, and so on. We could make a long list of such possible applications, which may be called *transactional*. There is hardly any reasonable transaction or application which has not been tried somewhere, and sometimes with outstanding ingenuity and acceptance. Most of these have grown in the face of demand. That is, those applications were tried first which were well known to those running the data center, or were of pressing urgency, or could be borrowed from a neighboring institution, or which the machine manufacturer could provide as an added inducement to using his wares, or which most closely resembled a manual process well-enough understood to be easily imitated with automated equipment. Seldom have management information applications emerged as a result of systematic study of the total problem of management in higher education. Indeed, it is easy to find situations in which systems developed quite separately, and with little if any interface, in the same institution: the registrar having a 407/EAM unit, the comptroller a 1401, and the counseling and testing center a scoring machine and some minimal EAM gear. And not far away may be a master computer center with large capacity not fully utilized. We can even point to one case where on the same campus two separate and mutually unknown efforts were being devoted to mechanizing class scheduling.

Examples of mutually exclusive systems abound: a payroll office may be using one set of codes and files for staff, a registrar's pupil-record office a completely different set of codes in class lists and grade reports, and an alumni office yet another set of codes. This is to say nothing of the fact that the computer center on the same campus adds yet another system of codes for faculty and student work, assigns different codes to work done on contracts than those used by the university contract officer and once again by the business manager. There is nothing inherently wrong with chaos if one never notices it or if one allows for it. Those concerned about system compatibilities have begun to realize that it is probably more sensible to design software for intersystem translation.

The forementioned instances of topsy-like growth of parallel, disconnected, uncoordinated, incompatible "systems" are intended, however, to suggest the lack of consideration given to approaching management *as a system*. But as Brown and Mayhew point out in their recent *American Higher Education*,[1] our higher-education system works reasonably well without systematic form or structure. Local autonomy, between and within institutions, is a matter of fierce pride. In short, anyone who offers to tinker with the information-system component of management may expose a nest of vested interests, tradition-based practice, actual as distinct from formal organizational lines, procedures whose original objectives have been forgotten, fear of automation, and a general distemper besides.

What is really driving the higher educator to think more systematically about his system, and especially to think about automating portions of it, is the pressure of rising costs, increasing demands for more and better data from boards of regents, state and federal agencies, foundations, and from planning and fiscal control agencies, combined with the generally increased complexity of management problems that derive from rapid growth.

The development of automated management practices in education (and this may be true in other areas) seems to follow a classic pattern: automation at first simply takes over and imitates what used to be done by hand. Then new and more elegant applications are developed as the relationships between the various files are perceived and as pioneer technicians experiment with massive solutions to problems like scheduling and resource allocation problems. At first, the academic manager may be inundated by more lists of figures and tables than he has ever seen. If he is able to stem this tide or demand better data reduction, he may begin to perceive the increased utility of information based on complete, accurate, and timely sources, and he may begin to conceive of new uses for management information. If he is fortunate, his information service officer will invent new reports, controls, and processes and teach the administrator effective applications.

It is indeed difficult to find very many examples of a broadly integrated and comprehensive management information system designed to serve the purposes of administration. With the cooperation and support of the American Council on Education's Commission on Administrative Affairs, I have been visiting a few colleges and universities to pursue this line of study. I have talked with presidents, administrative staff

[1] Hugh S. Brown and Lewis Mayhew, *American Higher Education*. New York: Center for Applied Research in Education, 1965.

members, and heads of computer centers and information processing systems. The following remarks are based on a small number of observations but are notable because of the consistency with which the same problems, attitudes, and trends emerge within particular environments.

THE CURRENT STATE OF COMPUTER UTILIZATION

Administrators are just beginning to be aware of the potential utility and power of truly integrated information systems. Those using such systems at all, and the minority of persons who have thought much about it, usually cite convenience and economy as the chief advantages. Many have been grateful for the solidity that clean data can contribute to an argument, a budget message, or an alumni fund-raising appeal. But there is also a growing interest in the possibilities of using simulation to test the effects of decisions, to arrive at better problem solutions by converging iterations, to project the shape of proposed programs, to forecast needs, and so on.

In the early days of university data centers, it was a widespread conviction that research and administrative units should be separate; that even within the administration separate facilities should be used for, say, grade reporting and payroll, to avoid peaking and queueing. But as computers become faster, as time-sharing systems become practical, as intercomputer system integration makes it possible to have a separate satellite that is all one's own part of the time and a feeder to a very large monster another part of the time, and as executive programs provide reliable scheduling and multiprogram processing so that both payroll and grade reports can be handled at the same time, the movement is toward the design of centrally planned and managed systems that meet the needs of research, instruction, and administration. A central system, it is perceived, does not imply a single large hardware center but may involve units placed for convenience of access and control at various points and yet with the potential of being combined into very large hardware complexes when large capacity or more sophisticated and complex processing is required. The existence of such linked complexes then raises some interest in the design of *true systems*. (Perhaps there is no such thing as an untrue system or a nonsystem; everything has a system somewhere in it. My own filing system, for example, functions for me; no one else can make any sense out of it, of course.)

There is increasing recognition that the computer capacity of a college or university is part of its total power to attract and hold students and faculty. It is safe to predict that within the next ten years a major college or university which does not have adequate computer facilities will be considered as unattractive as a college without a library. There have been instances already of outstanding scholars turning down offers to join a faculty because of inadequate computer facilities. We also know of instances in which the award of research grants or contracts has been conditional upon the existence of such facilities. Nor is it merely a matter of keeping up with the Joneses.

In large institutions the demand for computer services tends to become so great that the computer facility must expand. As costs rise (not per unit of computing work, but absolutely), it becomes necessary to pool the resources of administrative budgets and research contracts in order to afford equipment of sufficient power. As the number of users, especially students, grows and grows (not just in mathematics and the hard sciences), the need for easier access via remote terminals and more effective operating systems, with short turnaround, grows insistently. One even begins to hear it said that in humanities and liberal-arts programs there is growing realization that the citizen of tomorrow had better know as much as he can about computers.

Hence the demands for instruction in computer sciences grow apace. It is possible to find in college catalogues across the country a great variety of courses designed for special purposes; the engineer and the business administrator apparently need different kinds of course programming; there are courses covering the general functions of computers, the design of computers, computers in system analysis, and so on. It is hard to find a discipline in which the computer has not obtruded, even in art and music.

In the process of conversion to an automated system, the administrator is forced to think seriously about objectives. Since the computer programmer must receive precise specifications for what he is to do, someone has to stop and figure out what is wanted and why. This process alone, according to E. L. Katzenbach, is worth the price of the machine. The introduction of the computer into management may be the opening door not merely to facilitation of current practice but to the fundamental improvement of management itself. Preparing for the computer forces us to be painfully explicit about the purposes of administration.

The rapid advance of computer technology, and its implications for system design, has led to certain kinds of confusion and ambivalence on the part of administrators. Almost everyone has heard about time sharing, but this is often confused with the simple idea of providing remote input-output terminals, not necessarily the same thing. On the one hand, some assume (correctly) that the production of time-sharing programs can be quite expensive, and on the other hand some assume (incorrectly) that time-sharing systems are available as off-the-shelf items. Someday they may be, and a few, such as those of General Electric, almost are. The largest and most elegant systems, however, such as Project MAC's and those of the System Development Corporation, are either tied to specific one-of-a-kind hardware or are not adequately documented. Most major computer systems *eventually* will be delivered by vendors with at least the framework for a time-shared system, but we should not be overly optimistic about the rapidity with which these can be delivered or put into operation.

Another source of confusion involves the problems of purchase versus rental. The computer censuses show an increasing proportion of purchase, apparently because analysis shows economies, but there is much concern with obsolescence. The administrator inevitably wonders whether a few years hence he will have a dud on his hands, and he knows little about the market for used computers or about the value of exchange for a new model. There is also a tendency to forget that purchase does not eliminate periodic costs, such as maintenance contracts. Some administrators are waiting for computer development to "level off" before they take the plunge.

I have found at least one enlightened college president who recognizes that his college is long overdue for a computer center but who will not move until his faculty evidences sufficiently strong interest, especially in the *instructional* use of the computer. The small college (1000 and under) has a special problem; in the liberal arts there is an uneasy feeling that a humanities curriculum should include something about computers, but the small college often feels that a computer is too expensive. It need not be as expensive as many presidents think, especially with the current wave of very fine small computers, some of which can be purchased outright for less than $20,000, to provide both modest computing power and the possibilities of hands-on experience for students. Some small colleges are looking seriously at the possibility of sharing a commonly supported center, and many have profited by the use of such regional centers as the Western Data Processing Center at UCLA, the Dartmouth and Phoenix General Electric centers, the New England Education Data Systems, and the like. One value of the latter kind of experience is that the college ultimately gets involved with computer utilization and takes faster steps toward developing its own facilities.

There is no particular pattern for the genesis and expanded use of university computer centers or systems. In some cases the lead has been taken by a college of engineering; in others by a school of business administration; and in still others by one of the "hard" science departments. Medical schools are also leaders in the field; several medical educators have said with great conviction that no self-respecting medical school, even today, can do without a computer center. In some cases, as in medicine, physics, and other subjects requiring extensive on-line use in relation to experiments, separate facilities are a must. At Tulane University, for example, the computer complex, serving not only the medical school but several associated hospitals, is in use around the clock, monitoring laboratory work and surgery on a real-time basis, performing quick turnaround analysis of lab reports, and involving specially engineered equipment for recording data on tape for direct computer input. Dr. James Sweeney at Tulane has developed methods for scanning and digitalizing X rays to provide for faster and more sensitive diagnosis. In very few institutions, however, is there strong evidence of a faculty-wide comprehensive plan for the development of computer services. Other faculties than the one originally responsible for a center gradually climb aboard as they see what can be done, but in too many institutions this is left to chance. At Stanford University, special attention has been paid to acquainting a broad spectrum of faculty members with potential uses of the computer in their own disciplines.

In some administrative areas, automated systems have provided some surprise economies and monetary returns. At the University of Colorado, for example, there is a very strict control of research-contract budgets and expenditures, with periodic reports that provide for short-term controls which few colleges enjoy. In another university, alumni-fund contributions and appeals are so effectively automated that the system can be credited with raising a quarter of a million dollars a year. Computers have been used for designing rooting-section card stunts for football games, with huge savings in money, for handling football or concert series tickets, for mailing lists, and for the assignment of parking space. Some of these trivial and even frivolous applications can save or be the source of money.

One of the major problems hampering the advance of new and better integrated systems is the shortage of administrators who understand how computers can be used in management. Many computer center directors and technicians know little about administration, and others are not receptive to management appeals for help. Unfortunately, there are very few places to which an administrator interested in improving his understanding of these matters can turn for training or assistance. There is a great need, steadily increasing, for the establishment of centers which can provide direct assistance, consulting services, training and orientation programs, and general information about existing practices and possibilities. The Association for Educational Data Systems now has an office in Washington, D.C., supported largely by a grant from The Fund for the Advancement of Education, but as yet its resources are very limited and most of its users are in public school or state education agencies. The College and University Machine Records conferences provide a forum for the exchange of ideas and software. But these activities come nowhere near meeting the *realized* need, to say nothing of the greater needs perceived by those studying the problem. We hope that the study conducted by the ACE will result in stimulating the development of such centers throughout the nation. In the meantime, development of systems in each center involves the proverbial reinventing of the wheel, the inevitable duplication of work already done elsewhere at considerable expense. As rapidly as possible, we hope to eliminate this.

After a review of present practices, trends, and interests, it may be useful to describe some of the components and characteristics of computer centers and systems to come, within the next decade at least, in a typical institution of higher education. My example will be a state university with an enrollment of around 15,000, part of a statewide system, with the usual schools of medicine, law, librarianship, education, engineering, liberal arts, science, and so on.

THE COMPREHENSIVE MANAGEMENT INFORMATION SYSTEM

The Computer Center, administered by a director who reports to the university's president, is housed in a special facility that provides space for system analysis, programming, administrative and operating staff, as well as for the offices and classes of the Institute of Computer Sciences. The Institute provides instructional and consulting services for students and faculty and conducts advanced research in the design of computers and systems, in cooperation with the faculties of engineering, medicine, and mathematics. The Center is equipped with a large-scale computer with extensive time-sharing capabilities. Access to the large computer is facilitated by the location of remote terminals and teletypes throughout the campus: in the library, administrative offices, study carrels, the various professional schools, laboratories, and resident dormitories. In addition, the smaller satellite computers operated by the schools of medicine, engineering, and education, by the central library's Information Retrieval Center, and by the Instructional Materials Development and Resources Center for the monitoring of computer-assisted instruction, are all capable of being linked with the Center's computer on either a real-time or batch-processing basis. Linkage of either permanent or part-time input-output units is facilitated by use of the university's Centrex telephone network. In addition, through the "Telpac A" system, providing twelve channels connecting all seven of the state's institutions of higher education, it is possible to provide for intercomputer links among the institutions themselves and with the offices of the state's board of regents. The latter has access via this system to the entire data base for all its institutions for purposes of administration, budget control, and forecasting and planning.

Special libraries, such as law and medicine, use their own computer facilities for document disposition and retrieval and use the university's central computer in off-peak hours for the translation of foreign documents. Scholars in all faculties may use the services of the Information Retrieval Center to obtain periodic or special request listings of new documents selected according to a list of keywords supplied by the scholars and revised periodically in the light of automatically produced periodic summaries of the utility of keyword lists; that is, the computer system counts "hits" and "misses" and the number of times that each keyword produced a shelf listing that turned out to be useful.

The university counseling center provides several services through its installation of six input-output terminals. A student can register for courses through the teletype system, with automatic feedback if he requests a course for which he has not met preliminary requirements. Students can also request information about their past records with special code numbers designated to prevent unauthorized access to their records. They can receive certain routine counseling assistance respecting requirements for certification in various fields, employment potentials, admission requirements of other schools or of graduate divisions, and the like. For specialized testing, computer-based standardized tests can also be administered which are scored as taken, the test terminating when the computer determines that the student has answered a sufficient number of questions to provide a specified minimum reliability coefficient. Counselors receive automatic reports concerning students whose course work is falling below specified minimum levels. The university center provides computer program service for the scheduling of all classes and prepares preaddressed reports for mailing class schedules, grade reports, tests, and other notices (e.g., periodic billing for tuition, loan fund repayment, etc.).

The university's administrative (and especially institutional research) staff has access to all of the data banks associated with the university's operations: student personnel, professional staff, budgets, research contracts, facilities, accounting, maintenance, and so on. The by-products from the transactional system provide current and immediately available information, in either cathode-ray tube or hard-copy displays, for current administration and planning. A general-purpose CRT display system, which can receive inputs via light pen, teletype, or electronic tablet, is sufficiently flexible to permit the user to arrange data in a variety of tabular and graphic forms and then to obtain hard copies when he is satisfied with the results.

The president, who is responsible for presenting budgets and plans to the board of regents and ultimately to the legislature, not only finds that his computer-assisted system permits more accurate and useful estimates of current and anticipated needs and resources but that the legislature is more willing to rely on the validity of the information on which he bases his plans. The board of regents' direct access to necessary data through its linkage to all the state system's computer centers makes it possible to conduct statewide planning and evaluation studies without involving institutional officials in filling out forms or answering questionnaires. Indeed, many local institutional reports and statewide compilations are prepared and delivered automatically on a periodic schedule.

Is this so much blue sky? Hardly.

Almost without exception every technical development implied by the foregoing sketch of tomorrow's university is *already a fact* in either final or semifinal form and is available either in the public domain or through commonly accessible vendors. Our problem is not the technology of information processing. The creation of powerful management systems, with their associated instructional and research capabilities, requires only that we decide to move ahead, commit the required resources, create the human proficiency, establish the training and orientation programs, keep our eyes open to the still newer developments that burst upon the scene continually, and demand that our system designers and technicians put their best resources at our disposal to bring the management of higher education at least into our own decade of the twentieth century—if not, as we hope, into the future.

chapter 19

Developing EDP Systems: Issues and Recommendations

Dwight W. Allen
Don D. Bushnell

Since the time of the AEDS-Stanford Conference at the end of 1965, the computer has been gaining acceptance among a growing number of educators. As could be expected, the most systematic exploitation of computer potential has been in budgeting, accounting, bookkeeping, and pupil-personnel records—applications that have already been tested in business and industry and could most easily be adapted to the educational setting. The use of the computer in environmental simulation and planning, in the individualization of instruction, in testing and evaluation, and in research on teaching and learning is coming more slowly. This is not because of deficiencies in equipment or prohibitive costs; hardware has become more sophisticated and, with the expansion of time sharing, less expensive each year. Nor is there a lack of encouragement—such federal programs as Titles I, III and V of the Elementary and Secondary Education Act of 1965 can provide funds for supplementary educational programs or demonstration projects that

226

make use of computers for data storage and retrieval, for experimentation with individualized instruction, for new approaches to the educationally disadvantaged, and so on.

The most formidable block to educational progress through the significant application of computer technology is the lack of understanding of basic educational processes: the nature of the relationship between teacher and learner, for example, and the lack of accurate, retrievable data on the effectiveness of various *ad hoc* techniques that have been highly successful. Nevertheless there is much to be learned from well-tested applications already in the public domain. Some of the more stimulating research projects going on around the country (as described in Chapter 8) are exploring techniques of computer-mediated learning that will have profound implications for education in the future.

Many school districts—particularly the more affluent ones—are eager to make a realistic test of the latest procedures for teaching languages and advanced concepts in mathematics and the sciences, for automating libraries, for flexible scheduling, and so on. There is no lack of interest or of hardware. The problem for educators is to identify those applications that have been shown to be effective and practical not just in the laboratory but in pilot school settings.

Implementation should proceed from an enthusiasm well tempered by the experience of others. It is imperative that educators be kept in regular touch with developments in the process of field application—what subsystems have become obsolete as a result of advances in technology, what configurations have seemed the most fruitful, and so on. This is particularly important when advertising and popular magazine articles can make computers seem capable of solving almost any educational problem. The practicing educator may be tempted to see what is now essentially a research device as an instructional tool that can be plugged into his regular program. The acceptance of untested practices not only can lead to disillusionment, but also may divert the educator from those approaches that hold the most promise for productive change in teaching and administration.

It may be instructive to review some of the areas in which progress has been made as well as areas in which predicted developments have turned out to contain more complexities than expected. This review, which is based on the recommendations made by conference participants, should indicate some of the dangers of wholesale acceptance of relatively untested systems or techniques. Three areas of EDP development have come into prominence: computer-assisted versus computer-augmented instruction, the data bank or information utility, and the total systems approach to computerizing educational processes.

The Computer in the Classroom. Much attention has been given to experimental work in computer-assisted instruction, i.e., programmed sequences of instructional materials dispensed by the machine in response to the learning performance of the student. The advantages of this technique over the conventional book or mechanical teaching machine have been described: sequences of material are individually tailored and records of learning patterns are accumulated for research and revision of the programs. Promising work in this area is being done today by Suppes and Atkinson at Stanford University, Mitzel at Pennsylvania State University, and Silberman at System Development Corporation.

Some reservations about this approach concern the extent to which the author-programmer can fully anticipate the learning needs of the student. An explicit predetermined model of educational needs is required for the development of the instructional programs. The teacher too may be placed in a new and somewhat peripheral role as troubleshooter and attendant. More recently, interest has turned to computer-augmented instruction, involving the classroom computer terminal as an aid to the student in classroom instructional activity. Pioneering ventures into this area have concentrated on mathematics, the sciences, and other subjects with a mathematical base. The presence of the computer makes it possible for teachers and students to formulate their own experiments with advanced mathematical concepts and, by viewing the graphical and geometrical translations of algebraic processes, to gain a more intuitive understanding. In this manner, subject-matter areas not previously taught below the college level can be broached.

In a pilot program in Massachusetts, teacher and student reactions have indicated that both bright students, who proceed to do some original mathematics, and slower students, who respond well to the Socratic method, gain a feeling for mathematics and some insight into the subject through the use of the computer. As a tool or teacher adjunct, the computer can simulate events and procedures, demonstrate scientific experiments, and participate in learning games, which have been shown to have a strongly motivating effect, particularly on those students who have not responded well to standard classroom practices.

There is growing interest in the exchange of computer-ready instructional capsules that make use of the problem-solving mode or exemplify the "learning by discovery" approach. As remote time-shared terminals tied to a central computer grow less costly, the classroom computer terminal will become a feasible and desirable addition to standard school equipment. It could be recommended then that, although more conventional programmed instruction modes should continue to be improved, greater attention should be given to new methods that employ the full capabilities of the computer for instruction.

The Data Bank. Administrators have welcomed the appearance of the efficient computer to handle the myriad details of accounting and record keeping, and can look forward to having access to a central data file with a place for everything and everything in its readily located place. Efforts to begin to build centralized data banks whose purpose is not merely the storage of data but the facilitation of information exchange have indicated that the major problems concern the definition of what data to collect, what to throw away and when, and how to secure different types of information, some of which are highly sensitive. The advent of the computer has intensified some of the questions that have always plagued data collectors, and there is an urgent need for the establishment of some guidelines for information storage and retrieval.

The Systems Approach. As several of the previous chapters indicate, automatic data processing has frequently been introduced in a piecemeal fashion. Various types of incompatible hardware may exist on one campus or within one school district. Overlapping data files and incompatible languages and formats frequently make it impossible for one subsystem to communicate with another. The experience of the military and aerospace programs in the last few years has proved the value of the systems approach—that is, the planned, evolutionary develment of a unified information-processing system. When long-term total design principles are kept foremost, new hardware components can be plugged in or substituted for less effective ones without severe dislocations in overall operations. The information flow among subsystems is facilitated, and long-range planning, for example, can be carried out with greater reliability.

ISSUES AND RECOMMENDATIONS

The three areas just described—alternate strategies for computer-mediated instruction, data banking, and the systems approach—encompass many of the problems and issues identified at the AEDS-Stanford Conference. Some of these concerns relate to deficiencies in methods and techniques, or needed improvements in the communication process;

others refer to underlying philosophical issues that have yet to be resolved.

Developments in the computer field are rapid, and some of the conference recommendations are already being acted upon by university research centers and by such organizations as AEDS, with its National Center for Educational Data Processing. A systems study, "The Computer and Educational Progress in the School District of Philadelphia," has been completed by the Brooks Foundation in collaboration with Technomics, Inc., and a two-year study for a statewide data-processing system is now underway in New York state.

The issues and recommendations that follow represent the consensus of conference participants—leaders in educational administration and research and experts in instructional technology. They serve to emphasize the fact that, with the change agent itself undergoing constant change, the challenge is great for the educator who wishes to keep control of the aims and purposes that the computer is to effect.

THE COMPUTER AND THE CURRICULUM

Criteria must be established for determining the disciplines or areas within disciplines in which either of the distinctive forms of computer mediation, computer-assisted or computer-augmented instruction, is appropriate and feasible. Establishing what should be included and what should be excluded from a computerized instructional system can lead to generalizations about the applicability of computer mediation to various disciplines; further, the identification of areas in which the technology is inappropriate or misused can give impetus to the development of expanded media approaches in those areas.

Before introducing computer processes, careful statement must be made in specific terms of the various components of the total curriculum—not simply the text, but the whole instructional plan, including instructional modes, sequence and methods of presenting material, performance data, and so on. It is necessary to determine curriculum objectives; for example, what it is one wishes to teach students in groups or individually, irrespective of their particular abilities or the capacities of the computer.

The computer requires very specific types of questions for very specific types of answers. The educator who seeks to use the system for curriculum development must learn to state or define his curriculum objectives in a clear and unequivocal fashion—a valuable exercise in any case. The need for greater specificity means that persons involved in the process of curriculum development may need to call upon the skills of specialists from several disciplines.

There has been much concern with the changing role and functions of the teacher within the new instructional environment created by the introduction of the computer. Questions have been raised about his role in instruction, whether he is to be a diagnostician or a counselor, troubleshooter or referral agent. Some of these questions can be resolved when the senior teacher, as part of a curriculum development team, has an active role in building instructional units and testing and adjusting software to computer hardware.

The involvement of experienced teachers in materials production has major advantages:

1. Persons who have had several years of experience with various methods of conventional instruction will be better able to produce the numerous alternative approaches to the subject matter that are needed in an individualized program of study.

2. A certain face validity for the material is gained when teachers know that experienced colleagues have had a hand in its production.

3. Teachers who have become programmers and participated in materials development are more likely to accept and utilize the CAI system when it is introduced into their school.

Various subspecialties will be defined and developed in the new educational environment. Teachers will not be prepared along a general pattern, but may instead be trained for specific roles, those of educational engineer, data interpreter, tutor, etc. Many may have dual competencies as teachers and as computer specialists. High priority should be assigned to studies of the implications of educational uses of the computer for teacher-training institutions and the establishment of innovative in-service training programs.

Automation may deprive the teacher of many of the traditional methods by which he has tried to transmit not only content but the kinds of attitudes he feels should be inherent in a course of education. With more content being transmitted by computers and less by face-to-face teacher-student contact, some other mechanism must be built in for the teacher personally to reach each student and to inculcate human values and attitudes.

Hardware and Software. Because educators have not yet become fully cognizant of the tremendous potential of the computer, they have not begun to use their influence on manufacturers to shape computer technology to meet specific educational needs. They have neither co-ordinated nor, in some cases, defined their requirements for specific computer applications. *Unless educational needs make an impact on manufacturers, development of computer software and hardware will continue to fall short of pedagogical specifications.* Educational agencies and professional associations can be instrumental in communicating these requirements to commercial producers.

Hardware and software should be designed and implemented with strictly educational purposes in mind. It is important that user requirements determine the type of electronic hardware to be employed. Initial conceptualizations of experiments with new technology should not be limited by the fact that certain kinds of hardware—which may be inappropriate—are available.

Of primary concern in the development of hardware and software is the learner interface. The traditional definition of interface is the point of contact between tutor and student, between author and reader, or between instructor and on-the-job trainee. Through the development of the computer and its associated technology (the computer's type-writer keyboards, television display tubes, etc.), this interface or point of interaction can be extended to include many different instructional modes. Major considerations in developing such interfaces should be:

1. The specific needs of specialized courses.

2. Human acceptance and convenience of operations.

3. Articulation with noncomputer components.

4. Teacher ease in course presentation and alteration.

5. Economic feasibility.

Subject matter within various disciplines can shape specific requirements for the interface. For example, if one is teaching a student to operate a lathe, the visible analogs or the controls that the student will be required to manipulate on the lathe will probably be used as an interface device in the training environment. This will ensure transfer of training to the operational task for which the training was designed.

The means of response provided should be natural for the learner and appropriate to the instructional goals. If the task requires pointing at objects or displays, the child should be able to do so readily. If the arrangement of various elements or a free-hand diagram is required, a cumbersome translation into words should be avoided. If a rapid typewritten response is desired, the student should be able to compose it without artificial restrictions. *Vocal input as an important capability should be developed.*

Systems of real classroom utility must be designed to be usable by a broad range of teachers. Such systems would allow the teachers convenient means to arrange, rearrange, extract, and modify the presentation and organization of material. Only with well-designed systems allowing easy modification will teachers feel that their investment of time is worthwhile and that the use of technology has real value.

Economic feasibility is equally important in determining the particular characteristics of the interface between learners and information source. At present there are no cost comparisons upon which to base decisions. Until further experimentation with various kinds of equipment configurations has been done, we cannot know, for example, whether nonautomated systems do the job any less effectively than those that are computer supported.

Certain kinds of costs can and should be reduced. For example, International Telephone and Telegraph should be asked to consider various means for making wide-band transmission facilities available to educational data and instructional systems at considerably lower rates than those that are currently operating. Some precedent for this can be seen in the reduced rates granted by the Post Office Department for mailing educational materials.

Commercial publishers, too, will soon be called upon to put books, journal articles, and similar written materials into machine-readable form, and to publish computer-instructional programs. Since such materials will be modified by users, new techniques may have to be developed to compensate the original author in ways different from current royalty arrangements. Authors might be compensated on a one-time basis and all materials placed in the public domain, with intellectual responsibility for a given instructional program resting with the institution using it rather than the author preparing it. The development and publication of computer-ready instructional packages must be made economically attractive to author and publisher; at the same time the materials produced must come within the budget of prospective users.

The choice between two instructional systems depends on considerations of both learning effectiveness and costs. Cost trade-off studies with computerized instructional systems on a multidisciplinary basis are needed in order to establish justification for using computer equipment for instructional purposes in an applied, nonresearch manner.
Orientation to the Change Process. *Increased funding should be made*

available to programs that put into practice some of the applications of computer-based systems which have already been found useful and reliable. Support for the implementation of such programs should be given to some pilot schools that are not normally on the forefront of change. These demonstration centers should encourage educators to come and view programs in actual operation. Funds will be needed to make visitations possible.

For major research efforts, federal agencies and foundations should cooperate in their support of a small number of research and development centers to prevent the duplication of efforts at a very high cost. Research with computer-assisted operations must be realistically oriented. Rather than being conducted in laboratories isolated from educational situations, it should be placed in as natural a setting as possible.

A vital aspect of research and development is the communication link among persons directly involved to persons who are potential "energy centers" and to persons who will be sharing in the results of the project. The development of adequate communications requires a research effort in itself. To whom does one communicate what? What should the timing be? What audience is ready to comprehend what kind of information? *Studies of the effectiveness of present methods of information dissemination should be made, and new techniques and channels for automatic dissemination developed or investigated.* These could include remote audiovisual displays at conventions, closed-circuit and open-circuit television, and computer network systems (such as EDUCOM).

All persons affected by the operations of a new system will need to acquire an understanding of the automated system as it evolves in their district. Continuous in-service training can be conducted at several levels. Some persons will not require a technical knowledge of systems or procedures, but only a general understanding of EDP. More specific skills must be imparted to persons who will be directly involved with the EDP system—planners, counselors, instructors in computer-augmented courses, and support staff. Instruction in programming should be provided for persons in the system who will be responsible for programming operations.

To ensure acceptance of new systems, strategies must be designed to prepare future users for the advent of technological change. As one strategy, simulation seems to hold much promise. If the validity of existing simulation models for the training of teachers and administrators can be confirmed, support should be given to the development of new models to aid in staff orientation and educational decision making.

Through familiarization with the technique of modeling, staff members can develop and pretest their own solutions to their district's or institution's unique problems. The use of computer-simulated models can help solve objectively and rapidly at least some of the complex decision-making problems facing educators without direct hazard to students or to ongoing administrative activities.

Although not all aspects of the educational process can be simulated, many can be programmed for simulation models. Curriculum simulation provides the means for experimental manipulation of educational goals, and can result in an educational program more sensitive to the progress of each individual student. Alternatives can be generated for a major revision of the total program or for narrowly limited specialized projects. Wide-ranging computer-simulation experience can help educators gain a better grasp of the implications of innovation. In addition, by reducing the amount of experimentation a school must undertake before introducing significant changes, simulation can greatly reduce the time between the conception and the implementation of change.

Computer-based simulation can also serve as a training device for student teachers who will not be involved directly with curriculum areas requiring computer support. Simulation of typical learning problems in a population of students and of effective teaching strategies can be generated by computer for teacher education or in-service training. For example, the student-teacher in a simulated classroom may view a variety of classroom situations on a screen, and respond as he or she thinks is most appropriate. From a computer-sequenced bank of film cartridges, he receives the feedback to his response. Then he may be given an opportunity to practice his response in a micro-teaching setting.

A file of materials for teachers to use for brush-up or for study of new procedures can be developed from data already being fed into the system. With an early and adequate orientation to information processing, imaginative uses can be made of the system for upgrading teaching skills. *Experimentation with computer-based gaming and simulation should be continued along these and similar lines.*

EVALUATION AND MEASUREMENT

Evaluation of computer-mediated procedures in the aerospace program is simple compared to the problem of evaluating the computer-mediated curriculum. Bit-by-bit evaluation is not enough. It would be quite possible to build up a new curriculum in which every element has been demonstrated to be effective in achieving its own objectives, but still to produce a total curriculum far inferior to the one with which we began. The whole process may result in the gradual exclusion of many important goals and outcomes simply because they are not amenable to a computerized approach. In the past, emphasis has often been placed on those outcomes of education that lend themselves to objective measurement. When the definition of educational goals is based on the results of standardized tests, one will be dealing with the highly rational, cognitive elements and neglecting the less tangible but frequently more important educational outcomes. Attempts should be made to avoid this approach to the evaluation of computer-mediated units in the curriculum. *Continuous evaluation of the entire operation should be made not with reference to the effectiveness of each bit, but with the idea of reaching some judgment about the total educational product.*

Criteria for measuring student performance and for monitoring progress in computer-mediated curricula must be developed. Feedback on a daily and weekly basis to both teacher and administrator would make for a more sensitive program of individualization and would help determine whether educational objectives are being met. Ways must be found to define and assess quality of teaching; to monitor and evaluate behavior of pupils and experienced teachers for the purpose of identifying and exposing effective teaching techniques.

A central store of cumulative experience is needed to aid in curriculum development, i.e., to identify student needs, to form concepts for teachers, and to provide factual bases upon which to plan teaching strategies and predict outcomes. *Records should be maintained of what has succeeded and what has not and why, and mechanisms developed for the objective sharing of information about failures. Methods are needed for collecting and analyzing in the cumulative experience file affective data that can be used for developing individual courses of instruction, for troubleshooting, and for generating feedback methods suited to individual learning styles.*

In assessing the total education of the child, one must not only measure his immediate achievements but must take stock of his interaction with his peers, his parents, and his community. Evaluation should be made of data from sources outside the school environment. Identification of these data is difficult. An understanding of what really are the conditions in which children, particularly deprived children, are developing will make all the difference in the kinds of learning approaches to be programmed. Computer hardware makes the accumulation and analysis of so much data possible; but the methodology for doing so is yet undeveloped.

The Data Bank. At present, data banks are considered to be primarily a means of facilitating the flow of information for routine management uses. To improve educational programs, facilities must be coordinated nationally so that data banks can transmit these administrative and educational records for instructional purposes.

The establishment of a data bank system coordinated at the local, state, regional, and national levels is essential. Critical questions about the content, organization, and uses as well as the general effectiveness of such a utility for educational objectives should be answered. For example, how will conflicts of public interest and of administrators and researchers drawing on the data be resolved? Can systems of communication be established for effective participation by all appropriate users? What decision-making responsibilities will occur at various levels of government?

Many agencies are mutually concerned with determining what kind of information to gather, how to collect and analyze it, and how to disseminate appropriately. Coordination of the work of these diverse organizations can enhance the quality and scope of the information and significantly reduce the cost of gathering, processing, and distributing it. *To prepare for sound coordination, the whole range of users must be considered with particular attention to cost, division of effort in acquisition and processing, and dissemination techniques.*

Common coding and classification of data items are needed to allow easy transfer from one system to another. At the same time, data must be stored in terms of user, subject matter or context, frequency of use, and relative levels of privacy. When data from sources outside the school are stored for evaluation purposes there are important questions as to who should have access to such personal educational information and how it should be utilized.

Computer technology must be further refined to produce methods of storing massive amounts of data in on-line computer storage devices or reducing data into optimum storage arrays, and of determining strategies for the design, maintenance, and purging of data bases. It is too easy to generate great amounts of data and plug up the machine with them—once the information has been generated it gains a functional autonomy. The value of the data being collected must be appraised and studies made of other types of useful data that might be collected.

TOWARD AN ETHICAL BASE

Unlike the building trades or the industrial arts, electronic data processing and its attendant crafts do not yet have their "professional imperatives." All of the older technologies operate within a philosophical framework: the principles of architecture guide the building crafts and those of the plastic arts influence the manual trades. These technologies, then, have their principles of goodness and beauty.

Cybernetics may be evolving as the "architecture" of the computing field. The point has not been reached, however, where the planning and experimentation of the computer craftsman are always influenced by a strong professional ethic.

In education, the full ethical implications of the many uses of the computer may not be apparent for many years. A seemingly desirable development such as the student data bank may have unforeseeable harmful effects in the future. As Harvey Wheeler has noted in a recent issue of *Nation* magazine, "the more profound the innovation and the more universal its applications, the more difficult it is to forecast its future effects." [1]

We have suggested that an important measure of control can be achieved by modeling future developments. But while simulation and systems planning may be valuable tools for predicting feasibility and costs, they do not provide measures of human value. The burden of this kind of decision making falls upon the educational practitioner.

The age of automation may bring about a world so complex that only professionals of broad vision and knowledge can manage it properly. Many of the problems they will encounter, however, will be so specialized that the professionals will have difficulty in understanding them. The field of education is no exception. Experts in automation must be able to talk to educators, who in turn must have a general acquaintance with the problems and promises of automation. Only through such a dialogue can the educational applications of technology be motivated not by what is merely efficient and ethically neutral but by what is meaningful and good.

[1] Vol. 204, No. 1, January 2, 1967, p. 15.

Bibliography

A. INSTRUCTIONAL DATA PROCESSING

1. American Psychological Association, American Education Research Association & National Education Association Department of Audiovisual Instruction. Self-instructional machines and devices. *American Psychologist*, **16**, 1961, 512.

   A joint statement presenting eight guiding principles for evaluating machines and programs in relation to logical development and instructional goals.
2. *American Scholar*, special issue on The Electronic Revolution, **35**, Spring 1966, 2.

   Scientists, artists, and social commentators examine the psychological and philosophical implications of the electronic revolution for the future of society.
3. Anderson, Richard C. Two rules for manipulating the sequence of stimuli in concept learning tasks. Prepublication draft. Urbana, Ill.: Training Research Laboratory, University of Illinois, 1966.
4. Anderson, Richard C., & John Guthrie. *Stimulus Sequence and Concept Learning*. Experiment II, Monograph No. 2. Urbana, Ill.: Training Research Laboratory, University of Illinois, 1965.
5. APT educational program. *Computer Digest*, **1**, October 1966, 10, 27.
6. Atkinson, Richard C., & Duncan Hansen. *Computer-Assisted Instruction in Initial Reading*. Technical Report 92. Stanford, Calif.: Institute for Mathematical Studies in the Social Sciences, Stanford University, 1966.
7. Avner, R. A. *Heart-Rate Correlates of Insight*. CSL Report R-198. Urbana, Ill.: Coordinated Science Laboratory, University of Illinois, 1964.
8. Baker, Frank B. Concept attainment experimentation by computer simulation. Paper presented at the annual meetings of the American Education Research Association, Chicago, February 1965.

239

9. Baker, James D. COBIS—computer-based instruction system. *Newsletter*, The Greater Boston Chapter of the National Society for Programmed Instruction, **1**, 4, 1965.

COBIS has three principal features: (1) a light pencil is used as the medium of communication between student and computer in a multiple-choice format; (2) the student indicates his degree of certainty for each alternative by adjusting the length of bars of light next to each answer on a CRT screen; (3) the computer considers both the student's answers and his degree of certainty when branching to remedial sequences or further steps, and a special scoring system has been developed for this purpose. No "errors" are made by the student. He progresses through levels of certainty and the computer always acts in the direction of raising his certainty.

10. Baker, James D. Computer-based instructional systems. Paper presented at the Seventy-Third Annual Convention of the American Psychological Association, Chicago, September 1965.

11. Baker, James D. From the Diet of Worms to the bucket of worms: a protest concerning existing display dogma for information systems. Paper read at the Second Congress on the Information System Sciences, Hot Springs, Va., November 1964.

12. Baker, James D. *A Technique for Obtaining Non-dichotomous Measures of Short-Term Memory.* ESD-TR-64-678. Bedford, Mass.: Air Force Systems Command, Decision Sciences Laboratory, 1964.

13. Bales, Robert F., Arthur S. Couch & Phillip J. Stone. The interaction simulator. *Proceedings of a Harvard Symposium on Digital Computers and Their Applications.* Cambridge, Mass.: Harvard University Press, 1962, 305–314.

14. Benjamin, R. The uses of PLATO. *Audiovisual Instruction*, 1966, 16–23.

15. Bennett, James H., William B. Easton, James R. Guard & Thomas H. Mott, Jr. *Toward Semi-automated Mathematics: The Language and Logic of SAM III.* Princeton, N.J.: Applied Logic Corporation, 1964.

16. Berkeley, Edmund D. The romance of good teaching and the time-shared computer. *Computers and Automation*, **14**, September 1965, 12–17.

Demonstrates use of a remote console of a time-shared computer situated in a high-school mathematics classroom.

17. Berlak, H. New curricula and measurement of thinking. *Educational Forum*, **30**, March 1966, 303–311.

18. Biggs, J. M. The application of STRESS to the teaching of structural engineering. Unpublished paper. Cambridge, Mass.: Engineering Laboratory, Massachusetts Institute of Technology, 1965.
19. Bitzer, Donald L., & Peter G. Braunfeld. Description and use of a computer-controlled teaching system. *Proceedings of the National Electronics Conference,* October 1962, 787–792.

    Describes PLATO, an automatic teaching system which uses a single, general-purpose, digital computer programmed so as to tutor a number of students concurrently.
20. Bitzer, D. L., P. G. Braunfeld & W. W. Lichtenberger. Plato II: a multiple-student, computer-controlled, automatic teaching device. In John E. Coulson (Ed.), *Programmed Learning and Computer-Based Instruction.* New York: Wiley, 1962, 205–216.
21. Bitzer, D. L., S. Chan, R. Johnson & M. Walker. *Lesson preparation for the PLATO Tutorial Logic (Compiler Version).* Urbana, Ill.: Coordinated Science Laboratory, University of Illinois, 1965.
22. Bitzer, D. L., & J. A. Easley, Jr. PLATO: a computer-controlled teaching system. In Margo A. Sass & William D. Wilkinson (Eds.), *Computer Augmentation of Human Reasoning.* Washington, D.C.: Spartan, 1965, 89–104.
23. Bitzer, D. L., E. R. Lyman & J. R. Suchman. *RELAB, A Study in Scientific Inquiry Using the PLATO System.* Report R-260. Urbana, Ill.: Coordinated Science Laboratory, University of Illinois, 1965.
24. Blin-Stoyle, Audrey, & Donald Savage. Computerized business management games. *ICC Bulletin,* 3, July 1964, 145–151.
25. Board of Cooperative Educational Services (BOCES). Computer-controlled economics games for the elementary school. Unpublished report. Northern Westchester County, New York, 1964.
26. Brann, James. Now, teaching by computer. *Science Digest,* **59,** April 1966, 78.
27. Braunfeld, Peter G. Problems and prospects of teaching with a computer. *Journal of Educational Psychology,* **55,** 4, 1964, 201–211.

    Reports on the use of the computer-based PLATO II system to teach undergraduates some topics in computer programming. Examples of how data can be sorted, processed, and interpreted are given.
28. Brown, J. W. Student response systems. *Audiovisual Instruction,* 8, 1963, 214–219.

    Pictures and describes the characteristics of several student response systems now in production: SDC's CLASS, the Student Response Monitor, TeleQuest, Tele-Test Communications System, Teleprompter Classroom Responder, Edex Teaching System.

29. Buiten, R., & H. Lane. A self-instructional device for conditioning accurate prosody. *Trends in Language Teaching.* New York: Mc-Graw-Hill, 1965.

30. Bushnell, Don D. *The Automation of School Information Systems.* DAVI Monograph No. 1. Washington, D.C.: Department of Audio-Visual Instruction, National Education Association, 1964.

A collection of papers dealing with a wide range of computer applications to school problems—both instructional and administrative.

31. Bushnell, Don D. *The Computer as an Instructional Tool: A Summary.* SP-1554. Santa Monica, Calif.: System Development Corporation, 1964.

Describes developments in computer-based teaching machines, rapid information-retrieval systems, and the advances in computer technology for aiding teachers in the diagnosis of student learning needs and in selecting appropriate teaching strategies.

32. Bushnell, Don D. Computer-based teaching machines. *Journal of Educational Research,* **55,** 1962, 528–531.

33. Bushnell, Don D. Computer-mediated instruction—a survey of new developments. *Computers and Automation,* **14,** 3, 1965, 18–20.

Practical applications include use of the computer (1) as a simulation device, (2) as a mediating and controlling device for teaching machines, (3) for storing student learning problems, (4) as an instructional tool for teaching about computer operations.

34. Bushnell, Don D. Computers in the classroom. *Data Processing Magazine,* April 1962, 9–14.

35. Bushnell, Don D. Education: future computer applications. In Edith Goodman (Ed.), *Data Processing Yearbook.* Detroit, Mich.: American Data Processing, 1965, 207–212.

36. Bushnell, Don D. *The Effects of Electronic Data Processing in Future Instructional Systems.* Santa Monica, Calif.: System Development Corporation, 1963.

37. Bushnell, Don D. The role of the computer in future instructional systems. *Audio-Visual Communication Review,* Supplement 7, **11,** 2, 1963.

Deals with computer fundamentals, computer-based teaching machines, information-retrieval systems in education, computer-based simulation, the automated classroom, plus a look at the future of computer applications to instruction.

38. Bushnell, Don D., Richard de Mille & Judith Purl. The application of computer technology to the improvement of instruction and learning. In *Educational Implications of Technological Change* (Appendix, Vol. IV, of *Technology and the American Economy*). Washington, D.C.: U.S. Government Printing Office, 1966, IV: 1–28.

39. Carroll, John B. Computer applications in the investigation of models in educational research. *Proceedings of a Harvard Symposium on Digital Computers and Their Applications*. Cambridge, Mass.: Harvard University, 1962, 48–58.

40. Carter, L. F. Automated instruction. *American Psychologist*, **16**, 1961, 705–710.

41. Carter, L. F., & H. F. Silberman. *The Systems Approach, Technology and the School*. Santa Monica, Calif.: System Development Corporation, 1965.

    Traces the history of SDC research in programmed instruction. Describes development of the tutorial approach and progress in the fields of time-sharing applications, computer-based instruction in statistical inference, computer-based student counseling, computer simulation as a tool for education management, and field evaluation of an elementary Spanish course.

42. Chapman, Robert L., & Janeth T. Carpenter. Computer techniques in instruction. In John E. Coulson (Ed.), *Programmed Learning and Computer-Based Instruction*. New York: Wiley, 1962, 240–253.

43. Clapp, Doris J., D. P. Yens, H. H. Shettel & Sylvia R. Mayer. *Development and Evaluation of a Self-instructional Source in the Operational Training Capability Query Language for System 473L, USAF Headquarters*. Bedford, Mass.: Air Force Electronic Systems Division, Decision Sciences Laboratory, 1964.

44. Coleman, James S., S. S. Boocock, S. Nicholson & M. Inbar. *Research Program in the Effects of Games with Simulated Environments in Secondary Education*. Research Report No. 2. Baltimore, Md.: Department of Social Relations, The Johns Hopkins University, 1964.

    Initial work in the development of computer-based games to teach facts and skills in vocational self-direction, understanding of and participation in democratic processes, and family relations, as well as primary skills.

45. *College and University Business*, special issue on Teaching and

Technology: New Methods, New Media, **41**, October 1966, 4.
46. Connelly, M. E., & O. Federoff. *A Demonstration Hybrid Computer for Real-Time Flight Simulation.* Wright Patterson Air Force Base, Ohio: Aerospace Medical Division, Aerospace Medical Research Laboratories, 1965.
47. Cooley, W. W. Computer-measurement system for guidance. *Harvard Educational Review*, **34**, 1964, 559–572.
48. Coulson, John E. *Automation, Cybernetics, and Education.* Santa Monica, Calif.: System Development Corporation, 1965.
49. Coulson, John E. (Ed.). *Programmed Learning and Computer-Based Instruction.* New York: Wiley, 1962.
50. Coulson, John E., Donald P. Estevan, Ralph Melaragno & Harry F. Silberman. Effects of branching in a computer-controlled auto-instructional device. *Journal of Applied Psychology*, **46**, 1962, 389–392.
51. Coulson, John E., Ralph J. Melaragno & Harry F. Silberman. *Nonprogram Variables in the Application of Programmed Instruction.* Santa Monica, Calif.: System Development Corporation, 1965.
52. Cramer, Joe J. Cost accounting in the development and presentation of four different college courses by computer teleprocessing. In Harold E. Mitzel & Kenneth H. Wodtke (Eds.), *Computer-Assisted Instruction Laboratory.* University Park, Pa.: Pennsylvania State University, 1965.
53. Culler, Glen J. Function-oriented on-line analysis. In A. Barnum & M. Knapp (Eds.), *Workshop on Computer Organization.* London: Cleaver-Hume, 1963, 191–213.
54. Davis, Daniel J., & Lawrence M. Stolurow. *Computer-Based Systems —The New Research Aid.* Technical Report No. 6. Urbana, Ill.: Training Research Laboratory, University of Illinois, 1964.
55. Dick, Walter. The development and current status of computer-based instruction. *American Educational Research Journal*, **2**, 1965, 41–53.

    Includes learning principles, current computer-instruction projects, typical computer-instruction equipment, programs and programmed texts, research with computer instruction, programming and equipment improvements.
56. Dodes, I. A. *IBM 1620 Programming for Science and Mathematics.* New York: Hayden, 1963.

    An exhaustive text for the exceptional high-school student, presenting some numerical analysis and all details of programming a particular machine often used for instructional purposes.

57. Dunwell, S. W. *Using a Computer to Teach Programming*. Research Report RC-854. Yorktown Heights, N.Y.: IBM, Thomas J. Watson Research Center, 1965.
58. Dwyer, T. Computers on campus at U.D. *Business Automation*, February 1964, 38–41.
    University of Dayton's four-year curriculum leading to a B.S. in computer science.
59. Easley, J. A., Jr., H. Gelder & W. Golden. *A PLATO Program for Instruction and Data Collection in Mathematical Problem Solving*. Urbana, Ill.: Coordinated Science Laboratory, University of Illinois, 1964.
60. Estrin, G. Interactions between future computer developments and automated teaching methods. In John E. Coulson (Ed.), *Programmed Learning and Computer-Based Instruction*. New York: Wiley, 1962, 281–288.
61. Fattu, N. A. Evaluation of automated instruction. *Education*, 83, 1962, 406–411.
    Describes necessary steps in evaluating an automated instructional program. Thirty-item bibliography.
62. Feigenbaum, Edward A., & Julian Feldman (Eds.). *Computers and Thought*. New York: McGraw-Hill, 1963.
63. Feingold, Samuel. A flexible language for programming student/computer interaction. Informal research report. Santa Monica, Calif.: System Development Corporation, February 1966.
64. Feurzeig, Wallace. The computer that talks like a teacher. *Journal of Accounting*, 117, May 1964, 27–28.
    The Socratic system, developed by Bolt, Beranek and Newman, Inc., was applied to teach a problem in accounting as a demonstration at the Harvard Business School. A sample of the exchange between student and computer is included.
65. Feurzeig, Wallace. A conversational teaching machine. *Datamation*, 10, 6, 1964.
    A brief history and demonstration of the Bolt, Beranek and Newman Socratic system.
66. Feurzeig, Wallace. Toward more versatile teaching machines. *Computers and Automation*, 14, 3, 1965, 22–25.
    Capabilities, goals, and current problems important in the evolution of more complex teaching machines are considered in five categories: instructional objectives, student-computer interactions, teacher-computer interactions, computer-response generation, and natural-language input.

67. Fuerzeig, Wallace, Preston Munter, John Swets & Myra Breen. Computer-aided teaching in medical diagnosis. *Journal of Medical Education,* **39,** 1964, 746–754.

   Describes a novel computer teaching system applied to a problem in teaching medical diagnosis. A sample computer run illustrates some of the capabilities of the system.

68. Frye, Charles H. *Guidebook to Simulated Statistical Inference Program: SIMIN.* Unpublished report. East Lansing, Mich.: Learning Systems Institute, Michigan State University, 1964.

69. Geis, George L. *Validated Instruction.* Unpublished report. Ann Arbor, Mich.: Center for Research on Learning and Teaching, University of Michigan, 1965.

   Describes an ideal progression in the design and development of instructional materials and procedures. Advocates emphasis on final goals of instruction and on an iterative-tutorial development of materials involving alternate media and approaches.

70. Gentile, J. Ronald. *The First Generation of Computer-Assisted Instructional Systems: An Evaluative Review.* University Park, Pa.: Computer-Assisted Instruction Laboratory, Pennsylvania State University, 1965.

71. Gerard, R. W. Intelligence, information and education. *Science,* **148,** May 7, 1965, 762–765.

72. Glaser, Robert, William W. Ramage & Joseph I. Lipson (with Appendix by A. Edward Blackhurst). *The Interface between Student and Subject Matter.* Pittsburgh, Pa.: Learning Research and Development Center, University of Pittsburgh, 1964.

   Examines the dimensions along which subject matter can be presented to a learner and the dimensions along which he can respond to it. Subject matter and instructional factors in interface design for mathematics, reading, science, and the possibilities of a general-purpose student-subject-matter interface are considered. Examines interface equipment, goals, and tasks of research and development.

73. Goldberg, A. A. Computer-based resource units. *Educational Leadership,* April 1966, 23.

74. Graybeal, W. S. Planning for instructional improvements: curriculum testing project of George Peabody College for Teachers. *National Education Association Journal,* **52,** 1963, 22.

   To provide information for use in improving instruction, modifying curricula, and solving organizational problems, data-processing procedures have been developed for analyzing standardized test scores.

75. Greenberger, Martin (Ed.). *Computers and the World of the Future*. Cambridge, Mass.: M.I.T. Press, 1962.

76. Groen, Guy, & Richard C. Atkinson. *Models for Optimizing the Learning Process*. Technical Report 91. Stanford, Calif.: Institute for Mathematical Studies in the Social Sciences, Stanford University, 1966.

77. Gropper, G. L., & G. C. Kress. Individualizing instruction through pacing procedures. *Audiovisual Communications Review*, **13**, 2, 1965, 165–182.
    Summarizes the results of three studies bearing on the relationship beween pacing mode and performance.

78. Grubb, R. E., & Lenore D. Selfridge. Computer tutoring in statistics. *Computers and Automation*, **13**, March 1964, 20–26.

79. Gruenberger, F. Computer training and education. *Datamation*, May 1963, 35–36.

80. Gruenberger, F. Computing in the secondary schools. *Datamation*, May 1964, 77–79.
    A rationale for teaching computing in high school.

81. Guard, James R. *Automated Logic for Semi-automated Mathematics*. Princeton, N.J.: Applied Logic Corporation, 1964.

82. Hansen, Duncan N. Applications of computers to research on instruction. Paper read at the National Society of College Teachers of Education, Chicago, February 17, 1966.

83. Hansen, D. N., R. Atkinson & H. Wilson. *Illustrative Lesson for Initial Reading and Accompanying Macro Structures for CAI*. Stanford, Calif.: Institute for Mathematical Studies in the Social Sciences, Stanford University, 1966.
    Includes instructional material covering letter discrimination, vocabulary acquisition, decoding problems, syntactic and intonation practice with phrases, and syntactic and semantic practice with word, phrase, and sentence materials. The illustrative reading lesson intended for the Stanford 1500 CAI system includes instructional format and execution statements.

84. Harnack, R. S. Computer-based resource units. *Educational Leadership*, **23**, December 1965, 239.

85. Hartmann, T. F. Computer-assisted instruction; IBM Thomas J. Watson Research Center. *Audiovisual Instruction*, **11**, January 1966, 22–23.

86. Heilman, C. E. Challenge, enrich and motivate with computers. *Science Teacher,* **33,** March 1966, 21–25.
87. Heller, G. G. Organizing a local program in computing education. *Datamation,* January 1963, 57–59.
    How to get community support for a computer-sciences curriculum in local schools.
88. Hickman, W. L. Renaissance of teaching. *School and Society,* **94,** Summer 1966, 265.
89. Hirsch, Richard S., & Bruce Moncreiff. A simulated chemistry laboratory. Paper presented at the fifty-sixth National Meeting of the American Institute of Chemical Engineers, San Francisco, May 18, 1965.
90. Hodge, Carle. A chatty computer in Room B-3; Computest on IBM 1620 used in a California grade school. *EDUCOM,* March 1966, 3–7.
91. Hoffmann, Thomas R. Programmed heuristics and the concept of par in business games. *Behavioral Science,* **10,** 1965, 169–172.
92. Ingham, G. E. Simulated environments for individualized instruction. *Audiovisual Instruction,* September 1964, 9.
93. International Business Machines Corporation. 1401, 1440 or 1460 operating system for computer-assisted instruction, Systems Reference Library Form C24-3253-1. Endicott, N.Y.: IBM, 1965.
94. Karush, W., & R. E. Dear. *Optimal Stimulus Presentation Strategy for a Stimulus Sampling Model of Learning.* Santa Monica, Calif.: System Development Corporation, 1964.
95. Kemeny, J. G. A library without books for the year 2000 A.D. *Book Production Magazine,* October 1964, 67–70.
    Describes a computer-based library that will retrieve stored information units and reproduce them for the user. Anticipates a national library to which university libraries may have immediate access.
96. Koppitz, Werner J., & Marilyn Charap. German through computer-guided instruction. Research paper RC-758. Yorktown Heights, N.Y.: IBM, Thomas J. Watson Research Center, 1962.
97. Kopstein, Felix F. The amplified teacher: the guidance of learning through controlling functional automata. Unpublished. Princeton, N.J.: Educational Testing Service, 1965.
    The hypothesis is made that computers can amplify man's functional properties or behavioral capabilities. Implications of this hypothesis are explored with particular reference to a rationale for a coherent program of research and development in such areas as subject-matter structure, student-instructor information coupling,

measurement of progress, and motivation. Some social consequences of instructional automata are considered.

98. Kristy, Norton F. Simu-Tech trainer concept. Unpublished. Santa Monica, Calif.: Rand Corporation, 1965.

    Advocates intensive computer-based simulative training of Air Force electronicians. Predicts training time one-third as long as at present.

99. Kropp, R. P. Technology in instruction. *Improving College and University Teaching*, Autumn 1965, 13.

100. Licklider, J. C. R. Man-computer partnership. *International Science and Technology*, May 1965, 18–26.

101. Licklider, J. C. R. Preliminary experiments in computer-aided teaching machines. In John E. Coulson (Ed.), *Programmed Learning and Computer-Based Instruction*. New York: Wiley, 1962, 217–239.

102. Lippert, Henry T. Operational description of the Master Tutor of the Socrates System. Technical Memo No. 3. Urbana, Ill.: Training Research Laboratory, University of Illinois, 1965.

103. Lipsitz, L. Ten thousand homes tied to computer center. *Teaching Aids News*, 5, 12, 1965, 5–8.

    A coaxial community cable network, similar to community antenna systems, will connect 10,000 homes in Columbia City, Md., to a community digital computer which is "on call" for each member of the family. Some early projected uses of the system and its time-sharing capacity (allowing the near simultaneous use of the computer by 5000 people) are described.

104. Lyman, Elisabeth R. *A Descriptive List of PLATO Lesson Programs, 1960–65*. Report R-186 (revised report). Urbana, Ill.: Coordinated Science Laboratory, University of Illinois, 1965.

105. MacDonald, N. The role of computers in education. *Computers and Automation*, 13, 3, 1964, 13–14.

106. Maher, A. *Computer-Based Instruction* (CBI): *Introduction to the IBM Research Project*. RC-1114. Yorktown Heights, N.Y.: IBM, Thomas J. Watson Research Center, 1964.

107. Maron, M. E., & J. L. Kuhns. On relevance, probabilistic indexing and information retrieval. *Journal of the Association for Computing Machinery*, 7, 1960, 216–244.

108. Mayer, Sylvia R. *Human Engineering in the Design of Instructional Systems*. Technical Documentary Report No. ESD-TDR-64-454. Bedford, Mass.: Decision Sciences Laboratory, Electronic Systems Division, Air Force Systems Command, L. G. Hanscom Field, 1964.

    A conceptual model is proposed for use in the application of human engineering principles and techniques to the design of instructional systems. The trainee and instructor are viewed as operators within an information system. To illustrate this model and its application, examples are drawn from the literature and from current research on instructional systems. A preliminary human engineering guide is outlined which presents factors critical to design decisions for instructional systems.

109. Mayer, Sylvia R., & Roy Morgan. *Computer-Aided Programmed Techniques in Support of Military Information Systems.* Project 7682, Task 768204. Bedford, Mass.: Decision Sciences Laboratory, Electronic Systems Division, Air Force Systems Command, L. G. Hanscom Field, 1965.

Describes research and development on a model for computer-aided, programmed instructional subsystems for training men in the use of information systems.

110. Meier, Richard L., & Jane P. Doyle. *Simulation of the Concept of Community in Ecological Systems: The Moose-Beaver-Wolf-Environment System of Isle Royale Mental Health Research Institute.* Report No. 16. Ann Arbor, Mich.: University of Michigan, 1965.

111. Merrill, M. D. *Transfer Effects within a Hierarchical Learning Task as a Function of Review and Correction on Successive Parts.* Technical Report No. 5. Urbana, Ill.: Training Research Laboratory, University of Illinois, 1964.

112. Messick, David M., & Amnon Rapoport. Computer-controlled experiments in psychology. *Behavioral Science,* **9,** October 1964, 378–382.

113. Mitzel, Harold E., et al. *Experimentation with Computer-Assisted Instruction in Technical Education.* Semi-Annual Progress Report, Project No. 5-85-074. University Park, Pa.: Computer-Assisted Instruction Laboratory, Pennsylvania State University, 1965.

114. Mitzel, Harold E., & Kenneth H. Wodtke (Eds.). *The Development and Presentation of Four Different College Courses by Computer Teleprocessing.* University Park, Pa.: University of Pennsylvania, 1965.

115. Moncreiff, B. The Sumerian Game: teaching economics with a computerized program. *Programmed Instruction,* **4,** 1965, 10–11.

Describes a simulated environment for teaching economics to elementary-school students.

116. Moore, Omar Khayyam. *Autotelic Responsive Environments and Exceptional Children.* Hamden, Conn.: Responsive Environments Foundation, Inc., 1963.

117. Morrison, William. *Computer Processing of Responses in Verbal Training*. RC-1136. Endicott, N.Y.: International Business Machines, 1964.

118. Moss, Carl R. Engineering economics. In Harold E. Mitzel and Kenneth H. Wodtke (Eds.), *The Development and Presentation of Four Different College Courses by Computer Teleprocessing*. University Park, Pa.: Computer-Assisted Instruction Laboratory, Pennsylvania State University, 1965.

119. Newman, E. R. Paracomputers in psychological research. *Harvard Symposium on Digital Computers and Their Applications*. Cambridge, Mass.: Harvard University Press, 1962, 239–251.

120. Oettinger, Anthony G. *Technical Aids to Creative Thought* (Project TACT). Cambridge, Mass.: Computation Laboratory, Harvard University, 1964.

The question is asked whether the information desired from certain teaching, command-control, IR, and other systems, even if made available by machine, could be assimilated and understood. A research program is proposed that will use a computer system as a teaching and a study aid in at least one appropriately selected course of instruction. The direct objective is to enable the natural and effective use of a computer as an animated blackboard.

121. Page, E. B. Imminence of grading essays by computer. *Phi Delta Kappan*, 14, January 1966, 238–243.

122. Pask, Gordon. Adaptive teaching with adaptive machines. In A. A. Lumsdaine and R. Glaser (Eds.), *Teaching Machines and Programmed Learning*. Washington, D.C.: DAVI, National Education Association, 1960, 349–366.

123. Pines, Maya. What the talking typewriter says. *New York Times Magazine*, May 9, 1965.

Discusses the efficacy of the talking typewriter, or Edison Responsive Environment, for teaching reading and typing to children as young as three years of age. Possible therapeutic value is seen for autistic children.

124. Porter, J. C., M. W. Sasieni, E. S. Marks & R. L. Ackoff. The use of simulation as a pedagogical device. *Computer Digest*, 1, 8, August 1966, 40–42.

125. Ramo, S. A new technique of education. In A. A. Lumsdaine & R. Glaser (Eds.), *Teaching Machines and Programmed Learning*. Washington, D.C.: DAVI, National Education Association, 1960, 367–381.

126. Rapoport, Amnon. Sequential decision-making in a computer-con-

trolled task. *Journal of Mathematical Psychology*, **1**, 1964, 351–374.

127. Rath, Gustave J., Nancy S. Anderson & R. C. Brainerd. The IBM research center teaching machine project. In Eugene Galanter (Ed.), *Automatic Teaching: The State of the Art*. New York: Wiley, 1959, 117–130.

128. Reisman, A. Higher education: a population flow feedback model. *Science*, **153**, July 1, 1966, 89.

129. Richardson, Jesse O. Teaching mathematics through the use of a time-shared computer system. *Automated Education Letter*. Boston: Massachusetts Board of Education, December 1965.

   To test hypotheses: (1) method will give student the feeling of having his own computer, (2) spontaneity of the situation will lead to voluntary extracurricular participation in it, (3) learning will be superior in the computer-instructed group.

130. Ridgeway, J. Computer tutor. *New Republic*, **154**, July 4, 1966, 19.

131. Riedesel, D. Alan. Modern mathematics. In Harold E. Mitzel & Kenneth H. Wodtke (Eds.), *The Development and Presentation of Four Different College Courses by Computer Teleprocessing*. University Park, Pa.: Computer Assisted Instruction Laboratory, Pennsylvania State University, 1965.

132. Rigney, Joseph W. Potential uses of computers as teaching machines. In John E. Coulson (Ed.), *Programmed Learning and Computer-Based Instruction*. New York: Wiley, 1962, 155–170.

133. Roe, Arnold. *An Adaptive Decision Structure for Educational Systems*. Report 63–63. Los Angeles, Calif.: Department of Engineering, University of California, 1963.

134. Samuel, Arthur L. Programming computers to play games. In Franz L. Alt (Ed.), *Advances in Computers*, Vol. 1. New York: Academic Press, 1960.

135. Samuel, Arthur L. Time-sharing on a computer. *New Scientist*, **26**, May 27, 1966, 445, 583–587.

136. Sass, Margo A., & William D. Wilkinson (Eds.). *Computer Augmentation of Human Reasoning*. Washington, D.C.: Spartan, 1965.

137. Schurdak, John J. *An Approach to the Use of Computers in the Instructional Process and an Evaluation*. Research Report RC-1432. Yorktown Heights, N.Y.: IBM, Thomas J. Watson Research Center, 1965.

138. *Scientific American*, special issue on Information, **215**, 3, September 1966.

   Entire issue devoted to current computer technology and applications. Describes present state of the art, including hardware now available and being developed, design and mechanics of computer operation, and applications in science and education.

139. Shuford, E. H. Cybernetic testing. Paper presented at meeting of National Society for Programmed Instruction, Philadelphia, May 5–8, 1965.

140. Shultz, A. A. *Teaching Machines and Programmed Learning in the Soviet Bloc* (a survey of published literature, 1962–63). Report TT64-21587. Washington, D.C.: U.S. Department of Commerce, Office of Technical Services, Joint Publications Research Service, 1964.

141. Siegenthaler, Bruce M. Audiology. In Harold E. Mitzel & Kenneth H. Wodtke (Eds.), *The Development and Presentation of Four Different College Courses by Computer Teleprocessing.* University Park, Pa.: Computer Assisted Instruction Laboratory, Pennsylvania State University, 1965.

142. Silberman, Charles E. Technology is knocking at the schoolhouse door. *Fortune,* LXXIV, 3, 1966, 120–125.

143. Silberman, H. F. A computer-controlled teaching machine. *Behavioral Science,* 6, 1961, 259–261.

144. Silberman, H. F., & John R. Coulson. Automated teaching. In Harold Borko (Ed.), *Computer Applications in the Behavioral Sciences.* Englewood Cliffs, N.J.: Prentice Hall, 1962, 309–327.

145. Silberman, H. F., R. J. Melaragno, J. F. Coulson & D. Estevan. Fixed sequence versus branching automatic instructional methods. *Journal of Educational Research,* 55, 1962, 421–432.

146. Silvern, Gloria M. Programmed instruction materials for computer programming—a survey. *Computers and Automation,* 14, 3, 1965, 26–32.

    General background on programmed instruction and description of twenty-five instructional programs in computing and data processing.

147. Silvern, L. C. A general system model of public education K–12. *Teaching Aids News,* 4, 1964, 1–20.

148. Simmons, R. F., et al. *Synthex: The Computer Synthesis of Language Behavior.* Research and Technology Division Report for 1965. Santa Monica, Calif.: System Development Corporation, 1966.

149. Skinner, B. F. Reflections on a decade of teaching machines. *Teachers College Record,* 65, 1963, 168–177.

    Urges the development of educational technology out of Skinner's kind of behavior analysis and study of reinforcement behavior.

150. Skinner, B. F. Teaching machines. *Scientific American,* **205,** 1961, 90–107.

A psychologist whose research was largely responsible for the advent of teaching machines discusses uses and benefits of the machines in terms of automatic reinforcement, remedial teaching, and freeing the teacher for more creative activity.

151. Skinner, Donald D., & Robert N. Wells, Jr. *Michigan Inter-Nation Simulation Staff Manual.* Ann Arbor, Mich.: Center for Research on Learning and Teaching, University of Michigan, 1965.

152. Smallwood, R. D. *A Decision Structure for Teaching Machines.* Cambridge, Mass.: MIT Press, 1962.

153. Starkweather, John A. Computer simulation of psychiatric interviewing. Paper read at the International Business Machines Seventh Medical Computing Symposium, Poughkeepsie, N.Y. October 1965.

154. Starkweather, John A. COMPUTEST: a computer language for individual testing, instruction, and interviewing. *Psychological Reports,* **17,** 1965, 227–237.

The structure and operation of a computer language is presented, an arrangement which allows machine simulation of individual testing, instruction, and interviewing.

155. Stolurow, Lawrence M. *Computer-Based Instruction.* Technical Report #9. Urbana, Ill.: Training Research Laboratory, University of Illinois, 1965.

The SOCRATES system of computer-based instruction is described, with emphasis on the ways in which it is adaptive to the student.

156. Stolurow, Lawrence M. *A Model and Cybernetic System for Research on the Teaching-Learning Process.* Technical Report #4. Urbana, Ill.: Training Research Laboratory, University of Illinois, 1965.

The basic elements of a three-process learning theory are presented. These are: stimulus learning, response learning, and stimulus-response learning. It is then shown how these processes determine the requirements of an adaptive teacher.

157. Stolurow, Lawrence M., & D. Davis. *Teaching Machines and Computer-Based Systems.* Urbana, Ill.: Training Research Laboratory, University of Illinois, 1964.

158. Stolurow, Lawrence M., & Henry T. Lippert. *Automatically Translating Heuristically Organized Routines: Author I.* TM #21. Ur-

bana, Ill.: Training Research Laboratory, University of Illinois, 1966.

159. Stolurow, Lawrence M., & Henry T. Lippert. *SOCRATES II: System Data and Development Work.* TM #22. Urbana, Ill.: Training Research Laboratory, University of Illinois, 1966.

160. Strogoff, Alfred, R. E. Slaughter, E. G. Mesthene & H. Howe. Education and the new technology. *Senior Scholastic,* October 7, 1966, 89.

161. Suppes, Patrick. Accelerated program in elementary-school mathematics—the second year. *Psychology in the Schools, 3,* 1966, 294–307.

162. Suppes, Patrick. *Computer-Assisted Instruction in the Schools: Potentialities, Problems, Prospects.* Technical Report No. 81. Stanford, Calif.: Institute for Mathematical Studies in the Social Sciences, Stanford University, 1965.

163. Suppes, Patrick. Computer-based instruction in the elementary school. *Education Age, 2,* 3, 1966.

164. Suppes, Patrick. Computer-based mathematics instruction: the first year of the project. *Bulletin of the International Study Group for Mathematics Learning, 3,* 1965, 7–22.

   Describes in detail the equipment in the Stanford Computer-Based Laboratory for Learning and Teaching, outlines the work which has been done on the programs for grades 1, 4, and 6, and describes the program logic to be used on the computer.

165. Suppes, Patrick. Modern learning theory and the elementary school curriculum. *American Educational Research Journal, 1,* 1964, 79–83.

   A computer-based laboratory can facilitate applications of learning theory to the school curriculum. Implications of various theoretical propositions for instruction.

166. Suppes, Patrick, Max Jerman & Guy Groen. Arithmetic drills and review on a computer-based teletype. *The Arithmetic Teacher, 13,* 1966, 303–309.

167. Swets, J. A., & W. Feurzeig. Computer-assisted instruction. *Science, 150,* 1965, 572–576.

   Describes the Socratic system developed by Bolt, Beranek and Newman, Inc., for teaching "rich" materials and for "students who might be hampered by inability to demonstrate initiative under a relatively restricted procedure."

168. Swets, J. A., H. R. Harris, L. S. McElroy & H. Rudloe. Computer-

aided instruction in perceptual identification. *Behavioral Science,* **11,** 1966, 98–104.

169. Swets, J. A., S. H. Millman, W. E. Fletcher & D. M. Green. Learning to identify nonverbal sounds: an application of a computer as a teaching machine. *Journal of the Acoustical Society of America,* **34,** 1962, 928–935.

170. Theobald, Robert, & Ralph W. Tyler. Higher education and cybernation. *NEA Journal,* **55,** March 1966, 26–29.

171. Tondow, M. Computers in special education. *Exceptional Children,* **31,** November 1964, 113–116.

172. Uhr, Leonard. *The Automatic Generation of Teaching Machine Programs.* CAIS Report 44b. Ann Arbor, Mich.: Center for Research on Learning and Teaching, University of Michigan, 1965.

173. Uhr, Leonard. The compilation of natural language text into teaching machine programs. *AFIPS Conference Proceedings of the Fall Joint Computer Conference.* Washington, D.C.: Spartan, 1964, 26.

174. Uhr, Leonard. *Toward the Compilation of Books into Teaching Machine Programs.* Ann Arbor, Mich.: Center for Research on Learning and Teaching, University of Michigan, 1965.

175. Uttal, William R. On conversational interaction. In John E. Coulson (Ed.), *Programmed Learning and Computer-Based Instruction.* New York: Wiley, 1962, 171–190.

176. Uttal, William R. The automated laboratory. Symposium and Workshop on the Quantification of Human Performance, University of New Mexico, Albuquerque, August 1964.

177. Uttal, William R., Marilyn Charap & Anna Maher. *The Computer Tutoring of Stenotypy: A Preliminary Report.* RC-663. Yorktown Heights, N.Y.: IBM, Thomas J. Watson Research Center, 1962.

178. Ward, Lewis. Some computer applications in research and teaching in business administration. *Proceedings of a Harvard Symposium on Digital Computers and Their Applications.* Cambridge, Mass.: Harvard University Press, 1962, 265–272.

179. Western Data Processing Center. *Progress Report 7.* Los Angeles: Graduate School of Business Administration, University of California, 1965.

Users in the eleven western states, Alaska, Hawaii, Canada, and Mexico are conducting projects in this large IBM installation which include simulation and instructional uses (e.g., UCLA Marketing Game used as a classroom teaching aid) in addition to problem-solving uses in many fields.

180. Wing, Richard L. Computer-controlled economics games for the elementary schools. *Audiovisual Instruction*, 9, December 1964, 681–682.

181. Wodtke, Kenneth H., Harold E. Mitzel & Bobby R. Brown. Some preliminary results on the reactions of students to computer-assisted instruction. *American Psychologist*, 20, 1965, 520.

182. Wynn, R. Simulation: terrible reality in the preparation of school administrators. *Phi Delta Kappan*, 46, 1964, 170–173.

Describes recent rapid adoption of simulation training by graduate school-superintendent programs in sixty-five universities. Discusses advantages and limitations of the method and advocates increased use.

183. Zinn, Karl L. Computer assistance for instruction. *Automated Education Newsletter*, October 1965.

General, nontechnical discussion of CAI, with emphasis on the importance of the instructional materials. Topics discussed include: cost of computer time for instruction, size for efficient operation, requisite skills for authors, automated scoring of answers, advantages of computer presentation, appropriate subject areas, the role of the teacher, and author-instructor costs.

184. Zinn, Karl L. Functional specifications for computer-aided instruction systems. In E. Goodman (Ed.), *Automated Education Handbook*, Detroit, Mich.: Automated Education Center, 1965, IV: A21–32.

Presents justification for on-line computer systems in instruction and research on instruction. Specifies some requirements and desirable characteristics of an instruction system aided by a general-purpose computer.

185. Zinn, Karl L. Survey of materials prepared for instruction or instruction research via on-line computer systems. In E. Goodman (Ed.), *Automated Education Handbook*, Detroit, Mich.: Automated Education Center, 1965, IV: A34–40.

186. Zinn, Karl L. Teaching logics, tutorial strategies and training patterns in a computerized educational technology. CAIS Report 3.3. Ann Arbor, Mich.: Center for Research on Learning and Teaching, University of Michigan, 1965.

187. Zinn, Karl L. The uses of the taxonomy and computer assistance in assembling sets of objectives, test items, and diagnostic test sequences. Paper read at American Education Research Association Annual Meeting, February 18, 1966.

B. ADMINISTRATIVE DATA PROCESSING

188. Alcorn, B. K. Educational specifications vs. systems—does the tail wag the dog? *Journal of Educational Data Processing,* **2,** 1965, 99–102.

    Discusses three stages in data-systems development: specifications, systems, and field operations. Concludes that educational specifications must control the other stages if data are to mean anything.

189. Anderson, G. E., Jr. Data processing practice. *Nations Schools,* since 1964.

    Bimonthly articles discussing technical, teaching, administration, and personnel problems of data processing.

190. Anderson, G. E., Jr. Educational data processing—the state of the art. *Educational Data Processing Newsletter,* **3,** 8, 1964, 12–23.

    An overview of present educational uses of data processing and of trends for the future.

191. Anderson, R. C. The role of educational engineer. *Journal of Educational Sociology,* 1961, 377–381.

    Expansion of technology in education may force the creation of the educational engineer, who would translate research findings into social inventions. Describes role and qualifications.

192. Appleby, J. S., D. V. Blake & E. A. Newman. Techniques for producing school timetables on a computer and their application to other scheduling problems. *Computer Journal,* **3,** 1961, 237–245.

    Describes production of table for medium-sized school in 1½ hours. Brief discussion of other applications.

193. Asher, J. William, & Marvin Kurfeerst. The computer and information retrieval: school law, a case study. *Harvard Educational Review,* Spring 1965, 35.

    Through a description of the application of information-retrieval techniques to school law, the authors suggest the immense potential that electronic computers have for helping cope with the proliferation of knowledge.

194. Asprey, Winifred. Computers on the campus. *Journal of Higher Education,* December 1965, 36.

    A survey of computer activities in the liberal-arts college.

195. *Audiovisual Instruction,* **10,** May 1965.

    The entire issue is devoted to examining the systems approach to

planning in schools. Discussion commences with clarifying statements on educational systems, proceeds through a definitive ques-
tion-answer section, and concludes with nine case studies of specific systems-design applications.

196. Automation in the central office. *Overview*, 3, 1, 1962, 31–34.
Samples data-processing systems and gives two examples of their
use. Stresses systems development.

197. Behnk, W. E. Results of data processing survey. *Journal of Educational Data Processing*, 1, 1964, 6–8.
To aid school districts to budget use of data-processing equipment,
three tables are presented: (1) per pupil costs, machine rental and
miscellaneous expenses, (2) personnel costs, number of machines
and applications, (3) applications and number of schools using
equipment. Study by New York State Education Department.

198. Better processing of educational data. *American School Board
Journal*, 143, 1961, 40.

199. Biggs, V. B. EDP feeds Memphis system with food service data.
Nations Schools, March 1966, 77.

200. Blackford, G. S. Honour classes and individual timetables. *Cana-
dian Education and Research Digest*, 4, 3, 1964, 17–24.

201. Blakesley, J. F. A data processing system for scheduling university
students to classes using an intermediate-speed digital computer.
Unpublished M.S. thesis. Lafayette, Ind.: Purdue University, 1960.

202. Blakesley, J. F. Registration is now a matter of minutes. *College
and University Business*, 27, 1959, 39–44.

203. Bond, C. L. Computer: time-saver for busy directors. *Journal of
College Placement*, 23, April 1963, 61–63.

204. Bush, R. N., J. G. Caffrey, R. V. Oakford & D. W. Allen. Using
machines to make the high school schedule. *School Review*, 69, 1,
1961, 48–59.
Secondary Education Project at Stanford reveals two approaches:
(1) making schedule conform to a predetermined plan, (2) determining whether a conflict-free schedule exists.

205. Bushnell, Don D., & R. L. Howe (Eds.). *A Report of an Experiment—The State Pilot Project in Educational Data Processing*.
Malibu, Calif.: Educational Data Systems Corporation, 1964.
An extensive, detailed, practical description and discussion of
educational data processing based on a study of California schools.
Applications included attendance accounting, standardized tests,
report cards, cumulative records, student scheduling, and machine
procedure.

206. Calhoun, S. R., & P. E. Green. Simulation: versatile aid to decision-making. *Advanced Management, 23,* 4, 1958, 11–16.

Simulation proved helpful in four technical problem areas at Lukens Steel Company by permitting "experimentation" with new procedures without disruption of actual existing processes.

207. Christian Brothers , Data Processing Center. *Educational Data Processing: Student Records—General Handbook.* Lockport, Ill.: Lewis College, 1965.

A handbook on documents and procedures involved in an EDP system.

208. Cogswell, J. F., R. L. Egbert et al. *New Solutions to Implementing Instructional Media through Analysis and Simulation of School Organization.* Santa Monica, Calif.: System Development Corporation, 1964.

Outlines the use of systems analysis and computer simulation in investigating the effects of innovations and adjustments in school curricula. Four major steps are involved: (1) survey and selection of schools, (2) system analysis of the schools, (3) construction of a computer simulation vehicle permitting the construction of detailed models of the schools and the hypothetical changes, and (4) application of this simulation vehicle to the schools selected.

209. Cogswell, J. F., R. L. Egbert, D. G. Marsh & F. Yett. *Construction of School Simulation Vehicle.* Santa Monica, Calif.: System Development Corporation, 1963.

Preliminary development of school simulator program, involving school operations, organizational configurations, staffing patterns; for exploration, prediction, or control.

210. Cogswell, J. F., & D. P. Estavan. *Explorations in Computer-Assisted Counseling.* Santa Monica, Calif.: System Development Corporation, 1965.

A computer reviews student progress, collects comments from the student, reacts to student plans, and helps student to plan a schedule of courses. Comparison with live counselor responses indicates that automated interviews have potential value.

211. Computer services for schools: UPDATE. *School and Society, 5,* 1963, 274.

212. Computer to aid long-range planning of school systems. *School and Society,* March 1966, 122.

213. Computers in the central office. In *The Shape of Education for 1964–65,* Vol. 5. Washington, D.C.: National School Public Relations Association, 1965.

Review of trend toward automatic data processing. Estimates 50 per cent of school children are served by some form of ADP.

214. Computing in the university. *Datamation*, 8, 1962, 27–30.
State-by-state listing of university-operated educational data-processing equipment.

215. Counce, S., & R. E. Davis. Data processing in a large school system. *National Association of Secondary-School Principals Bulletin*, 47, 1963, 137–145.

216. Crisler, R. D., & T. D. Wogaman. Educational data processing at Richmond. *Journal of Secondary Education*, 38, 1963, 71–76.

217. Csima, J., & C. C. Gotlieb. Tests on a computer method for constructing school timetables. *Communications of the ACM*, 7, 1964, 160–163.

218. Cunningham, J. F., Jr. Machine data processing for educational administrators; problems and solutions. *Dissertation Abstracts*, 3, October 1962, 1241–1242.

219. Dahl, Don. Teacher test scoring and analysis. *Educational Data Processing Newsletter*, 3, July-August 1964, 18–25.

220. Dailey, J. W. What's ahead in educational data processing. *Educational Data Processing Newsletter*, 4, 4, 1965, 6–9.
Despite recency of educational data processing, current research promises rapidly expanding benefits to administrators. Lists of eleven new developments, including light pen, program packages, information retrieval, and real-time applications.

221. Darnowski, V. Teachers, administrators and data processing. *New Jersey Educational Association Review*, 38, 1965, 344–345.
The Project on Information Processing at Montclair, N.J., has produced a text on computers for junior-high-school students, a booklet on careers in the field, a high-school-level film on computers, and a bimonthly newsletter on high-school-level data-processing education.

222. Data processing and computing at Southern Illinois University. *International Computation Centre Bulletin*, 3, 1, 1964, 30–34.

223. DeJarnett, L. R. Automated circulation control at Southern Illinois University. *Educational Data Processing Newsletter*, 3, 4, 1964, 7–11.

224. EDP comes to New Jersey schools. *New Jersey Educational Association Review*, 38, 1965, 340–343.
Electronic data processing is now in use for grade records, grade-level rosters, transcripts, honor roll, attendance, scheduling, bus routing, locker assignments, parent lists, and health records.

225. Egbert, R. L. The computer in education: malefactor or benefactor. In *American Federation of Information Processing Societies, Proceedings.* Washington, D. C.: Spartan, 1963.

226. Evans, L. H., & G. Arnstein. *Automation and the Challenge to Education.* Washington, D.C.: National Education Association, 1962.

227. Faulkner, M. Computer sectioning and class scheduling. *Datamation,* June 1965, 35–37.

   Washington State University employs a computer to build low-conflict course schedules and optimize assignments of space, time, and instructors.

228. Flanagan, Thelma. Save time and dollars in school feeding. *Nations Schools,* **71,** 1963, 110.

   Advocates automated record storage, payrolling, and calculation of nutritional value of diets.

229. Florida Association for Educational Data Systems. *Florida Program Application Library.* Tallahassee, Fla.: Florida State Department of Education, 1963.

   A list of computer programs available for student accounting, test-result procedures, census report, cafeteria accounting, textbook accounting, teacher contracts, payroll procedures, budgetary accounting, property records, and school-supplies budgeting.

230. Flowers, J. F. The production of secondary school timetables by a digital computer: A progress report. *Educational Data Processing Newsletter,* **4,** 1, 1965, 6–10.

   Three major operations of scheduling are: determination of course requirements, production of master schedule, production of individual student schedules. Master scheduling for secondary schools without human intervention is not yet a reality.

231. Flowers, J. F. An educational information and data system. *Educational Data Processing Newsletter,* **4,** 5, 1965, 1–5.

   Lays out a practical system for educational data processing and contributory activities.

232. Fluckiger, W. L. Use of a service bureau for student registration. *College and University,* **38,** 1963, 190–196.

233. Flynt, R. C. M. The role of data processing. *Higher Education,* **20,** 3, 1963, 7–10.

   Describes data processing in educational administration, local operations, research, information retrieval, and public relations; indicates plans of U.S. Office of Education for future use of data-processing equipment.

234. Folkers, J. S. Construction of school timetables by a computer. *Communications of the ACM*, **6**, 1963, 421.

235. Foster, C. C. Using a computer for non-conflict scheduling of high school classes. *Michigan Education Journal*, **40**, 1962, 328–329.

236. Freeman, J. P. Starting an EDP program in a school system. *American School Board Journal*, **146**, 2, 1963, 34–35.

   A study of school system needs in Memphis and a description of applications in departments of business affairs, guidance and attendance, instruction, and plant management and operation.

237. Gerletti, R. C. Electronic data processing applied to AV centers. *Audiovisual Instruction*, **6**, 1961, 515–517.

   Space- and time-saving benefits of EDP make the audiovisual instructor more effective.

238. Goldberg, A. L. First steps in the systems approach. *Audiovisual Instruction*, May 1965, 10.

239. Gotlieb, C. C. Construction of class-teacher time-tables. *Communications of the ACM*, **6**, 1963, 23.

240. Grossman, A. The feasibility of establishing an integrated data processing system for pupil personnel records. *Educational Data Processing Newsletter*, **1**, May 1962, 16–25.

241. Grossman, A. A new approach to guidance research using an electronic computer. *California Journal of Educational Research*, 1962, 170–173.

   Advocates use of operations-research techniques in developing better decision-making methods for guidance programs and in sustaining programs.

242. Grossman, A., & R. L. Howe. Advantages of the regional approach to educational data processing. *Journal of Secondary Education*, March 1966, 41.

243. Grossman, A., & R. L. Howe. *Data Processing for Educators*. Chicago: Educational Methods, Inc., 1965.

244. Grossman, A., & R. L. Howe. R & D center for computerized educational data processing. In *Computer Applications Service*. Detroit, Mich.: American Data Processing, Inc., 1962, 214–222.

245. Grossman, A., & R. L. Howe. Revolution in record keeping through electronic data processing. *Clearing House*, **37**, 1963, 455–459.

   California State Department of Education has a research and development center to: (1) design data systems, (2) study existing data-processing equipment, (3) establish information clearing house, (4) furnish consultation, (5) develop proposals for local school district systems, (6) conduct simulation studies.

246. Guengerich, R. D. Cost and evaluation of three methods of program scheduling and progress reporting for high school students. *Dissertation Abstracts,* **24,** 1963, 1881–1882.
247. Guidelines for choosing business machines. *American School and University,* May 1965, 37.
248. Haines, G., F. Heider & D. Remington. The computer as a small group member. *Administrative Science Quarterly,* **6,** 1961, 360–374.

   Human reactions to change in the areas of decision making, organization, and information flow. Discusses appropriate management applications of computers.
249. Hamblen, J. W. Coordination of administrative, research, and instructional uses of data processing equipment in colleges and universities. *Educational Data Processing Newsletter,* **3,** 1964, 2:19–25; 3:8–16; 4:16–23.

   A detailed outline for setting up and operating a coordinated system.
250. Hartford, D. L., & B. A. Johnson. *Computers in College Student Scheduling.* Tallahassee Fla.: Florida State University, 1963.
251. Haussman, R. D., & G. J. Rath. Automatic teacher assignment—GPSS simulation. *Journal of Educational Data Processing,* **2,** 1965, 103–108.

   A successful simulation of the daily hiring and assignment of substitute teachers, indicating the kinds of data needed for a complete analysis.
252. Hogle, W. R. Accounting inventory and stock control applications of data processing equipment in school business management. *Dissertation Abstracts,* **23,** 1963, 2394.
253. Holzman, A. G., & W. R. Turkes. *Optimal Scheduling in Educational Institutions.* Pittsburgh, Pa.: University of Pittsburgh, 1965.

   A thorough and inclusive treatment of a wide variety of approaches to computer scheduling of classes and individual students.
254. How to determine your need for data processing. *School Management,* **7,** September 1963, 58–60.
255. How you can program school bus maintenance. *School Management,* May 1965, 9.
256. Howe, Robert L. First regional data processing center. *California Education,* January 1965, 11.

   Describes the regional center in Sacramento which will provide the capability for facilitating desirable changes in school operations. The center will process information on a total system plan.
257. Hubbard, R. E. An approach to institutional cost analysis. *Journal of Experimental Education,* **31,** 1962, 109–113.

Outlines procedure used in a computer-based campus-wide cost study at Wayne State University, 1960.

258. Hull, L. E., et al. Predicting course enrollments. *College and University*, **38**, 1963, 276–281.

259. Hunter, G. T. An information system for school management. *Educational Data Processing Newsletter*, **5**, 6, 1965, 1–10.
Valid decisions by school board officials depend on information about students, faculty, and operations. A data-processing system is indispensable.

260. Jennison, R. E. Foreign EDP. *Datamation*, January 1963, 28–29.
A brief description of educational data processing in other countries.

261. Johnson, M. C. Educational research by computer. *Michigan Educational Journal*, **41**, 1964, 12.

262. *Journal of Educational Data Processing*, **1**, 2, 1964.
This May 1964 issue is devoted to scheduling problems. GASP, SOCRATES, and CLASS are described. Articles by G. E. Anderson, Mary F. Gould, R. E. Holz, E. T. Smith, and C. F. Wilkes.

263. Kaimann, R. A. Project TUHL: an integrated educational data bank. *Computer Digest*, **1**, 6, June 1966, 7–9.

264. Kaimann, R. A., & J. P. Van Uxem. *Data Processing in Catholic Educational Administration*. Milwaukee, Wis.: College of Business Administration, Marquette University, 1965.
A compilation of papers and discussion sessions comprising the proceedings of the Invitational Conference for Diocesan School Administrators. Purposes were: (1) to provide administrators of diocesan schools and school systems with pertinent information about the application of data processing, (2) to gather factual information, (3) to learn about institutions, (4) to become acquainted with the potential for data processing in education.

265. Kenney, James B. A flow chart sequence for computer scheduling of high school classes—from registration to grade reporting. *Journal of Experimental Education*, Spring 1965, 33.
A series of flow charts designed to represent graphically the operations necessary to produce a schedule of classes for students of a secondary school by use of data-processing equipment.

266. Kinling, W. J. Dissemination of guidance information using data processing equipment. *Personnel and Guidance Journal*, **39**, 1960, 220–222.

267. Kleiner, D. A. Freedom for creativity—data processing in the schools. *Educational Data Processing Newsletter*, **3**, 8, 1964, 1–7.
Illustrates and discusses applications of data processing that re-

duce the clerical burden of teachers and administrators, allowing them more time for creative activities.

268. Kornfeld, L. What every schoolman should know about data processing. *School Management*, **6**, 1962, 59–68, 79–82.

A clear description of data-processing techniques and a discussion of applications, including student and business accounting.

269. Kornfeld, L., & G. L. McManis. Computer sharing for the small college. *Educational Data Processing Newsletter*, **4**, 5, 1965, 6–13.

Discusses improvements in administration potentially available to small colleges through computer sharing, made possible by recent advances in multiple-remote-input and transmission of information.

270. Kropp, R. P. Technology in instruction. *Improving College and University Teaching*, Autumn 1965, 13.

271. Larson, H. I. Education, sociology, and EDP. *Business Automation*, June 1963, 42–45.

Recommends increased use of data-processing equipment which should handle routine work, support research, and be treated as an additional intellectual resource of the whole community. Suggests that educators prepare the public for DP applications.

272. Lessons learned—discussion among the leaders of the Richmond, California state pilot project in educational data processing. *Educational Data Processing Newsletter*, **2**, 1963, July: 15–23; Aug.-Sept.: 1–9; Oct.: 1–8.

273. Lewis, J. W. Use of tabulating machinery as an aid to business administration of schools. In *National Association of Public School Business Officials Proceedings*, 1935, 80–91.

274. Lindquist, E. F. An evaluation of a technique for scaling high school grades to improve prediction of college success. *Educational and Psychological Measurements*, **23**, 1963, 623–646.

Suggests a logical analysis of and a method for scaling high-school grades for use in a large number of schools simultaneously. Reports an empirical test of the method conducted by American College Testing Program.

275. Little, T. C. New computer system saves teaching time at Richmond Schools. *Journal of Machine Accounting*, November 1964, 10–12.

A Virginia school system uses electronic data processing for attendance, payroll, accounting, cost analyses, inventory, personnel, and statistical analyses.

276. Lohman, M. A. The application of data processing procedure to

the testing of administrative policies by means of the reference data of the sequential simplex. *Dissertation Abstracts*, **23**, 1962, 1581.

277. Long, F. How improved grade reporting can help your district. *School Management*, **7**, 1963, 104–106.

278. Machine accounting and related services for school administration. *Nations Schools*, **61**, 5, 1958, 65–84.

The report represents a milestone in automation; describes early experiences of school districts and gives authoritative advice for changing to automated services.

279. McDonald, R. J. Administrative uses of electronic data processing in public schools. *Dissertation Abstracts*, **24**, 1964, 2758–2759.

280. Merz, A. F. Use of data processing equipment for educational records. *National Association of Secondary-School Principals Bulletin*, **46**, April 1962, 7–16.

281. Miles, E. P., Jr., & D. L. Hartford. *A Study of Administrative Uses of Computers in Colleges and Universities of the United States.* Tallahassee, Fla.: Florida State University, 1962.

282. Miller, C. L., & W. W. Seifert. Faculty and the computer; some problems and goals. *Journal of Engineering Education*, **50**, 1960, 839–845.

283. More on Iowa's UPDATE project. *Educational Data Processing Newsletter*, May 1963, 11–14.

284. Morrison, D. (Ed.). *Proceedings of the 9th Annual College and University Machine Records Conference.* Malibu, Calif.: Educational Data Processing Corporation, 1965.

285. Murphy, Judith. *School Scheduling by Computer—The Story of GASP.* New York: Educational Facilities Laboratories, Inc., 1964.

Describes how a versatile computer program saves administrative time and produces superior master schedules in both traditional and experimental school settings.

286. Murphy, R. M. Data processing system for the small high school. *National Association of Secondary-School Principals Bulletin*, **46**, April 1962, 19–21.

287. Oakford, R. V. Machine assistance for constructing the high school schedule; an industrial engineer's report. *Journal of Secondary Education*, **36**, 1961, 374–379.

Reports application of a flexible scheduling routine to nongraded high schools.

288. Oldehoeft, A. E. The roles of systems analysis, programming, and operations in an information system. *Educational Data Processing Newsletter*, **4**, 1, 1964, 15–19.

Illustrations of special roles and interrelations that are developing for persons involved in data processing, as the art develops.

289. Packer, R. E. Computers in education: a reference guide to projects and papers. *Computers and Automation,* **13,** 3, 1964, 27–28.

References and very brief descriptions are provided under the headings of educational computers, applications, and bibliography. Includes seventy-five references.

290. Patton, S. R. Considerations in educational data conversion and processing. *Educational Data Processing Newsletter,* **3,** 4, 1964, 12–15.

New optical devices for entering data into an EDP system without first converting it will make possible the development of a Total Information Service, which will respond to individual needs of students in administrative as well as instructional areas.

291. Pfaltz, John L. Post-registration course registration. *Data Processing for Education,* **3,** March 1964, 3–5.

292. Problems in establishing an EDP center. *Educational Data Processing Newsletter,* April 1963, 12–14.

293. Redfern, L. F. The calculating administrators. *State Government,* **36,** 3, 1963, 183–188.

294. Rhein, C. L. Automation of attendance records. *New York State Education,* **49,** February 1962, 14–16.

295. Rose, L. C. (Ed.). *Mechanization of Records and Office Procedures in Education.* Lafayette, Ind.: Purdue University, 1961.

296. Rosenstein, R. D., & S. R. Smith. Using computing machines to grade student analysis reports. *Journal of Chemical Education,* **39,** 1962, 620–621.

297. Saathoff, A. B. Automation in school accounting. *American School Board Journal,* **142,** 3, 1961, 17–19.

Describes change from manual to machine accounting in Oakland schools, discussing training and requisite effectiveness of needed personnel.

298. Schaefer, J. W. Communications today: computers tomorrow's answer. *American School Board Journal,* April 1966, 152.

299. School district plans a computer installation. *Data Processing Digest,* **10,** January 1964, 21–23.

300. School scheduling by computer: generalized academic simulation programs. *School and Society,* **6,** March 1965, 93.

301. Schure, A. Educational escalation through systems analysis. *Audiovisual Instruction,* May 1965, 10.

302. Simon, Herbert A. *The Shape of Automation for Men and Management.* New York: Harper & Row, 1965.

303. Sims, R. W. Educational data systems for Florida. *Educational Data Processing Newsletter*, 3, 4, 1964, 1–6.

Problems of establishing EDP systems. Advocates statewide systems, total availability of information, acceptance of unprocessed information by the system, top-management-level control of the system.

304. Smith, E. T. The computer in student scheduling (IBM "CLASS"). *Journal of Educational Data Processing*, 1, 1964, 53–60.

305. Smith, G. R. A computer program for the placement of student teachers. *Journal of Teacher Education*, 13, 1962, 431–432.

To make preliminary assignments on the basis of five characteristics of student teachers.

306. Smith, G. R. The computer program sketches curriculum design. *Elementary School Journal*, 63, 1963, 201–206.

A program designed to make curriculum recommendations based on probability statements that a group of pupils will understand a given set of ideas.

307. Spooner, P. A. Planning and controlling examinations by computer. *Data Processing* (British), 4, 1962, 140–148.

308. Spring, B. P. Plug-in schools: next step in educational design? *Architectural Forum*, 119, 1963, 68–73.

309. Stafford, C., & J. Bianchini. Scoring teacher-made tests with the new IBM 1620. *Educational and Psychological Measurements*, 23, 1963, 581–586.

At San Jose State College, California, students answer test questions by marking special cards with an electrographic pencil. Cards are punched and become direct input to the computer. Description of the program, which accommodates a wide range of tests.

310. Starkweather, W. *Electronic Data Processing of Admissions*. Amherst, Mass.: University of Massachusetts, 1963.

Describes need for EDP and procedures, including keypunching, coding, and computer programs.

311. Stout, E. M., & I. Halfter. Institutional research and automation. *Journal of Experimental Education*, 31, 1962, 95–98.

312. Students' progress measured electronically. *Input for Modern Management*, 1, 1, 1964, 18.

313. Stumpf, W. A. The new world of educational administration. *American School Board Journal*, February 1966, 152.

A summary of the changes taking place in the administration of large-city school systems including discussion of innovations, big-city administration, teacher militancy, integration, educational technology, record automation, and new federal relations.

314. Subcommittee on electronic computers. *Survey Report on Computer and Systems Applications in Admissions and Registrations.* Allentown, Pa.: American Association of College Registrars and Admissions Officers, 1963.

315. Sullivan, J. W. Education and automation. *Educational Data Processing Newsletter,* 4, 5, 1965, 14–22.

American society is undergoing a revolution based largely on computer technology. Education and individual students participate in that revolution when educational data systems are aware of individual student needs.

316. Thompdon, Victor A. Bureaucracy and innovation. *Administrative Science Quarterly,* June 1965, 10.

The relationship between bureaucratic structure and innovative behavior is examined by comparing the conditions within the structure with the conditions most conducive to individual creativity. The conditions within bureaucracy are found to be determined by a drive for productivity and control, and inappropriate for creativity.

317. Thompson, J. M. Analysis of guidance case studies using data processing procedures. *California Journal of Educational Research,* 12, 1961, 195–199.

318. Throop, H. L., Jr. Simplifying student population projections. *American School Board Journal,* 145, July 1962, 11–12.

319. Tillit, H. E. Schools and electronic data processing: an experiment. *International Computation Centre Bulletin,* 2, 1963, 162–173.

320. Total information service in Chicago schools. *School and Society,* 91, 1963, 328.

321. Turpen, N. C. Computer information system serves educators. *Journal of Machine Accounting,* November 1964, 4–9.

In Albuquerque schools, a system encompassing budget, curricula, staff, and scheduling has cut scheduling cost from $1.50 to less than $.40 per student.

322. Tyndall, D. G., & G. A. Barnes. Unit costs of instruction in higher education. *Journal of Experimental Education,* 31, 1962, 114–118.

323. Walton, W. W. Potentialities of the computer for measurement and prediction with respect to the college admission process. *Educational and Psychological Measurement,* Spring 1965, 25.

324. Weinberg, E. *Adjustment to the Introduction of Office Automation.* Washington, D.C.: U.S. Department of Labor, 1960.

A pioneer study of the introduction of electronic data processing in twenty offices in private industry, describing reactions of those affected.

325. Wells, W. D. Computer simulation of consumer behavior. *Harvard Business Review*, 41, 1963, 93–98.

Describes simulation and its potential for computer pretesting of market strategies by managers. Predicts controlled experiments in marketing that will save much time and money over present methods and will encourage novel plans through elimination of most of the real risk.

326. Welton, G. Data processing and the school schedule: a Burroughs approach. *Journal of Secondary Education*, 36, 1961, 382–384.

327. Wennerberg, C. H. An administrator looks at data processing. *Educational Data Processing Newsletter*, 3, 3, 1964, 1–7.

First steps and problems in establishing data processing in a large school district. Predicts better, not cheaper, education.

328. Whitlock, J. W. *Automatic Data Processing in Education*. New York: Macmillan, 1964.

329. Wilkes, C. F. Application of data processing to mark analysis and class size analysis. *Journal of Educational Data Processing*, 1, 1964, 18–27.

Description of techniques for analytical study of grading and class size on data-processing equipment below the computer level.

330. Wilkes, C. F. SOCRATES: a system for student scheduling. *Journal of Educational Data Processing*, 1, 1964, 46–52.

331. Williams, C. W. Scheduling students by computer. *Computer Application Service*, 3, 1964, 180–185. (*Data Processing for Education*, 3, May 1964, 3–8.)

332. Wogaman, Thomas D. Educational data processing. *American School Board Journal*, February, March, April 1966.

I. Reception of EDP in the schools. II. Changes in the schools. III. Lessons learned in the Richmond Project. A series of three important papers surveying the early use and the growing improvement in data processing for educational statistical work.

333. Wulff, B. H. Data processing for student scheduling: an IBM approach. *Journal of Secondary Education*, 36, 1961, 380–381.

334. Yasaki, Edward. Educational data processing. *Datamation*, June 1963, 24–27.

Reports a workshop on educational research; participants—AEDS, American Educational Research Association, California Educational Data Processing Association, and System Development Corporation.

335. Yates, F. H., Jr. State departments of education and data processing. *American School Board Journal*, 145, 1962, 14.

C. RESEARCH AND GENERAL APPLICATIONS

336. Baker, F. B. Generalized item and test analysis program—a program for the control data 1604 computer. *Educational and Psychological Measurement,* **23,** 1963, 187–190.

    A program that performs the major calculations and displays needed for the evaluation of a test.

337. Baker, F. B. Use of computers in educational research. *Review of Educational Research,* **33,** 1963, 566–578.

    Many aspects of computer application will affect educational research methodology. Fifty-three-item bibliography.

338. Becker, H. C., H. E. Longnecker, & L. C. Cusachs. Pictures of molecular orbitals. *Communications of the ACM,* 8, 1965, 542.

339. Berkeley, E. C. *The Computer Revolution.* Garden City, N.Y.: Doubleday, 1962.

340. Borko, H. (Ed.). *Computer Applications in the Behavioral Sciences.* Englewood Cliffs, N.J.: Prentice-Hall, 1962.

    A textbook for a university-level course in the use of computers in research.

341. Borko, H. The construction of an empirically based, mathematically derived classification system. In *Proceedings: 1962 Spring Joint Computer Conference.* Palo Alto, Calif.: National Press, 1962, 279–289.

    The development of an automatic classification system for a set of documents based on a mathematical treatment (factor-analysis) of the associations of keywords in the documents.

342. Brickman, William W., & Stanley Lehrer (Eds.). *Automation, Education, and Human Values.* New York: School and Society Books, 1965.

343. Bromberg, H. Survey of programming languages and processors. *Communications of the ACM,* **6,** 1963, 93–99.

    The survey indicates an evolution of programming languages from lower to higher levels of sophistication, with all levels still in use.

344. Caffrey, J. G., D. D. Bushnell, F. I. Converse & S. S. Stott. *Application of Electronic Data Processing Methods in Education: Preliminary Report.* Santa Monica, Calif.: System Development Corporation, 1964.

345. Caffrey, J. G., & C. J. Mosmann. *Computers on Campus:* A Report

to the President on Their Use and Management. Washington, D.C.: American Council on Education, 1967 (in press).

346. Cavanaugh, A. D. Institutional research and the computer. *Educational Data Processing Newsletter*, **2**, September 1963, 18–23.

347. Cogswell, J. F. A study of psycho-educational appraisal by digital computer. Santa Monica, Calif.: System Development Corporation, 1963.

348. Coleman, J. S. Analysis of social structures and simulation of social processes with electronic computers. *Educational and Psychological Measurement*, **21**, 1961, 203–218.

Analysis of interpersonal sociometric choices to reveal such social entities as cliques and personal influence.

349. Computer and educational research: a symposium. *Harvard Educational Review*, **31**, 1961, 235–263.

Discussants consider the use of a computer in establishing a data bank and a research information service; establishing and running a university data-processing center; planning large-scale research projects; modifying educational research methods.

350. Computer simulation of city traffic. *Communications of the ACM*, **5**, 1962, 224–226.

Reports simulations of automobile traffic performed by the National Bureau of Standards.

351. *Computopics, Special Issue*. Washington, D.C.: Association for Computing Machinery, 1965.

An annotated bibliography of career guidance materials in mathematics and the computer sciences; an annotated bibliography of computer science films.

352. Cooley, W. W., & P. R. Lohnes. *Multivariate Procedures for the Behavioral Sciences*. New York: Wiley, 1962.

FORTRAN (computer-coded) programs for some statistical procedures of particular interest to behavioral scientists.

353. Davis, R. H. *The Computer Is Neutral*. Santa Monica, Calif.: System Development Corporation, 1965.

The social and psychological implications of the computer revolution. In education, learning will be lifelong, university departments will become less insular, students will need more training for leisure activities, and students will have to be educated about the meaning of the computer revolution as well as about operating or utilizing computers.

354. Dixon, W. J. (Ed.). *BMD—Biomedical Computer Programs*. Los Angeles: School of Medicine, University of California, 1964.

A widely used, much-respected manual containing computer programs for modern statistical techniques applicable to many areas of research.

355. Egbert, R. L., & J. F. Cogswell. *System Design for a Continuous Progress School: Part 1.* Santa Monica, Calif.: System Development Corporation, 1964.

Examines the plan for a continuous progress school being developed at the Brigham Young University Laboratory School and uses the data for system analysis and simulation to construct an explicit descriptive model of a future CPS.

356. Egbert, R. L., & J. F. Cogswell. *System Design for a Continuous Progress School: Part 2—Surveillance and Detection System.* Santa Monica, Calif.: System Development Corporation, 1964.

Use of the computer to compare results of alternative treatments of the same statistical data.

357. Feigenbaum, E. A. An experimental course in simulation of cognitive processes. *Behavioral Science, 7,* 1962, 244–245.

Proposes a course in computer symbol manipulation as distinct from more traditional mathematically oriented programming courses.

358. Feigenbaum, E. A., & H. A. Simon. Performance of a reading task by an elementary perceiving and memorizing program. *Behavioral Science, 8,* 1963, 72–76.

A computer is programmed to learn to read by steps that resemble those used by human learners, and thus serves as a highly manipulative model of human learning.

359. Fein, L. Intellectual preparation for living in a rapidly automating society. *Educational Data Processing Newsletter, 3,* 6, 1964, 10–19.

Advocates development of theories of automated economies to be supported by labor, industry, and government.

360. Green, B. F., Jr. Using computers to study human perception. *Educational and Psychological Measurement, 21,* 1961, 227–233.

Computer generation of stimulus patterns for the study of human perception gives a high degree of control over a number of stimulus characteristics.

361. Green, B. F., Jr., et al. Baseball: an automatic question-answerer. In *Proceedings of the Western Joint Computer Conference.* New York: Institute of Radio Engineers, 1961, 219–224.

362. Grems, M. A survey of languages and systems for information retrieval. *Communications of the ACM, 5,* 1962, 43–46.

A survey of progress in the field of information retrieval.

363. Griffin, Marjorie. *The Library of Tomorrow*. San Jose, Calif.: IBM Corporation, Advanced Systems Development Division Laboratory, 1963.

Describes a fully automated library of the future which uses machines to index, store, and retrieve information. Suggests that technical writers may have to operate under constraints to make information compatible with machine format.

364. Gullahorn, J. E., & J. T. Gullahorn. *A Computer Model of Elementary Social Behavior*. Santa Monica, Calif.: System Development Corporation, 1962.

Computer simulation of a two-person interaction.

365. Hartley, J. Research report. *New Education*, 2, 1, 1966.

Outlines the limitations of generalizing about the effectiveness of programmed instruction following one evaluation study. Generalizations from pooling such studies together are discussed. Matches 112 unselected studies comparing programmed with conventional instruction against suggested minimum criteria for experiments of this kind. Emphasis is placed on the internal evaluation of what leads to and what prevents efficient performance.

366. Heller, G. C. A computer curriculum for the high school. *Datamation*, 8, 1962, 23–26.

Describes efforts to increase the supply of programmers by introducing computer programming at the high-school level.

367. Hovland, C. I., & E. B. Hunt. Computer simulation of concept attainment. *Behavioral Science*, 5, 1960, 265–267.

A description of one of the earliest attempts to simulate human concept-learning behavior.

368. Hunt, E. B. *Concept Learning: An Information Processing Problem*. New York: Wiley, 1962.

Overview of theoretical and practical implications of an information-processing approach to concept learning; an introduction.

369. Jacobs, J. N., K. A. Johnson & J. S. Abma. *An Evaluation of Programed Instruction for Teaching Facts and Concepts*. Report No. AMRL-TR-65-222. Wright-Patterson Air Force Base, Ohio: Aerospace Medical Research Laboratories, 1965.

370. Laughery, K. R., & L. W. Gregg. Simulation of human problem-solving behavior. *Psychometrika*, 27, 1962, 265–282.

A detailed account of the process of developing a computer program to simulate the behavior of a single human problem solver.

371. Leeson, D. N., & D. L. Dimitry. *Basic Programing Concepts and*

the IBM 1620 Computer. New York: Holt, Rinehart & Winston, 1962.

372. Leone, F. C., et al. *Abstracts of Statistical Computer Routines.* Cleveland, Ohio: Case Institute of Technology, 1961.

   Lists many statistical programs available for a wide variety of computers.

373. McCracken, D. D. *A Guide to FORTRAN Programming.* New York: Wiley, 1961.

   The most-used formula language for computer programming, out of which modified languages have been developed.

374. Naur, P. (Ed.). Revised report on the algorithmic language ALGOL 60. *Communications of the ACM,* 6, 1963, 1–17.

   Describes efforts to develop a language that could be used both for programming and for standard publication.

375. Newell, A., et al. (Eds.). *Information Processing Language-V Manual.* Englewood Cliffs, N.J.: Prentice-Hall, 1961.

376. Oettinger, Anthony G. Automatic processing of natural and formal languages. In W. A. Kalenich (Ed.), *Proceedings of AFIPS Congress, 1965,* Vol. I. Washington, D.C.: Spartan Books, 1965.

377. Oettinger, Anthony G. A vision of technology and education. *Communications of the ACM,* 9, 7, July 1966, 487–490.

   Views potential uses of educational technology and raises questions about the modes of social response and adaptation likely to be evoked by such future developments.

378. Packer, R. E. Computers, education, and the government. *Computers and Automation,* 14, 3, 1965, 14–17.

379. Page, E. B. *Project Essay Grade, II, IA.* Two research proposals. Storrs, Conn.: Bureau of Educational Research, University of Connecticut, 1965.

380. Peres, S. H., & P. H. Arnold. Identifying programmer behavior. *Datamation,* 9, 1963, 40.

381. Perlis, A. J. Programming of digital computers. *Communications of the ACM,* 7, 1964, 210–211.

382. Roster of school, college, and university computer centers. *Computers and Automation,* 11, 6, 1962.

383. Ryans, D. G. *The Application of Programmed Instruction and Auto-instructional Devices in Colleges and Their Relation to a Theory of Instruction.* Santa Monica, Calif.: System Development Corporation, 1963.

   Examines the purposes, essential characteristics, and potential utility of programmed instruction and recommends that research and practice with respect to programmed instruction be viewed within a context provided by a theoretical model. Discusses the use of autoinstructional materials and the essential features of programmed instruction.

384. Selfridge, O. G., & U. Neisser. Pattern recognition by machine. *Scientific American, 203,* 1960, 60–68.

385. Silvern, Leonard C. A component-type general-purpose teaching machine of optimum capability for curriculum development. *Human Factors, 3,* 1961, 286–298.

386. Smith, Gary R. The computer program sketches curriculum design. *The Elementary School Journal, 63,* 1963, 201–206.

Describes a program designed to make curriculum recommendations based on probability statements that a group of pupils will understand a given set of ideas.

387. Smith, R. E. Examination by computer. *Behavioral Science, 8,* January 1963, 76–79.

388. Stolurow, Lawrence M. Implications of current research and future trends. *Journal of Educational Research, 55,* 1962, 519–527.

Predicts increase in autoinstructional programming; more initiative in communicating with teachers; more research on effectiveness of different programmed methods; research contributing to a theory of teaching; more book formats and computerized setups; dynamic individualized programming.

389. Tomkins, S. S., & S. Messick. *Computer Simulation of Personality.* New York: Wiley, 1963.

390. Uhr, L. "Pattern recognition" computers as models for form perception. *Psychological Bulletin, 60,* 1963, 40–73.

391. Walsh, J. E. Computer-feasible method for handling incomplete data in regression analysis. *Journal of the Association for Computing Machinery, 8,* 1961, 201–211.

392. Wayne, M. E., Jr., & D. J. Hall. Data processing: automation in calculation. *Review of Educational Research, 30,* 1960, 522–535.

Reviews state of computer art. Ninety-six-item bibliography.

393. Westley, Bruce H., & Harvey K. Jacobson. Instructional television and student attitudes toward teacher, course, and medium. *Audiovisual Communication Review, 11,* 1963, 47–60.

A study of student attitudes. The data suggest that the presence of television teacher may actually enhance the position of the classroom teacher in the eyes of his pupils.

Selected Conferences on Educational Data Processing

1. AEDS National Center for Educational Data Processing Workshop Program.
   Workshop 1: NEA Building, Washington, D.C., October 25–26, 1966. *A Critical Look at Educational Data Processing.*
   Workshop 2: NEA Building, Washington, D.C., November 14–15, 1966. *A Forum on the Practical Problems Involved in the Automating of Large City School Systems.*
   Workshop 3: University of Utah, Salt Lake City, December 6–7, 1966. *An Introduction to Educational Data Processing.*
   Workshop 4: University of California at Irvine, January 17–18, 1967. *Developing Information Systems in Colleges and Universities.*
   Workshop 5: New Orleans, February 9–10, 1967. *The Regionalization and Sharing of Facilities for Educational Data Processing.*
   Workshop 6: University of Iowa, Iowa City, February 27–28, 1967. *Instructional Programs in Data Processing in Secondary, Technical Schools, and Colleges.*
   Workshop 7: Florida Atlantic University, Boca Raton, April 5–6, 1967. *Automating Pupil Personnel Records.*
   Workshop 8: Statler-Hilton, Detroit, May 1967. *An Overview of Developments across the United States in the Area of Educational Data Processing.*
   Workshop 9: New York City, May 18–19, 1967. *Standards for Educational Data Processing.*

2. Association for Educational Data Systems—*Second Annual Meeting.* April 19–22, 1964, Santa Barbara, Calif.
   Discussions:
   Neil Young (Chairman), Getting started in data processing.
   Murray Tondow (Chairman), Acquiring a computer for school application.

William G. Katzenmeyer (Chairman), Test scoring and analysis.

Robert Hewes (Chairman), Scheduling.

Richard V. Andree (Chairman), Teaching secondary school students about computer mathematics.

Robert Howe (Chairman), Establishing an information exchange in educational data.

J. Richard Haish (Chairman), New products and their school applications.

Alvin Goldberg (Chairman), Training technical and professional personnel in EDP operations.

Robert Sims (Chairman), Relationships between state and local EDP installations.

G. T. Hunter (Chairman), The school computing center and/or the service bureau.

Peter McGraw (Chairman), Attendance accounting systems.

3. Association for Educational Data Systems—*Third Annual Meeting.* May 9–11, 1965, Miami Beach, Fla.

Discussions:

Amos Kimberling (Chairman), Developing a state and regional data processing center.

Morris Rubinoff (Chairman), Advanced developments in data processing.

Bruce K. Alcorn (Chairman), Establishment of a master student file.

Earl T. Klein (Chairman), Automation and educational opportunity.

William G. Katzenmeyer (Chairman), Test scoring and analysis.

John W. Sullivan (Chairman), Curricula for teaching educational data processing in colleges and universities.

Robert Gates (Chairman), and Peter McGraw, Meet the experts on E.A.M.

William J. Emerson (Chairman), Role of the intermediate unit in educational data processing.

G. E. Anderson, Jr. (Chairman), Scheduling.

Andres Llana, Jr. (Chairman), Industrial computer applications and their application to the needs of the educator.

Don D. Bushnell (Chairman), New developments in computer-assisted instruction.

William J. English (Chairman), Role of the junior college in an educational data processing center in a unified school system.

John Caffrey (Chairman), Time-sharing demonstration.

John P. Freeman (Chairman), Accounting and financial applications of educational data processing.

Ivan N. Seibert (Chairman), Getting started in educational data processing at the state level.

John W. Hamblen (Chairman), The role of the university data processing and/or computing center.

Murray Pfeferman (Chairman), Establishing an information exchange in educational data processing.

Sylvia Charp (Chairman), Use of computer mathematics in teaching secondary school students.

John E. Stecklein (Chairman), Data systems applications to institutional research.

Irvin A. Gaydos (Chairman), Role of a systems analyst in educational data processing.

Thomas Kurtz (Chairman), Use of the remote console to teach computer mathematics—a demonstration.

4. Association for Educational Data Systems—*Fourth Annual Convention*. May 1–4, 1966, Philadelphia.
   Discussions:

   Thomas P. Stephens (Chairman), Local school district applications.

   Malcolm H. Gotterer (Chairman), The application of management science techniques.

   G. Ernest Anderson, Jr. (Chairman), Recent and future equipment developments.

   Ralph Van Duseldorp (Chairman), State education agency developments.

   Paul Shoemaker (Chairman), The advantages and disadvantages of regional centers.

   Gene Callahan, University and college administration developments.

   Robert Marker (Chairman), Iowa educational information center presentation.

   Wesley N. Dorn (Chairman), An analysis of recent federal legislation affecting educational data processing.

   Don F. Morrison (Chairman), Total systems concepts in education.

   Stanley Patton (Chairman), Total information service presentation, Chicago City Schools.

   Robert D. Gates, (Chairman), The impact of recent federal legislation on educational data processing.

Frank Dunn (Chairman), Scheduling and sectioning.

William W. Wayson (Chairman), The training and retraining of present education administrators.

Donald L. Hartford (Chairman), The teaching of ADP and computerized instruction in colleges of education.

Sylvia Charp (Chairman), The teaching of ADP and computerized instruction in secondary and vocational schools.

Simeon P. Taylor III (Chairman), The development and utilization of data transmission.

John W. Sullivan (Chairman), Security and confidentiality of information.

William G. Katzenmeyer (Chairman), Management tools, executive reports, and planning.

5. California Educational Data Processing Association—*Third Annual Conference*. November 14, 1963, Los Angeles.
   Topics:
   (*a*) Systems analysis and the parable of the restaurant spindle.
   (*b*) New developments in student scheduling.
   (*c*) Management of input data.

6. California Educational Data Processing Association—*Fourth Annual Conference*. November 5, 1964, San Francisco.
   Papers:
   John Caffrey, Student scheduling: problems and progress.
   Kojiro Kawaguchi, Input problems.
   Murray Tondow, Development of a curriculum for computer education in high school.
   Martin de Rodeff, The qualifications and role of the professional EDP director.
   Robert Whittaker, Data transmission from local schools to district offices.
   Dwayne Orton, Effect of data processing on education.
   John Ivan, Beginning EDP—the ABC's.
   Harry Ward, Small computer programs.
   Robert Rolens, Card and form design (output).
   Don Crisler, Scheduling production in a data center.
   Alvin Grossman and Robert Howe, Progress report—state department of education.

7. California Educational Data Processing Association—*Sixth Annual Conference*. November 15–16, 1966, San Francisco.

Topics:
  (*a*) The task of organizing and implementing the total information system.
  (*b*) EDP curriculum instruction.
  (*c*) Computer assisted instruction.
  (*d*) Counseling students—job opportunities.
  (*e*) Pupil personnel records and guidance services.
  (*f*) Automating school business services.
  (*g*) Audio visual and library services.
  (*h*) State and national programs in data processing.
  (*i*) Educational research—computer based.

8. California State Department of Education—*Conference on Electronic Data Processing and Computing in Secondary Education.* November 20–22, 1964, University of California, Davis.
   Papers:
   Ned Chapin, Electronic data processing and computing: their challenge to secondary education.
   Robert Albrecht, A modern day medicine show: a laboratory approach to secondary mathematics.
   Jess Peckenham, Use of computers in the Oakland school curriculum.
   Bryce Yourd, A vocational business data processing program.
   Marc Brann, A computer course for low achievers in high school.
   Thomas Clements, Junior college and joint high school–junior college curricula in computer sciences.
   Leland Baldwin, Financing a data processing and computing program.
   Don D. Bushnell, The future of electronic data processing and computing in secondary schools.
   Workshops were held on curricula, methods, materials, and administration, in relation to computers. There were eight tutorial sessions on computer-related topics.

9. Harvard Graduate School of Education and United States Office of Education—*Educational Data Bank Conference.* December 3–5, 1964, Boston.
   Topics:
   Paul R. Lohnes, Application of the Markov model to the data bank.
   Ralph F. Berdie, Principles governing data collection.
   Julian Stanley, Experimental rigor applied to surveys.

Donald P. Mitchell, Good data do not guarantee useful conclusions.

John B. Carroll, Opportunity and need for micro-data, e.g., item responses in addition to summary test scores.

Frank L. Field, Danger of usurping rather than facilitating decision making that should be done by students.

Benjamin S. Bloom, Various dangers of distortion of research goals by existence of the data bank.

10. National Council of Teachers of Mathematics—*Conference on Computer-Oriented Mathematics and the Secondary School.* May 24–25, 1963, Washington, D.C.
Topics:
(*a*) The growing need for trained personnel in all fields of computer research.
(*b*) Need for direct contact with computers in high school.
(*c*) Need for greater emphasis on mathematics for future computer scientists and programmers.
(*d*) Possibility of training some terminal high school students as lower echelon programmers.
(*e*) The status of computer education in Philadelphia.
(*f*) Possibility of introducing algorithms in algebra courses.
(*g*) Favorable response to Saturday computer courses for teachers.
(*h*) Description of computer courses offered or planned.
(*i*) Cooperation between educators and computer technologists.
(*j*) Willingness of industry to help, if asked by educators.

11. New England Educational Data Systems—*Summer Institute.* June–July 1964, Cambridge, Mass.
A six-week course providing technical training for association members. The program has three aims: to teach coordinators how to manage data in their schools; to train them in the use of computers; and to teach computer program writing.

12. Office of Naval Research, Personnel and Training Branch, Invitational Conferences in Computer-Assisted Instruction.
Fall 1965, University of Illinois, Training Research Laboratory.
Spring 1966, Bolt, Baranek and Newman, Cambridge, Mass.
September 1966, System Development Corporation, Santa Monica, Calif.

13. Phi Delta Kappa and Indiana University—*Fourth Annual Phi*

Delta Kappa Symposium on Educational Research: Simulation Models for Education. November 1962, Indianapolis, Ind.

Papers:

Nicholas A. Fattu, An introduction to simulation.

Michael R. Lackner, Toward a general simulation capability.

Herbert W. Karr, A quick look at Simscript.

William R. Dill and Neil Doppelt, The acquisition of experience in a complex management game.

Kalman J. Cohen and Richard M. Cyert, Simulation of organizational behavior.

Donald L. Bitzer, PLATO: An electronic teaching device.

14. Stanford University, School of Education—*Workshop on Flexible Scheduling.* July 20–24, 1964, Stanford, Calif.

The workshop concentrates on new basic designs for the secondary school curriculum, procedures for constructing modular schedules, preparation of input data for presentation to high-speed computers for the generation of master schedules, the interpretation of output data from the computer, and data-processing techniques associated with the use of computers in scheduling.

D. W. Allen and R. N. Bush, chairmen.

15. Stanford University, School of Education—*Workshop on Flexible Scheduling.* July 19–23, 1965, Stanford, Calif.

D. W. Allen and R. N. Bush, chairmen.

16. Stanford University, School of Education—*Workshop on Flexibility for Vocational Education through Computer Scheduling,* July 18–22, 1967; *Performance Criterion Conference,* November 7–8, 1967.

17. United States Office of Naval Research and System Development Corporation—*Conference on Application of Digital Computers to Automated Instruction.* October 10–12, 1961, Washington, D.C.

Twelve papers discussed "Theory and experimentation in programmed learning." Nine of these dealt with experimental hypotheses about allocation of items, size of step, and similar specifics; the papers were by H. F. Silberman; R. E. Dear and R. C. Atkinson; J. G. Holland; N. A. Crowder; R. Glaser; L. J. Briggs, R. A. Goldbeck, V. N. Campbell, and D. G. Nichols; A. Roe; D. A. Cook; and J. Senders. E. R. Keislar and J. D. McNeil described an application in primary mathematics and science. A. A. Lumsdaine reviewed theoretical and practical problems; and L. F. Carter discussed probable changes in the thinking of educators due to automation.

Six papers discussed "Computer-based instructional systems." J. W. Rigney called for systematic work on abilities and methods of presentation of subject matter in preparation for realizing the potential of computers as teaching machines. W. R. Uttal described and evaluated "conversational interaction" between student and computer. J. E. Coulson described and evaluated System Development Corporation's Computer-based Laboratory for Automated School Systems (CLASS). D. L. Bitzer, P. G. Braunfeld, and W. W. Lichtenberger discussed University of Illinois' PLATO II, a computer-based teaching device. J. C. R. Licklider described computer-based foreign-vocabulary learning and concluded that it will be possible to develop computer-based instruction that greatly increases the student's concentration. R. L. Chapman and J. T. Carpenter discussed the interaction between science and technology in the development of computer-based instructional routines.

18. University Council for Educational Administration—*Career Development Seminar: Computer Concepts and Educational Administration.* April 25–29, 1965, University of Iowa, Iowa City.
   Topics:

   Willard R. Lane, The need for better taxonomy and theory on which to base rational method and organization in education.

   R. H. Davis, Social, psychological, and educational implications of the computer revolution.

   Judith Murphy, Master scheduling done by GASP in two school systems.

   D. N. Michael, Computer preemption of middle echelon decision making will greatly change management roles and business and social organization.

   F. Yett, Specifications for educational simulation.

   E. F. Lindquist, Major aspects of the Iowa Educational Information Center, and hopes and needs for the future.

   R. W. Marker, Problems associated with computer-based educational information systems, as revealed at University of Iowa.

   J. A. Ramseyer, Training and role of educational administrators and education of students for society are changing under the impact of computer technology.

19. University of California at Los Angeles, Department of Education, and System Development Corporation—*Lake Arrowhead Colloquy:*

Application of Electronic Data Processing Methods in Education.
November 17–20, 1963, Lake Arrowhead, Calif.

A broadly based conference of educational data-processing specialists, teachers, curriculum and guidance specialists, administrators,
psychologists, and research workers determined areas of common
problems and interests, and unresolved issues relating to electronic
data processing in education, and produced the following recommendations:

1. Encourage research to identify educational problems arising
   from impact of electronic data processing.
2. Conduct studies of hardware and software requirements.
3. Support studies of how to get full value from an EDP system
   and how to develop systems that will respond to a wide range
   of demands.
4. Support studies to determine smallest workable information
   units for common inter- and intraschool district use.
5. Support studies leading toward total EDP systems compatibility.
6. Support studies to determine software needs not likely to be met
   on time by commercial suppliers.
7. Support projects in which educational innovations may be
   coupled with automated data processing.
8. Make funds available for more conferences like the present one.
9. Support projects to identify, develop, and disseminate programs
   of formal education and direct experience needed by educators
   and EDP personnel for mastery and collaboration in and between their respective domains.
10. Establish a national clearing house to promote exchange of in-
    formation and materials.

20. University of Oregon School of Education—*Conference on Com-
    puters in Education.* March 9–11, 1964, Eugene, Ore.
    Papers:
    John Caffrey, The use of the computer in allocating educational
    resources.
    Robert Trocchi, Demonstration of long-distance computer inter-
    rogation by telecommunication.
    Rollin Thompson, Teaching computer technology in schools and
    colleges.
    Murray Tondow, The role of computers in pupil-appraisal sys-
    tems.
    Don D. Bushnell, The computer in the classroom.

Selected Conference Presentations on Educational Data Processing

1. American Association of School Administrators—*Centennial Conference*. February 15–19, 1964, Atlantic City, N.J.
   Topics:
   Don Russell (Chairman), Who's doing what with data processing in education?
   John Caffrey (Chairman), Requirements for educational information systems.

2. American Association of School Administrators—*97th Annual Convention*. February 13–17, 1965, Atlantic City, N.J.
   Address: Peter McGraw, Instructional and accounting uses of data processing in education.

3. American Documentation Institute—*Annual Meeting: Parameters of Information Science*. October 5–8, 1964, Philadelphia.
   Paper:
   Don D. Bushnell, Information retrieval systems for schools of the future as extrapolated from current research.

4. American Documentation Institute—*Symposium on Education for Information Science*. September 7–10, 1965, Arlington, Va.
   Topic 1: Contributions toward information science theory. M. Belth, R. A. Fairthorne, F. Goodman and L. Heilprin, W. J. Paisley and E. B. Parker.
   Topic 2: Operational constraints in design of information science systems. C. L. Bernier, H. Ohlman, M. Rigby, W. F. Seibert.
   Topic 3: Pedagogical aspects. M. Barnett, R. M. Hayes, D. J. Hillman, A. M. Rees, R. S. Taylor.
   Topic 4: Administrative problems. A. J. Goldwyn, V. Slamecka.
   Topic 5: A university course on information retrieval theory. M. Kochen.
   Topic 6: Computer sciences in the information sciences curriculum. B. F. Cheydleur, H. J. Koller, G. Salton, W. J. Stuart.

288

5. American Educational Research Association, *Annual Convention.* February 16–18, 1967, New York.

Symposium: The computer and the teaching-learning process. K. Zinn (Chairman), R. Harnack, P. Nachtigal, H. Silberman, D. Stotler, R. Glaser.

Symposium: Natural languages and the computer for education in the humanities. A. B. Ellis (Chairman), W. A. Sedelowe, D. Paulus, M. P. Smith, Sally Y. Sedelowe, E. B. Page.

Address: Herbert Simon, Computers and cognition.

Symposium: Applications of computers. R. T. Hartnett (Chairman), J. F. Vinsonhaler, B. G. Wingersky, P. R. Lohner, J. M. Sparks.

6. American Management Association—*Second International Conference and Exhibit.* August 9–12, 1966, New York.

Topics:

Emmanuel G. Mesthene, Knowledge, action, and the direction of change.

Ralph W. Tyler, Evaluation—the ultimate reality.

Harold Howe II, Educational realities—the requirements for progress.

Symposium: Training teachers to cope with change. B. Brown, H. Simon, P. C. Horne, Col. D. Ofiesh, K. Komoski, R. Gates.

Symposium: New curricula development to cope with change. B. E. Donovan, O. K. Moore, L. Spencer, Susan Markle, G. F. Winfield, E. Brice.

Symposium: Dial "E" for education—the realities of the school of tomorrow. Katherine LaBelle, H. Wilke, L. Campion, W. Humphrey, D. Horsman, P. Lewis, C. Palmer.

Symposium: Games and simulation—with and without computers: new tools for education and training. D. D. Bushnell, C. C. Abt, Saranne Boocock, R. L. Hunt, N. Kristy.

Symposium: The realities of computer-assisted instruction. R. L. Bright, H. E. Mitzel, R. E. Grubb, L. M. Stolurow.

Symposium: Broadcast communications: past, present, and future. C. R. Carpenter, R. L. Hilliard, Rev. J. Culkin, S. J., S. N. Siegel, N. L. Halpern.

Also problem-solving workshops in computer-assisted instruction, programmed instruction, and instructional television.

7. American Federation of Information Processing Societies—*Fall Joint Computer Conference.* November 12–14, 1963, Las Vegas.

Topics:

(*a*) California project in developing a prototype for a statewide integrated educational data processing system.

(*b*) System school modeling and a computer-based school system.

(*c*) Progress of the National Defense Education Act projects.

(*d*) Method of teaching computing to secondary school students.

(*e*) Role of computers in education.

(*f*) Demonstration of problem solving with the computer.

8. American Federation of Information Processing Societies—*Fall Joint Computer Conference.* November 30–December 2, 1965, Las Vegas.

   Topic 1: Alvin Grossman, California plan for communication network of regional data processing centers for the exchange of administrative and educational information.

   Topic 2: Murray Tondow, Use of automated program for counseling and guidance.

   Topic 3: Alan Isaacs and Dale Wolgamuth, Registration information as a basis for a total educational data processing system.

   Topic 4: Impact of computers on society: computers and education.

9. American Psychological Association—*72nd Annual Convention.* September 4–9, 1964, Los Angeles.

   Topic: Robert L. Egbert (Chairman), The role of computer simulation in education.

   Papers:

   John F. Cogswell, New solutions to implementing instructional media through analysis and simulation of school organizations.

   John Forkes, Operational gaming and decision simulation: an attack on some chronic human problems in educational organization.

   Benjamin Kleinmuntz, Simulation of counselor's diagnostic judgment.

   Frank A. Yett, Simulation in professional staff control.

   Thomas Steel, Reaction and prognostication: education and the next generation of computers.

   R. Stewart Jones, Innovations in teaching educational psychology.

   Frank R. Baker, The role of digital computers in the teaching of educational psychology.

   Philip Lambert, The place of a synoetics laboratory in the teaching of educational psychology.

10. American Psychological Association—*73rd Annual Convention.* September 3–7, 1965, Chicago.

Paper: K. H. Wodtke, H. E. Mitzel, and B. R. Brown, Some preliminary results on the reactions of students to computer-assisted instruction.

Topic: M. Stolurow, J. A. Swets, E. H. Shuford, Jr., C. E. Helm, J. E. Coulson, Complex learning studies in the computer-based laboratory.

Topic: E. B. Page, A. Diagon, H. Garber, A. Ellis, J. A. Davis, Essay grading by computer: measurement frontier?

11. American Psychological Association—*74th Annual Convention,* September 2–6, 1966, New York.

Topic: Programmed instruction.

Papers:

Leslie J. Briggs, A procedure for the design of multimedia instruction.

John T. Flynn and James H. Morgan, A methodological study of the effectiveness of programmed instruction through analysis of learner characteristics.

Gerard C. Kress, Jr., The effects of pacing mode and administrative setting on programmed learning.

Paul I. Jacobs, Programmed progressive matrices.

Symposium: Perspectives in educational psychology: from Thorndike to CAI. E. B. Page (Chairman), R. E. Grinder, M. W. Travers, J. B. Carroll.

Symposium: What are counseling centers doing now to equip themselves for working with the campus changes of 1980? D. G. Danskin (Chairman), J. D. Black, L. D. Fols, C. H. Haagen, C. E. Kennedy, Jr., T. Magoon, E. R. Sinnett.

Symposium: Information processing and counseling and decision making. C. Wrenn (Chairman), A. M. Martin, T. Magoon, J. Cogswell, R. Hummel, Saranne S. Boocock, T. Hilton.

Symposium: Computer methods for psychological assessment. J. Veldman (Chairman), P. J. Stone, R. Gorham, R. F. Peck.

12. American Textbook Publishers Institute—*Information Storage, Retrieval, and Dissemination Seminar.* November 4–5, 1964, New York.

Papers:

Isaac D. Welt, Definitions and basic concepts.

Luther Evans, Conflicting philosophies as to the answer to the information problem.

Basil Doudnikoff, Satellite information storage and retrieval systems.

Peter Scott, Reproduction and storage mechanisms.

13. Association of School Business Officials—*49th Annual Meeting and Education Exhibit*. November 3–8, 1963, Denver.
   Topics:
   (*a*) Planning and implementing new data processing installations.
   (*b*) Applications and procedures in specialized areas.

14. Association of School Business Officials—*50th Annual Meeting and Education Exhibit*. October 17–22, 1964, San Francisco.
   Topic 1: Donald L. Ferguson, Development and implementation of data processing services for moderately sized school districts.
   Topic 2: James W. Whitlock, Growth in data processing installations for educational services and training of needed personnel.
   Topic 3: R. Meade Abbott, Automation of data processing is really not new.
   Topic 4: Gray N. Taylor, Problems and solutions for cooperative data processing centers among school districts.
   Topic 5: Robert D. Gates, What has been done in electronic data processing systems in Florida.

15. Data Processing Management Association—*International Data Processing Conference and Business Exposition*. June 23–26, 1964, New Orleans.
   Paper:
   Paul Serote, Various roles of the computer at educational institutions.

16. Data Processing Management Association—*International Data Processing Conference and Business Exposition*. June 29–July 2, 1965, Philadelphia.
   Topic:
   A. Kushner, R. A. Samans, M. M. Stone, J. McGinnis, W. E. Wadsworth, J. Paul, C. T. Whittier, J. W. Geckle, J. M. Adams, Jr., Advances in data processing education.

17. Data Processing Management Association—*International Fall Data Processing Conference and Business Exposition*. November 3–5, 1965, Dallas, Tex.
   Topic:
   P. Minton, L. Katz, D. Teichroew, J. W. Cowee, I. Harrison, J. E.

Pearson, E. Sweringer, J. A. White, Contributions to data processing and computing from universities.

18. International Federation for Information Processing—*Congress 65.* May 24–29, 1965, New York.
    Panel on Education:
    R. A. Buckingham (United Kingdom), J. Arsac (France), W. F. Atchinson (U.S.A.), F. L. Bauer (Germany), G. E. Forsythe (U.S.A.), and G. G. Heller (U.S.A.).
    Topic:
    I. L. Auerbach (Chairman), Man as an information processing system.
    Papers:
    H. von Foerster (U.S.A.), W. S. McCulloch and W. L. Kilmer (U.S.A.), and D. M. MacKay (United Kingdom).

19. National Education Association Department of Audiovisual Instruction—*Convention: The Media Specialist and Educational Change.* April 24–30, 1965, Milwaukee.
    Topic:
    Educational data processing for the audiovisual specialist.
    Papers:
    Patricia Patsloff, P. P. McGraw, P. Lambert, D. D. Bushnell, and F. Benham.

20. Southeastern Psychological Association—*12th Annual Meeting.* March 31–April 2, 1966, New Orleans.
    Paper:
    Gerald H. Whitlock, Programmed learning: some nonconfirming research.
    Topical discussion:
    Wilson H. Guertin (Chairman), Computer applications: present and future.

21. Southwestern Psychological Association—*13th Annual Meeting.* April 21–23, 1966, Arlington, Tex.
    Symposium:
    Computer simulation: From percepts to concepts and beyond. L. W. Gregg (Organizer), Benjamin Kleinmuntz (Chairman).
    Papers:
    Selby H. Evans, A model for perceptual concept formation.
    Kenneth R. Laughery, Simulation of short-term memory processes.

Lee W. Gregg, Formal and informal properties of stochastic and simulation models of concept learning.

John C. Loehlin, A computer model of idle ideation.

22. University of Georgia and System Development Corporation—*Joint Conference on Application of Electronic Data Processing in State and Local Government.* March 29–31, 1965, University of Georgia, Athens, Ga.

Topic:

James Kenny (Chairman), Education and computer-assisted systems.

Papers:

John Caffrey, Computers and decision making in education.

Charles K. Pullen, Coordination of educational data processing and research.

Address:

James Whitlock, Automatic data processing system: a tool for improving education research.

23. Western Psychological Association—*45th Annual Meeting.* June 14–19, 1965, Honolulu, Hi.

Topic:

Computer-aided learning and instruction.

Participants:

D. Hansen, H. Silberman, L. Stolurow, and A. Hickey.

24. Western Psychological Association—*46th Annual Meeting.* April 28–30, 1966, Long Beach, Calif.

Papers:

Harry C. Mahan, Adjunct programming of the basic psychology course for oral presentation via tape recorder.

R. C. Wilson, R. M. Berger, J. W. Rigney, A comparative validity study of three computer programmer interest keys for the Strong Vocational Interest Blank.

Dallis Perry, William Cannon, Development of a computer programmer key for the Strong Vocational Interest Blank.

Index

295